A Book Of

BUSINESS COMMUNICATION

For
M.B.A. and M.P.M. (Semester - I)
Also Useful for M.M.M. (Semester - I)
As Per Pune University's Revised Syllabus
Effective from June 2013

Mrs. Radha Raj
M.A. (Economics)

N2958

BUSINESS COMMUNICATION (FOR MBA, MPM, MMM)   **ISBN 978-93-5164-039-4**

Second Edition : August, 2015
© : Authors

The text of this publication, or any part thereof, should not be reproduced or transmitted in any form or stored in any computer storage system or device for distribution including photocopy, recording, taping or information retrieval system or reproduced on any disc, tape, perforated media or other information storage device etc., without the written permission of Authors with whom the rights are reserved. Breach of this condition is liable for legal action.

Every effort has been made to avoid errors or omissions in this publication. In spite of this, errors may have crept in. Any mistake, error or discrepancy so noted and shall be brought to our notice shall be taken care of in the next edition. It is notified that neither the publisher nor the authors or seller shall be responsible for any damage or loss of action to any one, of any kind, in any manner, therefrom.

Published By :
NIRALI PRAKASHAN
Abhyudaya Pragati, 1312, Shivaji Nagar
Off J.M. Road, Pune – 411005
Tel - (020) 25512336/37/39, Fax - (020) 25511379
Email : niralipune@pragationline.com

Printed By :
Repro Knowledgecast Limited,
Thane

✦ DISTRIBUTION CENTRES

PUNE
Nirali Prakashan : 119, Budhwar Peth, Jogeshwari Mandir Lane, Pune 411002, Maharashtra
Tel : (020) 2445 2044, 66022708, Fax : (020) 2445 1538
Email : bookorder@pragationline.com, niralilocal@pragationline.com

Nirali Prakashan : S. No. 28/27, Dhyari, Near Pari Company, Pune 411041
Tel : (020) 24690204 Fax : (020) 24690316
Email : dhyari@pragationline.com, bookorder@pragationline.com

MUMBAI
Nirali Prakashan : 385, S.V.P. Road, Rasdhara Co-op. Hsg. Society Ltd.,
Girgaum, Mumbai 400004, Maharashtra
Tel : (022) 2385 6339 / 2386 9976, Fax : (022) 2386 9976
Email : niralimumbai@pragationline.com

✦ DISTRIBUTION BRANCHES

JALGAON
Nirali Prakashan : 34, V. V. Golani Market, Navi Peth, Jalgaon 425001,
Maharashtra, Tel : (0257) 222 0395, Mob : 94234 91860

KOLHAPUR
Nirali Prakashan : New Mahadvar Road, Kedar Plaza, 1st Floor Opp. IDBI Bank
Kolhapur 416 012, Maharashtra. Mob : 9850046155

NAGPUR
Pratibha Book Distributors : Above Maratha Mandir, Shop No. 3, First Floor,
Rani Jhanshi Square, Sitabuldi, Nagpur 440012, Maharashtra
Tel : (0712) 254 7129

DELHI
Nirali Prakashan : 4593/21, Basement, Aggarwal Lane 15, Ansari Road, Daryaganj
Near Times of India Building, New Delhi 110002
Mob : 08505972553

BENGALURU
Pragati Book House : House No. 1, Sanjeevappa Lane, Avenue Road Cross,
Opp. Rice Church, Bengaluru – 560002.
Tel : (080) 64513344, 64513355,Mob : 9880582331, 9845021552
Email:bharatsavla@yahoo.com

CHENNAI
Pragati Books : 9/1, Montieth Road, Behind Taas Mahal, Egmore,
Chennai 600008 Tamil Nadu, Tel : (044) 6518 3535,
Mob : 94440 01782 / 98450 21552 / 98805 82331,
Email : bharatsavla@yahoo.com

niralipune@pragationline.com | www.pragationline.com

Also find us on   www.facebook.com/niralibooks

Preface

> *"The basic building block of good communications is the feeling that every human being is unique and of value."*
> — *Unknown*

Good communication skills differentiate a good leader from the 'also ran' person.

Today's students are tomorrow's managers. Very soon they will graduate and start their job search. They will write their resume, send them to organisations with interesting cover letters and land good jobs as well. But effective communication skills are not limited to this level of activity. These skills will be with the managers all the way during their work life.

In these days of intense global competition, organisations prefer to employ team workers, managers who can lead teams and deliver desired results. Good communication skills are the hallmarks of a successful leader. As James Humes says, "The art of communication is the language of leadership."

The importance of communication in a manager's work life can be seen from the fact that he spends on an average, almost 80 per cent of his time communicating to run his team, department or company. He would be constantly interacting at various levels with his subordinates, peers and superiors. The purposes range from project or performance review, giving instructions, understanding, brainstorming, and giving information. His communication is not limited by organisational boundaries. He needs to talk to or correspond with customers, suppliers, service providers, academic and research institutions, trade unions, business associations, government departments and the public at large. To borrow Lee Iacocca's words, "You can have brilliant ideas, but if you can't get them across, your ideas won't get you anywhere."

Unfortunately, there is no such thing as 'one size fits all' in this field. A good teacher or a book on communication can only give tips, but it is up to the manager to use them and work on them. Communication strategies, methods and skills required at various operational and organisational levels vary. That is perhaps why American author and composer John S. Powell made his famous statement – *"Communication works for those who work at it."* He also said, *"The only real mistake is the one from which we learn nothing"*, meaning that one should take every opportunity to keep learning, even from one's mistakes. This applies to communication skills as well, as people are continuously getting exposed to different cultural groups which have their own nuances.

Communication is not just talking. It involves a number of skills, such as organising, explaining, convincing, listening, reading, silence, body language, writing, audio-visual presentation and adopting newer technological developments.

A couple of decades ago, perhaps, no one had imagined that there would be *virtual offices* and *virtual teams* in various locations all over the world. Creating web pages and writing email is just passé. By using features on cell phones like *voice mail*, managers stay in touch all the time. Cloud computing, joining the 'cloud' is another buzz term which can help businesses and managers access everything from data backup to customer relationship management systems, leading to greater collaboration among team members and improving productivity, particularly for businesses with employees scattered all over the world. Impromptu meetings or meetings without prior notice can be held to discuss and sort out issues. Instant messaging is another feature to help managers stay connected. In these virtual teams, the manager would not even have an occasion to meet the team members but they have to come together in *virtual meetings* irrespective of the time zones they are in. Terms like social media and sharing of computer screens so that literally and figuratively the team members are on the 'same page' wherever they are located have increased office efficiency manifold. The matter is read, edited and modifications accepted or rejected on a continuous basis without even a second lost. Such revolutionary developments in communication technology open up newer ways of communicating in business as well as in personal life. Managers will have to stay abreast of all these developments and adopt them with all necessary care.

Failure to develop good communication skills and practices can result in grave misunderstandings and can damage the manager's career and affect organisational efficiency. As Northcote Parkinson says, "The void created by the failure to communicate is soon filled with poison, drivel and misrepresentation." *I earnestly urge management students to understand the significance of effective communication. In the ultimate analysis, their commitment to work and passion to succeed should be seen in the way they conduct themselves.*

I wish them good luck.

Radha Raj

Acknowledgements

Business Communication is one of my most favourite subjects. I am truly grateful to Nirali Prakashan for giving me an opportunity to write a book on this. I sincerely thank Shri Dineshbhai Furia and Shri Jignesh Furia, the publishers, for making this happen. I consider this as a privilege.

I thank Mrs. Nirja Sharma and Mr. Prasad Chintakindi for the care with which they have studied the script and their attention to each and every detail.

I would also like to thank Mr. Akbar Shaikh, Miss Chaitali Takle and Miss Neha Banswadekar who have painstakingly attended to all the details to make this book appear good.

I am also grateful to all the staff members of Nirali Prakashan, who were involved in the publication of this book.

Radha Raj

Syllabus ...

(MBA : Semester I)

1. Introduction to Managerial Communication (3 + 7)

1.1 Introduction to Managerial Communication: Principles of effective communication, Target group profile, Barriers of Communication, Reading Skills, Listening, Feedback.

1.2 Principles of Nonverbal Communication: Professional dressing and body language. Role Playing, Debates and Quiz. Types of managerial speeches - Presentations and Extempore - speech of introduction, speech of thanks, occasional speech, theme speech.

1.3 Group communication: Meetings, group discussions.

1.4 Other Aspects of Communication: Cross Cultural Dimensions of Business Communication Technology and Communication, Ethical & Legal Issues in Business Communication.

2. Managerial Writing (2 + 5)

Business letters, Routine letters, Bad news and persuasion letters, sales letters, collection letters, Maintaining a Diary, Resume/CV, job application letters, proposals. Internal communication through - notices, circulars, memos, agenda and minutes, reports. Case Studies. Exercises on Corporate Writing, Executive Summary of Documents, Creative Writing, Poster Making, Framing Advertisements, Slogans, Captions, Preparing Press Release and Press Notes

3. Effective Presentations

Principles of Effective Presentations, Principles governing the use of audiovisual media.

4. Interview Skills (2 + 3)

Mastering the art of giving interviews in - selection or placement interviews, discipline interviews, appraisal interviews, exit interviews, web /video conferencing, tele-meeting.

5. Report Writing (2 + 4)

Objectives of report, types of report, Report Planning, Types of Reports, Developing an outline, Nature of Headings, Ordering of Points, Logical Sequencing, Graphs, Charts, Executive Summary, List of Illustration, Report Writing.

(MPM : Semester I)

1. Introduction to Business Communication (5 + 1)

Meaning, Importance and Objectives - Principles of Communication, Forms of Communication, Communication Process, Barriers of Effective Communication, Techniques of Effective Communication, Importance of Effective Communication in Organisation, Organisational Structure and Communication Process.

2. Other Communication Skills (5 + 1)

Body Language, Gestures, Postures, Listening Skill, Observation, Cross Cultural Dimensions of Business Communication Technology and Communication, Ethical and Legal Issues in Business Communication.

3. Effective Presentations (5 + 1)

Principles of Effective Presentations, Principles governing the use of Audiovisual media.

4. Business Correspondence (5 + 1)

Importance of Effective Writing, Essential Features of Business Writing, Business letters: Application Letters, Inquiries, Circulars, Acknowledgements, Complaints, Claims and Adjustments, Job application letters - Biodata, Covering Letter, Intervier Letters, Letter of Reference, Memos, Minutes, Email etiquettes: Formal and Informal emails, E-mail Writing.

5. Reports (5 + 1)

Types of Business Reports - Format, Choice of Vocabulary, Coherence and Cohesion, Organisation reports by individual, New report introduction, Report writing, Basic features of a report, Types of reports, Planning the Report, Writing the report, Difference between Report and Proposal, Writing Business Proposals.

Contents ...

1. Introduction to Managerial Communication — 1.1 – 1.128

2. Managerial Writing — 2.1 – 2.52

3. Effective Presentations — 3.1 – 3.16

4. Interview Skills — 4.1 – 4.22

5. Report Writing — 5.1 – 5.14

Appendix: Business Correspondence (Only for MPM) — A.1 – A.28

Case Studies — C.1 – C.8

Annexure — P.1 – P.2

Chapter 1...

Introduction to Managerial Communication

Contents ...

1.1 Principles of Effective Communication
    1.1.1 Introduction
    1.1.2 Distinction between Management Communication, Organisational Communication and Corporate Communication
    1.1.3 Role and Importance of Managerial Communication
    1.1.4 Characteristics of Present Day Organisations
    1.1.5 Characteristics of Business Communication in a Dynamic Work Place
    1.1.6 Communication Process
    1.1.7 Characteristics of Effective Business Communication
    1.1.8 Communication Gap
    1.1.9 Principles of Communication
    1.1.10 7 C's of Effective Business Communication
    1.1.11 Other Variations of Principles of Effective Business Communication
    1.1.12 Significance of the Principles or Tenets of Effective Business Communication
1.2 Target Group Profile
    1.2.1 Principles for Understanding the Target Audience
1.3 Barriers to Communication
    1.3.1 Major Barriers to Communication
    1.3.2 Levels in Barriers to Communication
    1.3.3 Causes of Barriers in Downward Communication
    1.3.4 Causes of Barriers in Upward Communication
    1.3.5 Barriers in Horizontal Communication
    1.3.6 Role of the Organisation
    1.3.7 Challenges for Organisation
1.4 Reading Skills
    1.4.1 Introduction
    1.4.2 Need to Develop Good Reading Skills
    1.4.3 Reading Techniques
1.5 Listening

- 1.6 Feedback
- 1.7 Principles of Non-verbal Communication
    - 1.7.1 Introduction
    - 1.7.2 History
    - 1.7.3 Significance
    - 1.7.4 Characteristics of Non-verbal Communication
    - 1.7.5 Types of Non-verbal Expressions
    - 1.7.6 Forms of Non-verbal Communication
    - 1.7.7 Principles of Non-verbal Communication
    - 1.7.8 Professional Dressing
- 1.8 Body Language
- 1.9 Role Playing
- 1.10 Debates
    - 1.10.1 Quiz
- 1.11 Group
    - 1.11.1 Defining 'Group'
    - 1.11.2 Characteristics of a Group
    - 1.11.3 Group Communication
    - 1.11.4 Characteristics of Group Communication
    - 1.11.5 Purpose of Group Communication
    - 1.11.6 The basic types of Group Communication
    - 1.11.7 Importance of Group Communication
    - 1.11.8 Facilitation of Group Communication
    - 1.11.9 Positive Factors for Group Communication
    - 1.11.10 Negative Factors for Group Communication
    - 1.11.11 Methods of Reaching Group Decisions
    - 1.11.12 Indications of Breakdown of Group Communication in an Organisation
- 1.12 Meetings
- 1.13 Techniques for Facilitating Discussions
- 1.14 Brainstorming
- 1.15 Negotiations
- 1.16 Group Discussion
- 1.17 Other Aspects of Communication
    - 1.17.1 Cross Cultural Dimensions of Business Communication
    - 1.17.2 Cross Cultural Business Communication
- 1.18 Technology and Communication
- 1.19 Ethical and Legal Issues in Business Communication
    - Points to Remember
    - Questions for Discussion

Learning Objectives ...

➢ To develop an understanding and awareness of managerial communication
➢ To get acquainted with the principles of effective communication, target group profile, barriers of communication, reading skills, listening and feedback
➢ To discuss the principles of non-verbal communication and its various aspects
➢ To be aware of what role playing in and the various types of managerial speeches
➢ To learn about group communication and other aspects of communication

Synopsis

Importance of Communication

- Communication is essential for the development of the individual, organisation, society, and the country.
- Raises awareness at all levels. Business communication meets the information needs of the organisation.
- Motivates the people in the organisation to work towards a purpose.
- Good communication is essential for proper planning and coordination of all organisational activities. It helps the administration in maintaining proper work flow, arriving at quick and well-informed decisions and in implementing them.
- Good all-round communication helps in effective team building and better job performance.
- A Manager's/ Executive's success depends on his ability to understand the needs and requirements of his superiors, subordinates and customers and use this knowledge effectively.
- Effective and timely communication promotes cordial relations and work culture and creates a healthy and happy environment within the organisation and its contacts outside.
- Without communication skills, it is not possible to maintain good human relations.

People in organisations usually spend over 75 per cent of their daily time on communication through writing, reading, listening, speaking, discussions etc. Effective communication is an essential component for organisational success. Needless to say, a person who has excellent communication skills apart from core subject expertise, stands a better chance of succeeding. Communication skills hold the key to better career prospects. Those who do not get selected for a post or a promotion may be having excellent technical knowledge, but without the ability to communicate and interact with others, they are less effective in the organisation. Communication skills are as important as technical qualifications for youngsters aiming at a bright career. Poor communication skills, low confidence levels and improper body language can impede their progress, especially in these days of stiff competition. Managers have to demonstrate good command over the language, and develop good verbal and non-verbal communication skills.

Organisations also play a very vital role in maintaining a conducive environment. They can promote a sound organisational culture and install and maintain an appropriate communication infrastructure. It can motivate the employees at all levels to operate effectively, be open to new ideas and work cohesively towards the vision and goals of the organisation. All barriers to effective communication should be removed, so that the organisation functions as a well-orchestrated entity.

1.1 Principles of Effective Communication

"Communication works for those who work at it." — **John Powell**

Studies show that managers spend about 50 to 80% of their time communicating, but their job description would not show communication specifically as an area of responsibility.

1.1.1 Introduction

The crucial role of communication in an organisation can be seen from the following statements:

- **Scott and Sprige** underline the importance of communication in an organisation by saying that *"Communication is the process involving the transmission and accurate replication of ideas reinforced by feedback purporting to stimulate actions to accomplish organisational goals."*

- **Chester Barnard**, *"In an exhaustive theory of organisation, communication would occupy a central place because the structure, extensiveness and scope of organisations are almost entirely determined by communication techniques."*

- **Simon**, *"The question to be asked of any administrative process is: How does it influence the decisions of the individuals without communication, the answer must always be: It does not influence them at all."*

1.1.2 Distinction between Management Communication, Organisational Communication and Corporate Communication

Managerial Communication forms a significant part of the larger discipline of communication studies. It deals with various issues and influences that affect communication within an organisation and ways to make it effective.

Organisational Communication deals with the consideration, analysis and criticism of the role of communication in the context of the total organisational environment and activities.

The term 'organisational communication' has a much wider connotation, as it is concerned with various aspects of an organisation, such as its goals, strategy, policies, structure, culture and behaviour as an organisation, and the overall environment in which its employees function. The entire range of these organisational issues determines the effectiveness of managerial communication.

From the perspective of public relations, the term 'Corporate Communications' is used to cover the three distinct sets of tasks of an organisation requiring different levels of interdependent planning and communication activities. Together, these three communication activities knit the organisation into a whole. The three levels of communication are:

- **Management communications,** i.e., communications between the management and its internal and external audiences. This level of communication relies heavily on inputs from the other two, viz., marketing and organisational communication.
- **Marketing communications** consist of product or service advertisement through various media including direct mail, personal selling and sponsorship of various causes and events relevant for the growth of the business.
- **Organisational communications** relate to employee communication, public relations and corporate image building, investor relationships, environmental communications etc.

According to this, Corporate Communication is the sum total of all communications within the organisation and with outside agencies and the public. It implies the development of a common strategic framework with a coherent approach to the development of communications in the organisation. It is concerned not only with the effectiveness of individual managers or the organisation, but also with the image of the organisation. It is perceived as an integrative communication structure linking all stakeholders to the organisation for projecting a shared vision, viz., the corporate brand.

1.1.3 Role and Importance of Managerial Communication

Communication can best be summarised as the transmission of a message from a sender to a receiver in an understandable manner. It is a central activity in all human and organisational activities. In organisations, it goes beyond transmission of a message or the message itself. It is the mutual goal oriented exchange of understanding between the sender and the receiver, in an effective manner. Peter Drucker, one of the greatest management thinkers of our time says: *"For managers in big organisations ... this ability to express oneself is perhaps the most important of all the skills a person can possess."*

It is often said that business is communication and communication is business. It brings home the significance of communication in an orgnisation. In order to run a business efficiently and successfully, people in the organisation must communicate using a business language that the receivers understand and respond to positively. It is essential to people who work in cooperation with others and need to coordinate their activities. It is essential for transfer of knowledge from one person to another and to communicate various issues like, jobs to be performed, methods to be used, responsibilities, suggestions, agreements, situational factors, work status, etc. The process of communication in an organisation is a continuous one, whether it is internal or with outside stakeholders. Effective communication creates a positive environment for the organisation to succeed and grow.

Communication is the major force in shaping the organisation. It is the *crucial link between the organisational purpose and the participants* in the organisation who make it work. It defines the superior-subordinate relationships. Thus, it has a *behavioural component*. Communication is the only means by which a person can influence others and hence, it is one of the most important topics in the study of *organisational behaviour*. (The importance of other elements in organisational behaviour like organisation structure, decision making process, motivation, stress levels etc., cannot be ignored.) The behaviours observed in an organisation are important indicators in the communication process of the organisation and in its overall success. The manner in which individuals perceive and talk to each other at work about different issues is a major determinant of the success of a business.

In every organisation, communication is initiated with some purpose. External communication with shareholders, customers, suppliers or members of the society is as important as communication within the organisation. Business administration is a collective enterprise. Without communication, between two different departments, there will be no co-ordination. The strength of an organisation is its teamwork and without communication, teamwork is not possible.

It has been proven that poor communication reduces quality, weakens productivity, and eventually leads to frustration, anger and a lack of trust among individuals within the organisation. In the day-to-day activities of the organisation as well as in implementing any activity of strategic importance effective communication becomes one of the most crucial prerequisites. It is reported that managers on an average, spend about 75 per cent of their time in communicating, exchanging information, giving instructions or presenting their points of view. Hence, from a business perspective, effective communication is an absolute imperative, because it commonly *defines the difference between success and failure or profit and loss*. Every business person needs to understand the fundamentals of effective communication and practice them, as good communication skills make the biggest relative contribution to the functioning of an effective manager.

1.1.4 Characteristics of Present Day Organisations

1. Globalisation and Diversity which has resulted in widening of interaction among people from all parts of the globe
2. Advances in technology and use of increasingly varied assets and processes in industry and business
3. Increasing pressure on efficient utilisation of resources because of increasing competition

4. Higher consumption levels induced by growing population and rising aspirations of consumers, especially in the developing world
5. Use of more complex decision making processes
6. Accelerating pace of change in business, such as team based organisations that demands ever increasing need for motivating people and obtaining their cooperation
7. Age of Information Technology, requiring newer communication skills

The basic functions of management (Planning, Organising, Staffing, Directing and Controlling) cannot be performed well without effective communication. Organisational communication involves constant flow of information. Organisations these days are very large. They involve a number of people. There are various *levels of hierarchy* in an organisation. The greater the number of levels, the more difficult is the job of managing the organisation. Communication here plays a very important role in the process of directing and controlling the people in the organisation. There should be effective communication between superiors and subordinates in an organisation, and between the organisation and the society at large (for example between management and trade unions). It is essential for the success and growth of an organisation.

1.1.5 Characteristics of Business Communication in a Dynamic Work Place

Business Communication is *goal oriented*. It is regulated by certain *rules and norms*. These rules, regulations and policies of a company have to be communicated to people within and outside the organisation. Effective business communication helps in *building the goodwill* of an organisation.

Feedback is an integral part of business communication. Immediate feedback can be obtained and misunderstandings if any can be avoided if the communication process is effective. It is very essential for employees of an organisation to develop good, responsive communication skills.

Communication can be said to be *effective* if the message is correct, complete and properly communicated to elicit the required response from the receiver. It is therefore necessary to acquire proper communication skills. In any organisation, a variety of *communication situations* arise. There may be letters of enquiry, complaints, orders and so on. It may be towards negotiating business deals, or even lobbying with the government for a favourable decision. Replies to business letters have to be very tactful, courteous and positive and not offensive. Business relations must continue in spite of lapses, drawbacks, misunderstandings etc. These skills must therefore be developed for the success of the business.

Without *effective communication* it is impossible to pass on information, educate and train employees for better performance and motivate them. It would be impossible to advice them, warn them or raise their morale. By adopting suitable communication strategies and practices, *good relationships* can be developed within the organisation and with outside agencies like the customers, suppliers, financiers etc. Absence of communication or prevalence of communication gap would result in misunderstandings, whereas, frequent, positive communication helps in creating more goodwill for the organisation. For instance, a letter acknowledging the customer who places large orders and pays his bill regularly can go a long way in retaining his goodwill and loyalty.

The business executive is concerned with better understanding among all stakeholders. He is interested in overcoming barriers to communication at all levels. As such, communication skills are needed at all levels relevant to the positions held by them. This is shown in the following diagram.

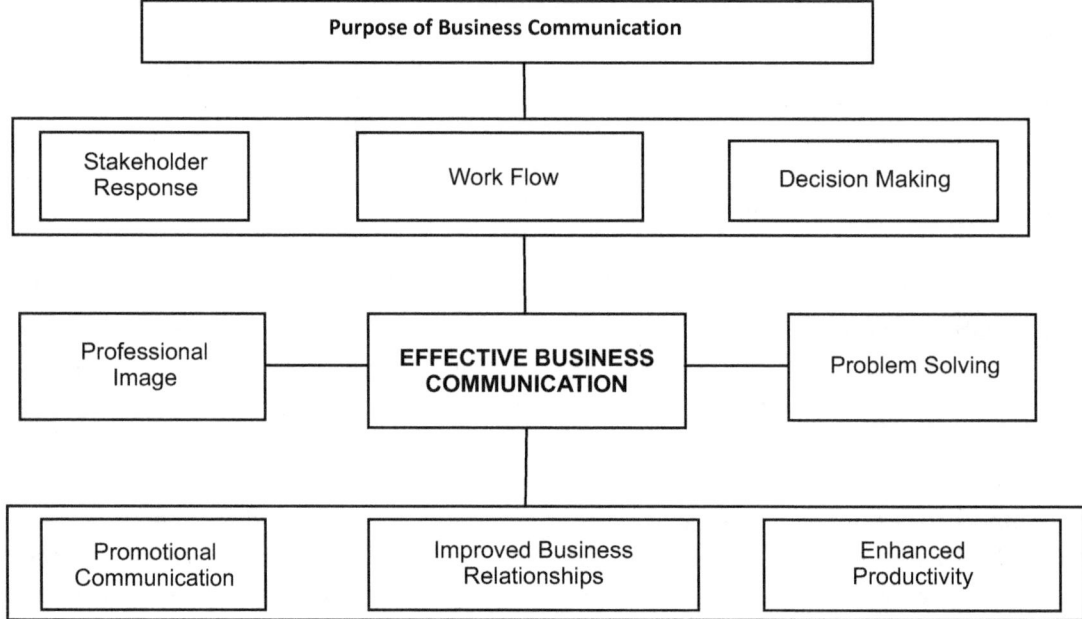

Fig. 1.1: Purpose of Business Communication

1.1.6 Communication Process

The manner in which individuals in an organisation perceive each other at work and communicate about different issues is a major factor determining the success of the organisation. It goes without saying that poor communication reduces the effectiveness and efficiency of the organisation and if due care is not taken, it can weaken all departments. Quality suffers, productivity gets affected, and eventually the situation can go out of control leading to reduced trust among individuals within the organisation, frustration and anger. This can finally get reflected in poor performance of the organisation in the market.

The communication process is the guide toward realising effective communication. It promotes sharing of a common meaning between the sender and the receiver. Individuals who understand and follow the communication process will have paved their way for becoming more productive in every aspect of their profession and set an example for the others. Effective communication leads to all round understanding, trust, shared goals and high achievements.

The communication process is made up of four key components, viz., encoding, medium of transmission, decoding, and feedback. There are also two other very important factors in the process, the sender and the receiver. The communication process begins with the sender and ends with the receiver.

1. **The Encoder:** All communication begins with the sender. The sender could be an individual, group, or organisation who initiates the communication and hence the onus of leading the process in to an effective course and getting the desired response rests with this source. The message is not a mere bunch of words, but goes beyond. As Davis has said, " The motto should be: Don't start talking until you start thinking," Considering the purpose of communication and the nature of the person to whom the idea is to be communicated, the sender reduces it to its essential components. Much depends on the sender's knowledge, skill, perceptions, experiences, attitudes, and cultural background, as they influence the initial message. "The written words, spoken words, and non-verbal language selected are paramount in ensuring the receiver interprets the message as intended by the sender" (Burnett & Dollar, 1989).

2. **Symbols Used:**

   "When we speak, the speech is a message; when we write, the writing is the message, when we paint, the picture is the message, and when we gesture, the movements of our arms and the expression on our faces are the messages."

   The first step in sending the message is encoding, or translating information into a message in the form of symbols that represent ideas or concepts that the receiver understands. The symbols can take on numerous forms such as, languages, words, or gestures. The encoding process begins when the sender decides what he/she wants to transmit. As stated earlier, this decision is influenced by what he/she knows or believes about the receivers, and the content he/she would include in the message to meet the receiver's requirements. While doing so, the ender or the encoder should use the symbols the receiver is familiar with. An effective encoder will view the message he/she is sending from the perspective of the decoder or the receiver. The sender then encodes the thought into some form of a logical and coded message, which may be oral or written. The most common form of encoding is the use of words. The message may be transmitted in verbal form or by letter, telegram, email etc. As the sender plans the issuance of his message, he/she considers the knowledge the receiver has of the subject matter and other background information.

The four conditions that influence the encoded message according to *Berlo* are:

(a) Skill,

(b) Attitudes,

(c) Knowledge and

(d) Socio-cultural system.

A person's success in communicating is dependent on his writing, speaking, reading, listening, analytical, reasoning and interpretation skills. Attitudes, too, influence one's behaviour.

3. **Channel:** To begin transmitting the message, the sender uses some kind of channel (also called a medium). Most channels are either oral or written, but currently visual channels are becoming more common as technology expands. Common channels include the telephone, and a variety of written forms such as memos, letters, and reports, sent through various data transmitting services. The effectiveness of the various channels fluctuates depending on the characteristics of the communication. For example, when immediate feedback is necessary, oral communication channels are more effective because any uncertainties can be cleared immediately. In a situation where the message must be delivered to more than a small group of people, written channels are often more effective, though teleconferencing and videoconferencing permit both voice and data to communicated among individuals and groups. Oral and written channels could be used to supplement each other.

   The choice of the channel determines the effectiveness of the receiver's understanding. The sender may ask himself/herself a number of questions in this regard:

   - Is the message going to someone inside or outside the organisation?
   - Is it urgent?
   - Is immediate feedback extremely important?
   - Is it necessary to create a document or a permanent record?
   - Is the content complicated, controversial, or private?
   - What oral and written communication skills does the receiver possess?
   - Which is the channel preferred by the receiver, so that the desired feedback can be obtained without undue loss of time?

4. **Decoding:** The channel selection is followed by decoding done by the receiver. The message is received and examined by the decoder, who then interprets it and assigns some meaning to it. The decoding or processing stage corresponds to interpretation of the symbols sent by the sender. In this process, the receiver translates the message to his/her own set of experiences and assigns meaning to the symbols. The communication is successful when the receiver interprets the sender's message the way it was intended.

5. **Receiver:** The receiver is the individual or group of individuals to whom the message is directed. The manner or extent to which this person or group of persons comprehend the message and interpret it will depend on a number of factors, such as: (a) the extent or depth of knowledge they possess about the subject, (b) their receptivity to the message, and (c) the mutual understanding and trust between the sender and the receiver. As in the case of the sender, the manner in which the receiver interprets is influenced by his/her knowledge, skills, perceptions, experiences, attitudes and culture.

6. **Feedback:** This is the final link in the chain of the communication process. After receiving a message and interpreting it, the receiver signals his/her response to the sender. The signal may take the form of a desired action, spoken comment, a long sigh, a written message, a smile, or some other action. "Even a lack of response, is in a sense, a form of response" (Bovee & Thill, 1992). The feedback helps the sender confirm whether the receiver has interpreted the message correctly or not. It is a key component in the communication process as it allows the sender to evaluate the effectiveness of the message. The receiver of the message now becomes the sender and the original sender, the receiver. One round of the cycle of communication is completed by the decoding of the feedback by the original sender. Based on that, the sender may consider corrective action if there is a misunderstood message. If the feedback is relevant and encouraging, it is known as positive feedback. Feedback such as yawns, signs of inattention etc., can be perceived as punishing and is known as negative feedback. "Feedback plays an important role by indicating significant communication barriers: differences in background, different interpretations of words, and differing emotional reactions" (Bovee & Thill, 1992).

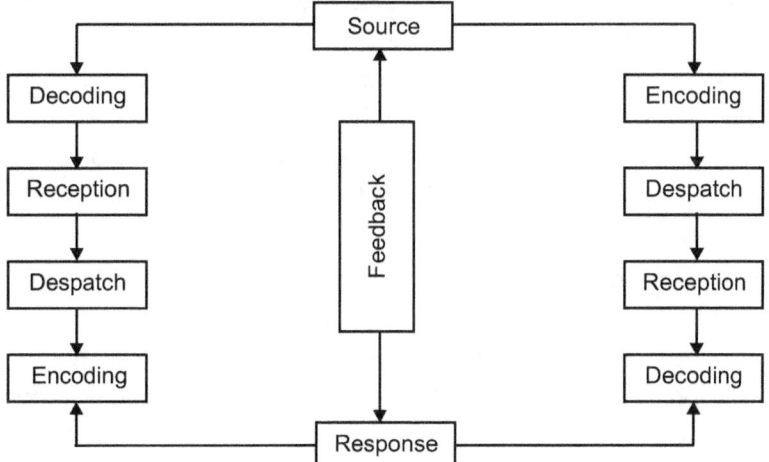

Fig. 1.2: Communication Process

1.1.7 Characteristics of Effective Business Communication

The following figure represents the characteristics of a good communication process in an organisation.

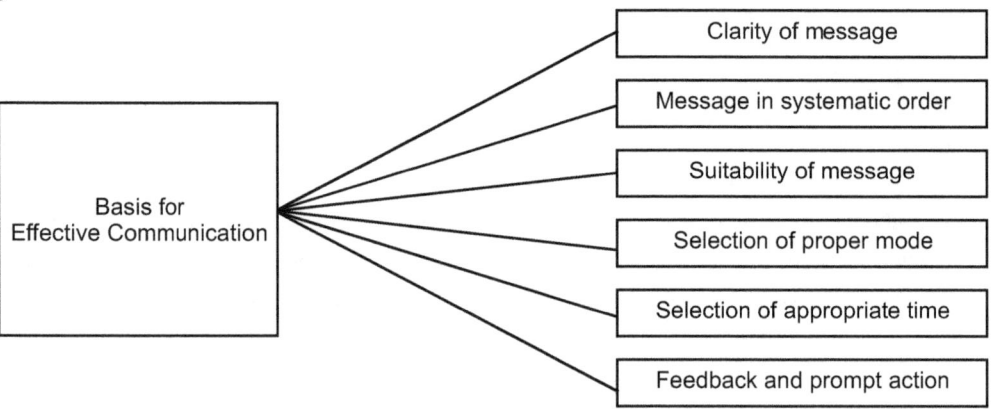

Fig. 1.3: Basis for Effective Communication

1. **Clarity about the Purpose of Communication:** Before beginning the process of communication the sender should be clear about the purpose, and the objectives, sift out all irrelevant material and make the message precise, intelligible and effective. The ideas should be worded precisely. The message should be clear and to the point and presented in a manner which is easy to understand, so that the receiver can respond correctly. Vague ideas and ambiguity should be avoided at all costs, to make communication effective. To get correct feedback, the sender must send correct information. Sending the correct information in a precise manner and highlighting the crucial facts will ensure that the message is easily understood. There should be consistency in expression and consistency in all the messages. Any type of contradictory words should be avoided. For instance, if the sender gives a particular view point in one message and in the next, he changes it altogether without explaining the underlying reason for this shift, he will have created confusion in the mind of the receiver. Any information to be conveyed, should be adequate and to the point. Unnecessary explanations or information should be avoided, as that will distract the attention of the receiver.

2. **Systematic Arrangement of the Message:** The message to be conveyed, whether spoken or written, must be organised in a systematic manner. If the points to be communicated are not properly ordered and the receiver is required to go back and forth while trying to understand the meaning, such a communication can only create confusion and frustration in the mind of the receiver. This will lead to unwanted doubts, calls for clarification etc. In written messages, proper attention should also be given towards neatness, type-spacing, paragraphs, style, and layout of the matter.

3. **Understanding the Needs of the Receiver:** The message to be conveyed should be suitable to the background, status and needs of the receiver. The message should be encoded in language, pictures or symbols which can be easily understood. For instance, persons with difficulties in hearing or sight should be treated appropriately such that the message is understood by them.

4. **Selection of Proper Media:** Different media of communication are available and in these days of information technology, the range is ever-widening. If one wants to place order for goods, one can go personally, send a messenger, write a letter, send a telegram or telephone the message, or opt for on-line shopping.

5. **Selection of Appropriate Time:** Many messages fail to achieve result because they do not reach their destination at an appropriate time. The sender has to assess the time it takes for the message to physically reach the receiver and also the time required for the receiver to take necessary action. For instance, the intended receiver may be ill or on vacation, the company at the receiving end is being restructured, it may be the holiday season at the receiver's end, there may be natural calamities like hurricanes, snow blizzards etc., disrupting the entire communication process. Thus, there are various situations requiring the sender to be aware of the circumstances of the receiver, time the messages and follow it up if required.

6. **Feedback and Prompt Action on Receiving Response:** Communication should be such as to make the receiver understand the purport of the message and send response as per the requirement and need of the sender. Feedback from the receiver helps to ascertain that the message has been understood in the manner desired by the sender. It indicates if there are any misunderstandings or doubts in the mind of the receiver. The sender can take remedial action on the basis of this. If the message is understood properly, proper feedback will be given. It should be remembered that, "communication is not a substitute for good management, but it is required for good management to operate effectively and efficiently".

1.1.8 Communication Gap

A favourable communication situation is said to exist when the sender receives correct or expected feedback from the recipient. If the feedback is not clear or correct, it results in a communication gap and can indicate the following:

- The message has not been clearly or properly understood by the receiver.
- The message was not correct, hence not understood properly by the receiver.
- The language in which the message was sent was not understood by the receiver.
- The media selected was not the most effective one.
- The timing of the message was not properly thought out.

Therefore, while sending a message, it is imperative that the sender takes into consideration the receiver's circumstances to elicit proper response.

1.1.9 Principles of Communication

1. **Principle of Completeness and Adequacy:** Whatever is to be communicated should be adequate and complete in all respects. Insufficient or inadequate statements of communication may create misunderstandings in the mind of the receiver resulting in delays. Consequently, original plans may not be successfully executed. The adequacy of the information also depends upon the power of understanding of the receiver of the message.

2. **Principle of Consistency:** The message communicated should be consistent with overall objectives, policies, programmes and procedures of the organisation. There should not be any difference between the communicator's statement and his action.

3. **Medium of Communication:** The choice of the medium depends on the circumstances. For instance, if the goods are required urgently, a telephonic order can be placed to be confirmed by a letter. As long as the message is clear and contains enough descriptions, technical or otherwise, it would be effective. Unnecessarily difficult, complicated and technical words should be avoided. If the message has legal implications, it would be proper to create a written document. For long messages, written letters are more appropriate, while, for short messages, telephone or other verbal means of communication should be used. In certain cases, to ensure better impact, the sender may adopt or supplement the message, by using an informal channel.

4. **Principle of Timeliness:** Sending messages in time and at the right time to be received at the other end is also important. If the message is sent too early, it is likely that it will slip out of the receiver's memory. On the other hand, if it is too close to an expected result, it may cause disruptions.

5. **Principle of Information:** In the beginning, the sender of the message must have perfect clarity in his own mind about what is to be communicated, the facts and figures, his source of information etc. Where there is proper understanding there is effective communication. The communicator as well as the receiver should sincerely participate in the process of communication. There should be a perfect understanding between both the parties.

6. **Principle of Channel or Media Adaptation:** Appropriate channels of communication should be available. The choice of any communication channel depends upon the content or matter of the message to be conveyed and importance and urgency of the matter.

7. **Principle of Appropriate Time Element:** The sender of the message must take into consideration the element of time while conveying the message. If the time is unsuitable for the receiver, it may result in failure.

8. **Principle of Integration:** The communication structure within the organisation should be well-integrated, so that each person knows his/her line of communication and the channel to choose from. For instance, departmental structure of an organisation places some duties and responsibilities at various levels in each department. Once this sort of demarcation is understood, the question of stepping into each other's jurisdiction will not arrive. For instance, the purchase department and quality department are responsible for choosing and approving a material, component or sub-assembly. It should be clear who will correspond with the supplier in case of quality issue. It is necessary to prepare an integrated system of communication so that there is minimum confusion and the enterprise can achieve its goals. Communication in an organisation functions almost like blood vessels and arteries in the human body. As it is a means to an end, it should be free from any personal prejudices.

9. **Principle of Flexibility:** Any organisation, no matter how big or small it is, should have a system of communication, which is reviewed and kept updated. It should be flexible enough to suit the changing requirements of the organisation, emerging working techniques as well as new communication systems or methods without much resistance and difficulties.

10. **Principle of Informality:** Managements cannot afford to be very rigid and very formal. Cordial relationships within the organisation often call for developing informal channels and methods to supplement the formal framework of its communication system.

11. **Principle of Feedback:** Communication is not a substitute for good management but it is the lifeblood of good management. There should always be scope for feedback, suggestions and even constructive criticism from the receiver of the message. Such openness can lead to expression of creative ideas. The ambience of the organisation should be such that the seniors can convey the required messages or orders and get a proper response from the receiver without fear or favour. Managements should adopt and encourage a system of communication that promotes a free and frank atmosphere in the company leading to the constant flow of information in all directions.

12. **Conciseness:** The sender of the message should reflect on the message being sent, for its simplicity and conciseness. This simplicity should be reflected in its wording and tone, the overall situation of the reader and also the result expected. This will make the receiver take the communication seriously. It means that the sender is conscious of the entire communication environment. He/she should mean what they say, say it effectively and take responsibility for the statements made in the message. It should be devoid of unnecessary details that may either distract or confuse the receiver. This will save a lot of time wasted in seeking clarifications.

13. **Attractiveness:** The presentation of the message should be attractive enough to draw the attention of the receiver. This depends on the nature of the message that is being sent. If it is a production or sales target to be communicated within the department, a simple statement would serve the purpose better. If it is a technical report or presentation, the receiver would be looking for technical details. In such a report, graphs, charts and sketches can carry the message much better than a wordy description.

14. **Correctness:** Accuracy and authenticity of the message is a significant factor in transmitting messages. The source of information should be known to the sender and mentioned in the message where necessary. Incorrectness of any message may create confusion in the mind of the listener or reader and may ultimately spoil the relations in the group or organisation. It is, therefore, necessary for the sender to take charge, and set forth details which are correct and authentic. Passing on the blame to someone else if the relationship sours, spoils the image of the organisation.

15. **Consideration:** When any message is prepared, one has to consider the feelings, emotions and sentiments of the receiver. It is necessary to understand the background of the person, who receives the message. This will ensure better impact of the message.

16. **Courtesy:** The idea of courtesy in transmitting the message includes polite manners and expressions. As far as possible, harsh expressions should be avoided while preparing the message as well as while acknowledging the message received.

17. **Careful use of Body Language:** Body language plays a vital role, particularly in oral communication. It adds many explained ideas into expressions. Facial expressions and eye contact contributes in transmitting the messages.

These principles of communication are depicted in the following diagram:

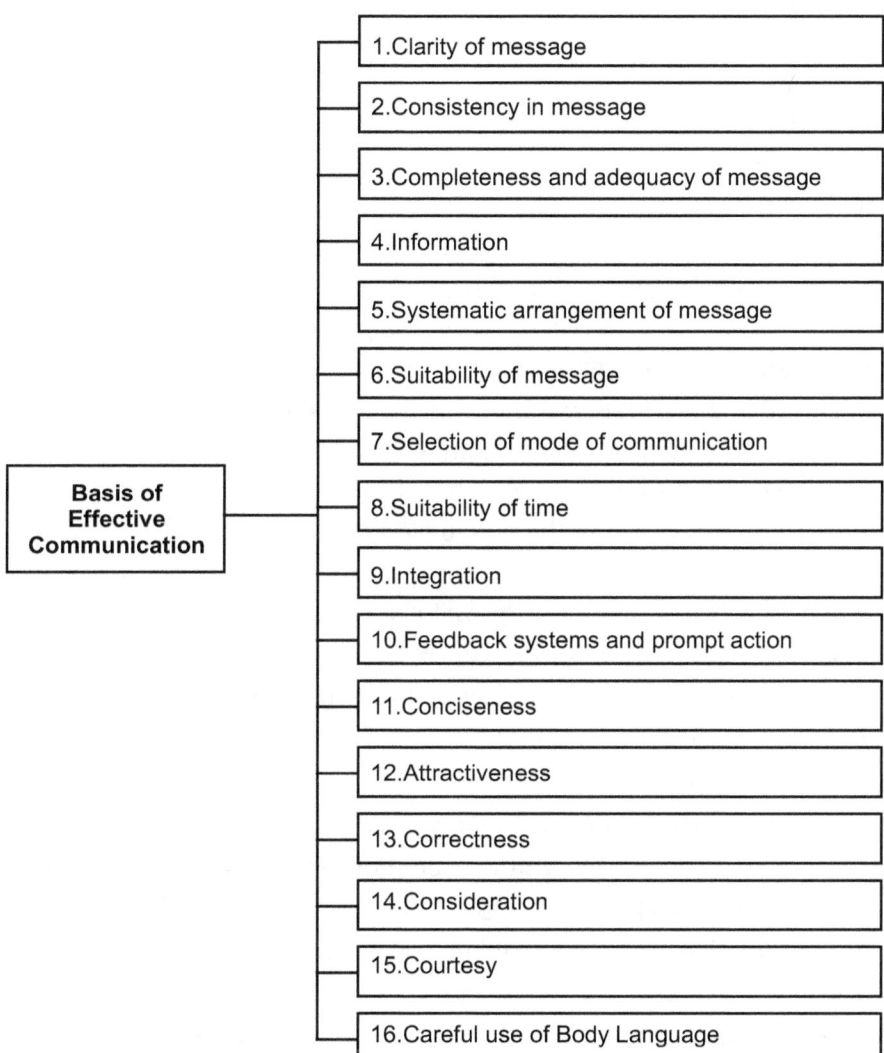

1.1.10 7C's of Effective Business Communication

The message is said to be effective when the receiver understands the same meaning that the sender had intended to convey. For any communication in business, in order to be effective, it must have seven qualities.

The 7Cs of Communication were first enunciated in 1952 by University of Wisconsin Professors Scott M. Cutlip and Allen H. Center in their classic work *'Effective Public Relations'*.

The original 7 Cs of Cutlip and Center are:
1. Correctness
2. Clarity
3. Conciseness
4. Completeness
5. Consideration
6. Concreteness
7. Courtesy

1. Correctness: While sending the message, the sender has to check the following for correctness. *A little time taken to review the message before it is sent can go a long way in creating a good image of the organisation.*

    (a) Facts being stated and the authenticity of the source and whether the facts can be defended, veracity of the numbers and amounts being incorporated in the message and their source, whether it is too wordy, whether it contains visual representations to strengthen the message etc.

    (b) Adequacy of the information being provided, information that needs to be withheld, whether the message will clarify the matter or create confusion in the mind of the receiver, and whether the communication serves the purpose.

    (c) Correct pronunciation of the receiver's or any others' names and proper spellings if it is a written communication.

    (d) Correct mention of all titles.

    (e) Use of non-discriminatory language.

    (f) Making sure that in the written communication, the spelling, punctuation and grammar and acceptable writing mechanics to be followed.

    (g) The technical terms used should fit the receiver's level of education or knowledge.

    (h) The message is sent at the correct time.

While adding any supporting material, the test of a good communication is in answering the following:

    (a) Will the inclusion of the material make it easier for the receiver to understand?

    (b) Will it help the message achieve its purpose?

    (c) The sender should be in a position to justify the use of each word. It helps if the encoder has comprehensive knowledge about the decoder of the message. The encoder should know the status, knowledge and educational background of the decoder.

    (d) Another point to be remembered is that generally the receiver, if he/she is busy, will not go beyond the first paragraph. Hence, it is necessary to put forth the reference, subject being addressed and the issue in the opening paragraph, with all clarifications like 'why', 'when' etc., in the following paragraphs. Secondly, the editing software does not check all spellings. A second reading of written material is very essential.

> *When the communication is correct, it fits the requirements of the receiver. Correct communication is also error-free communication. Correctness in message helps in building better understanding between the communicating parties.*

  2. **Clarity:** Clarity demands the use of simple language and easy sentence structure in composing the message. The style of communication should be aimed at making the message understood easily. Clarity demands the use of simple language and easy sentence structure in composing the message. The following points should be remembered:
   (a) Minimum number of ideas in each sentence and paragraph,
   (b) Use of short, familiar and conversational words
   (c) Construction of sentences and paragraphs to maintain unity of the idea. The points should be sequenced properly, so that there is no moving back and forth to get the whole idea. This will ensure that there is no confusion in the mind of the decoder.
   (d) Appropriate readability should be achieved by using formal or informal language as required by the situation.
   (e) Where necessary, examples, illustrations and visual aids should be included.

Clarity means being clear about the purpose of the communication and the message itself. If the encoder is not sure, the decoder will not be sure either. When there is clarity in presenting the message, it is easy for the receiver/decoder to comprehend the meaning being conveyed by the sender/encoder. The receiver should not have to 'read between the lines.' The meaning should be clear, and visible up-front and not hidden for the receiver to interpret it as he/she pleases.

Clear messages make use of exact, appropriate and meaningful words. To achieve this, the encoder should have complete clarity of thoughts and ideas in his mind. Only then can he/she present it effectively and also select additional presentation tools to enhance the meaning of message. When the communication is coherent, it becomes logical. All points are connected and relevant to the main topic and the tone and flow of the text is consistent. *A little time taken to think out and plan the message and the manner in which it should be conveyed can reduce confusion, frustration and embarrassment. Clarity makes comprehension easier.*

  3. **Conciseness:** A concise message saves the time of both the sender and the receiver. It is achieved by using including only relevant material and brief, to the point sentences. Any short forms or abbreviations should be explained and then used. Conciseness means that the message is focused and there are no unnecessarily wordy expressions and repetitions.

Unnecessary display of politeness should be avoided. What can be communicated effectively in say, three sentences, should not require six sentences.

While aiming at conciseness, it is necessary to make sure of the following:

(a) Are there any adjectives or "filler words" that can be deleted? This is true for both verbal and written communication. For instance, in verbal communication, mannerisms creep in, such as using fillers like , "you see," "kind of," "literally," "basically," or "I mean," etc.

(b) Unnecessary sentences should be removed.

(c) Repetitions should be avoided. It is not necessary to state the same point several times, in different ways. It means that the sender is underestimating the understanding capacity of the receiver and this can irritate that person.

Achieving conciseness does not mean that there is any compromise on completeness. It is only aimed at avoiding unwanted words or what is known as 'packing material' or 'taking the receiver in circles', which can irritate the receiver. It is achieving efficiency in communication. Conciseness means 'meaning what is said' in the message. It is communicating the message effectively, using the least possible number of words without losing the meaning to be communicated. While being concise, it is necessary to keep in view the other C's as well. Concise communication has the following advantages:

(a) It is both time-saving as well as cost-saving, as it eliminates wordy explanations.

(b) A concise message is crisp and non-repetitive in nature.

(c) When the message is short and complete, there are less chances of making grammatical errors and the need for editing is reduced.

(d) It addresses the issue without the use of excessive and needless words. Thus, the receiver gets to the point immediately. There is no scope for confusion about what the sender wants to communicate.

(e) A concise message is more appealing and comprehensible to the audience.

The general pattern regarding the length and structure of the message should be followed, as it is necessary to sustain the attention of the receiver.

> *Spending some time in planning the message, both verbal and written, and editing the written message can go a long way in making it effective. Conciseness saves the time of both the sender and the receiver without sacrificing on the content.*

4. Completeness: The communication must be complete. It should convey all the facts required by the audience. It involves consideration of all facts and figures to be communicated and also anticipating the response of receiver/ receivers. Hence, it is essential for the sender to understand the background and expectations of the receiver and his/her mindset and convey the message accordingly. If the message is not complete, it will fail to

convince the receiver. Giving partial information would not work in a highly competitive environment. The significance of a complete communication can be seen from the following:
- (a) It develops and enhances the reputation of an organisation.
- (b) It saves cost and time involved in giving additional information every time it is asked for to complete the message.
- (c) A complete communication always gives all the information required by the receiver and hence, leaves no questions in the mind of receiver. It also includes contact name, details, dates, times, locations etc., apart from the main subject.
- (d) It helps in better decision making by the audience/ readers/ receivers of message as they get all desired and crucial information and do not have any doubts to be clarified later. It includes a "call to action", so that the receiver knows exactly what is expected.
- (e) It helps in impressing the audience, influencing them and persuading them in favour of the issue being discussed or the organisation.

Completeness means that the message must contain all the necessary information to bring the required response. The sender should anticipate and answer all the issues or questions that the receiver may raise, with facts and figures. Only if and when necessary, further details can be added.

In a complete message, the receiver has everything he/she needs to be informed and, if applicable, take action. Completeness brings the desired response.

5. Consideration: Consideration means that the sender reads the message from the receiver's point of view and circumstances. It is putting oneself in the place of the receiver while composing a message. It refers to the use of 'You' attitude, emphasises positive pleasant facts, visualising reader's problems, desires, emotions and his response. The points to be noted are:
- (a) The focus should be on YOU instead of I and WE.
- (b) The decoder should show the benefits of following the message and taking suitable action. That will sustain the decoder's interest in the message.
- (c) The emphasis should be on the positive aspects and the entire communication process should display a pleasant demeanour.
- (d) The encoder should take adequate care to win the confidence of the decoder by applying integrity and following basic ethics.

It should be remembered that consideration requires understanding human nature.

6. Concreteness: Concreteness is being clear, definite, specific and focused. It is the opposite of being obscure, vague or general. The facts and figures should be specific. They should be verified and substantiated. The objective is to gain the confidence of the decoder and ensure appropriate action. The following are the essential aspects of concreteness:
- (a) Facts and figures in the message are specific.
- (b) Direct action verbs are used.
- (c) Vivid image building words are used, strengthened by appropriate comparisons. Care should be taken to ensure that these comparisons add to the meaning and not confuse the decoder.

Concreteness reinforces the confidence level of the decoder.

7. Courtesy: In business as in personal communication, care should be taken to ensure that the receiver's feelings are not, for if that happens, the result could be either break in communication or further rancorous or bitter exchange of messages. The outcome for the business would be disastrous. Hence, in business, almost everything starts and ends in courtesy and strengthening goodwill. Courtesy does not mean merely thinking about the receiver but also valuing his/her feelings. It also does not mean being unnecessarily weak or cowardly. Showing courtesy involves:

(a) Using polite words and gestures,
(b) Being appreciative, thoughtful and tactful,
(c) Showing respect to the receiver,
(d) Being sincere,
(e) Not using hurtful, insulting, irritating or discriminatory expressions,
(f) Accepting mistakes and apologising gracefully.

> *Courteous communication is friendly, open, and honest. There are no apparent or hidden insults nor are there passive or aggressive tones. At the same time, it does not indicate weakness on the part of the sender. Courtesy in communication builds goodwill and strengthens relations.*

The 8th C: Consistency: To the above 7 Cs, the eighth one is often added, viz., Consistency, i.e., the message is relevant to the topic and does not contain any extraneous information that distracts the attention of the receiver and distorts the intended message.

1.1.11 Other Variations of Principles of Effective Business Communication

(a) **The Eight Cs of Communication:**
1. **Credibility:** The message should ensure that the receiver develops confidence in the sender.
2. **Context:** The message should make the receiver understand what is required of him/her and give appropriate feedback. The decoder should be in a position to confirm, not contradict or argue with the encoder.
3. **Content:** The content must have meaning to the receiver. It should be relevant and timed appropriately.
4. **Clarity:** The message must be direct and easy to comprehend. Words must mean the same thing to the receiver as they do to the sender.
5. **Continuity:** There should be consistent to the stand or view point of the encoder and every time it is referred to, the same stand should be continued.
6. **Consistency:** The message must be consistent with the goals of the organisation and the objectives it has to fulfil.
7. **Channels:** The sender must use channels that the receiver is comfortable with, so that the latter can respond by words or suitable action.

8. **Capability of Audience:** The sender should be aware of the background and status of the receiver and frame the message in such a way that he/she uses the least amount of effort to understand the message. Only then will it be effective.

(b) 10 Cs of Communication:
- Clear,
- Concise,
- Correct,
- Conscious,
- Complete,
- Considerate,
- Courteous,
- Consistent,
- Concrete, and
- Connected

(c) The 7 Tenets of Communication of Legend Inc, an American Advertising Agency

(The Original 7 Cs as documented by Legend Inc in their Project Log as The Seven Tenets of Communication which is referenced to Scott M. Cutlip, Allen H. Center, Effective Public Relations - excerpts)

1. **Credibility:** Communication begins in a climate of trust and belief. This climate is built by the performance of the sender who should reflect an earnest desire to serve the receiver. The receiver will then have high regard for the competency of the sender.
2. **Context:** An advertising/communications programme must square with the realities of its environment. Your daily business activities must confirm, not contradict, the message.
3. **Content:** The message must have meaning and relevance for the receiver. Content determines the audience and vice versa.
4. **Clarity:** The message must be put in simple terms. Words used must have exactly the same meaning to the sender as they do to the receiver. Complex messages must be distilled into simpler terms, and the farther a message must travel, the simpler it should be.
5. **Continuity and Consistency:** Communication is an unending process. It requires repetition to achieve understanding. Repetition, with variation, contributes to learning both facts and attitudes.
6. **Channels:** Use established channels of communication—channels the receiver uses and respects. Creating new channels is difficult.
7. **Capability of Audience:** Communication must take into account the capability of the audience. Communications are most effective when they require the least effort on the part of the recipient.

8. **Four Ss of Communication:** Besides the 7 Cs, the following four principles have become popular:

   (a) **Shortness:** Shortness 'economises' on words. Message should be as brief as possible. While delivering lengthy messages, the sender will have ample opportunity to make mistakes, and the receiver may also lose patience.

   (b) **Simplicity:** Simplicity impresses. The term KISS stands for 'keep it simple and short.' It is better to avoid high sounding, pompous and complex words, phrases and ideas. By having clarity of thought, and using simple, common and popular vocabulary, the sender can ensure that the receiver understands the message and gives proper feedback. It is said that confused persons employ confusing words that leave the receiver confused.

   (c) **Strength:** Strength of the message helps in convincing the receivers and getting proper response. This means that the sender has to put together all the necessary facts and figures and anticipate the questions while framing the message. The message should speak for the sender's conviction. Half-hearted statements, giving falsehoods etc., erode the credibility of the sender.

   (d) **Sincerity:** The quality of sincerity adds to the credibility of the sender. It appeals to everyone who receives the message.

1.1.12 Significance of the Principles or Tenets of Effective Business Communication

Since the first enunciation by Cutlip and Center, various versions of these principles have emerged, indicating the importance of effective business communication. All these efforts highlight the fact that to make the communication process in a business successful, the encoder needs to take utmost care while sending a message. Random and careless messages without much thought can only damage relationships and prove detrimental for the organisation. The objective of the communication process is totally lost. This brings us to the need to understand another crucial topic, the very opposite of effective communication, viz., Barriers of Communication that can disrupt the entire process and the means of overcoming them.

1.2 Target Group Profile

'Nothing is so simple that it cannot be misunderstood... '

Freeman Teague, Jr.

Communication is the key factor in the success of any organisation. It is the fabric of a company that helps employees succeed at their job, relate to the public and conduct business with customers and other businesses. Effective communication is an essential component of organisational success whether it is at the interpersonal, intergroup, intra-group, organisational, or external levels. Managerial communication involves formal and

informal communications throughout the organisation and with the other organisations with which it works. Communication in an organisation is at several levels, such as:
- Communication to employees,
- Communication with employees
- Communication from employees, and
- Communication with other stakeholders.

Whatever the level, effective communication requires a thorough understanding of the recipient. The recipient, while sending the feedback or response, should be able to judge the sender and his/her expectations and respond accordingly.

A look at the following diagram indicates the importance of understanding the target group (audience), whether it is oral or written communication and while effectively using non-verbal clues or body language. It is necessary to ensure that the receiver understands and interprets the message just as it is intended by the sender. Otherwise, it can create misunderstandings, a lot of back and forth of explanations, delays as a result or even breakdown of communication.

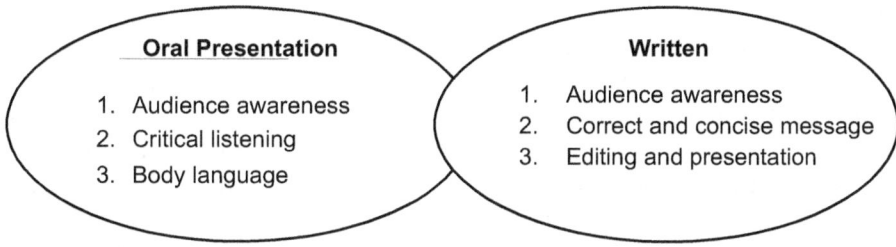

Fig. 1.4

Some leaders tend to think that they have communicated once they have passed on the message. However, it should be remembered that a message has NOT been communicated unless it is understood by the receiver. In other words, the receiver has decoded the message and given a feedback to the sender indicating that the receiver has understood the message and its level of importance, and also the action expected from him/her. It is not just the responsibility of the sender. **All parties involved must participate to complete the information exchange.** Many physical and psychological barriers exist which act as **filters**. These filters may muffle the message. It is necessary to identify the filters and address them. It is necessary to ensure that:
- The message reaches the receiver in its correct form.
- The audience agrees to the message, and
- They respond accordingly and give necessary feedbacks by way of required response or action expected of them.

The choice of words or language in which a sender encodes a message will influence the quality of communication. Because language is a symbolic representation of the sender's thought process, there is always room for interpretation and distortion of the meaning. Hence the sender of the message has to be careful. *The same word could mean different things for different people.*

1.2.1 Principles for understanding the Target Audience

- The educational, training and knowledge level of the recipient. In a communication to a team of technical persons where feedback and action is desired, all facts and figures should be laid out in an understandable and orderly manner. On the other hand, while communicating with lay persons in a business, giving too much technical details will defeat the purpose. The speaker must be very careful about his selection of words and content. For instance, when the teacher uses very difficult or strange words the students may not comprehend them.
- The communicator will also determine the extent of usage of graphics, charts, maps, diagrams etc., depending on the above considerations.
- The gender of the recipient may also determine the choice of words in a message as also the body language.
- Level at which communication takes place: In an organisation, communication between employees depends on the direction of message flow – upward from employee to superiors, superiors to employees and among employees at the same level.
- Stakeholders involved: Again, when outside stakeholders are involved, apart from the immediate objective, maintenance of goodwill and broad interest of the organisation will become the overriding concern. For instance, when a customer intends to purchase a mobile phone, he will be more inclined to purchase the handset from that store where the salesman gives an impressive demonstration of suitable products after understanding the requirements and the budget of the customer. It depends on the skill of the salesman to understand the target audience and communicate in a manner to influence the listeners so that they respond to him in a way he actually wants i.e. purchase the handset and increase his billing.
- Nature of the audience – whether active or passive. It is necessary to understand whether the audience is active and is contemplating a response or is a passive receiver of the message and is not expected to offer any feedback.
- Perceptional differences: There could be differences in the perceptions of the communicator and the recipient, which in turn may also depend on the socio-economic and cultural background, gender, age, education, exposure, experience and attitude of the receiver. Due to various factors, persons can develop biases. The sender of the message, while deciding on the choice of words, language and tone of a communication should remember this.
- Timing of the communication: An understanding of the target audience will also indicate the right timing of the message. The receiver may be spending a lot of time on the shop floor with a lot of noisy operations going on. There may be other distractions. The recipient may be going through a trying time and is emotionally drained when he gets a communication which may impede his understanding of the message or its timing and urgency properly. Similarly, when one or both of the persons in the process of communication is indisposed or when there is any kind of discomfort on either part, communication becomes ineffective.

> In a political meeting, the leader delivers a speech to the audience in his constituency urging for votes. He tries to convince the crowd in the best possible way he can so that he emerges as a winner. What is he actually doing?
>
> He is delivering his speech in a manner that the listeners are willing to absorb and would get convinced enough to cast their votes in his favour, or in other words respond in the same manner the speaker wanted them to. Here the leader or the speaker or the sender is the centre of attraction and the crowd is simply the passive listeners. However, the speaker will not be effective if he does not know the general background of the audience, their burning issues and their expectations. While addressing a constituency comprising of less privileged persons, if he talks of larger policy issues, he will have wasted his opportunity and the audience would go back without any inputs or guidance about the politician's intentions to solve their immediate problems.
>
> The politician must understand the needs of the people in his constituency. It could be reduction in fuel prices, better transport system, safety of girls, improvements in the school system etc., and then design his speech. His speech should address all the major issues and focus on providing the solutions to their problems. His tone and pitch should also be modulated enough for the people to hear and understand the speech properly. Stammering, getting nervous in between, mumbling, not facing the audience etc., can add to the general confusion. Blank expressions, confused looks and monotonous pitch all through the speech can nullify its effects of a superbly written speech. To get the desired result, the speaker should know where to lay more stress, and where to highlight in order to influence the listeners.

In the ultimate analysis, success of a communication process depends on the proper understanding of the target audience.

1.3 Barriers to Communication

> *"To effectively communicate, we must realise that we are all different in the way we perceive the world and use this understanding as a guide to our communication with others."*
> — ***Anthony Robbins***

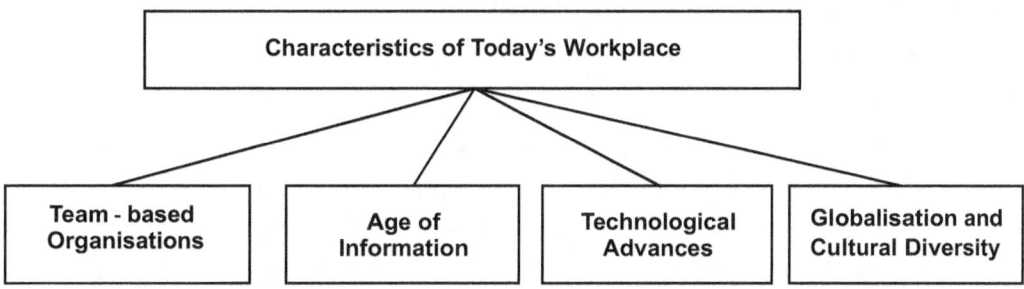

Fig. 1.5: Characteristics of Today's Workplace

1.3.1 Major Barriers to Communication

The three corners of the barriers to communication are:
1. The thought of the sender and the receiver
2. Their speech or delivery of the message, and
3. Their action

Invariably gaps in communication develop as the sender's thought, speech (oral, non-verbal or written) and action do not match with those of the receiver's, or in other words, when the size of the triangle becomes big. Thus, barriers to communication arise from the inherent process of sending / receiving of messages among humans. If the triangle is smaller in size, it means that there is no trust deficit in the individual, group or organisation.

> *The ability to communicate is the primary factor that distinguishes human beings from animals. And it is the ability to communicate well that distinguishes one individual from another.*

Imperfections creep in from different levels of thinking of individuals which act as mental filters. As we have seen, these mental filters are influenced by

- Age,
- Socio-cultural background,
- Experience,
- Wrong choice of words,
- Wrong choice of media, channel, timing etc.

Managers need to overcome these barriers so that they can function more effectively in the organisation and the organisation should recognise the need for this and provide all necessary policy, training and technology deployment to make managerial communication effective.

1.3.2 Levels in Barriers to Communication

Barriers to effective communication within an organisation happen at the following three levels: Personal barriers, Group barriers and Organisational barriers.

- **Personal:** *Communication capability* is a personal skill. The sender of the messages must use words and phrases that the receiver is familiar with so that the latter can understand and respond to them. The sender therefore, has to develop this capability carefully and with diligence. In the absence of suitable choice of words, the message may not invoke the desired response from the receiver. Each area of specialisation requires a unique language format that is peculiar to that profession.

> A manager who has to interact with farmers to sell agricultural inputs or machinery should be in a position to understand issues like crops, cropping pattern, sowing and harvesting seasons, their working patterns, financial issues, attitude of the farmers with respect to change, role of opinion leaders, group dynamics etc., apart from their manner of greeting. However, while reporting back in his office, he will follow the requirements and protocol within the organisation.
>
> Similarly, a scientist interacting within his/her community would use technical terms which are understood by both the parties, but the same scientist, while interacting with lay persons, school children etc., would make the language simpler and easy to understand, with examples from day-to-day life situations.

- *Within the organisation*: Business leaders have to orchestrate the efforts of different kinds of employees, investors, consumers, suppliers etc. They have to handle people with different aspirations and requirements while achieving their goals. Within organisations, communication barriers at various levels can pose serious disruptions in this.

1.3.3 Causes of Barriers in Downward Communication

(i) The attitude of the seniors. They may override the interests of the subordinates due to lack of awareness about them or because of personal biases or preferences. In such cases, messages will not flow freely between the superiors and subordinates, thus affecting the efficiency of the organisation

(ii) Inflexibility of the superiors if they prefer to conform to the organisation structure and the line of communication set forth in it

(iii) Feeling of insecurity. The superiors can then become defensive, and may view any upward communication as a challenge to their authority and importance. They may ignore any communication from the subordinates and even withhold necessary information thus jeopardising work in the organisation

(iv) Lack of confidence in the subordinates and fear that the subordinates would misuse information may make the superiors maintain a distance from them.

(v) The superiors may be hard pressed for time. They may be overburdened with work and consequently have no time to provide information downwards, upwards or horizontally.

(vi) Lack of awareness regarding the critical importance and significance of maintaining a smooth flow of information in all directions within and outside of the organisation.

1.3.4 Causes of Barriers in Upward Communication

(i) Unwillingness to communicate if the subordinate feels that giving a particular piece of information to the superiors may be embarrassing. He/she would then withhold it or delay the communication as much as possible or even modify it so as to protect his/her interests. This can mislead the superiors.

(ii) Lack of proper incentive by way of appreciation may prevent the subordinates from participating in the communication process. It can have a snowballing effect in the organisation. Thus, suggestions from the subordinates with respect to product improvement, improvements to processes and systems can be ignored, thus affecting the growth of the organisation. In fact, the subordinates may have their finger on the pulse of the market and understand the competitive environment much better than the superiors who would be one step removed from them. New recruits in the field of finance may come with a better understanding of the latest practices. Very often, upward communication can spell the success or failure of the organisation to capture growth opportunities.

1.3.5 Barriers in Horizontal Communication

Interpersonal barriers to communication within a group of employees, such as a department or team having members from different specialist functions occur under the following circumstances:

(i) The receiver has developed preconceived notions about the sender based on gender, looks or dress. It may also be that the sender has not been impressive while introducing the subject or initiating the discussion.

(ii) At the outset, the credibility of the sender is low. The receiver will then ignore the message. The sender can overcome these obstacles by preparing the message in such a way that it is acceptable to the receiver.

(iii) The sender may delay sending the message due to prior commitments or sheer lethargy. All attempts to rectify the situation may be ignored by the receiver.

(iv) The receivers also have the responsibility of listening to the speakers free from prejudice, positive temperament and commitment. If the receiver is preoccupied with something else and is concerned with other issues, he may fail to comprehend the message and register it in his mind. Thus, the receiver fails to react to the message.

A message that has to pass through *several layers of organisation structure* or many stages before it reaches the target may lose its accuracy. For oral messages, the distortion can happen at every stage of its transmission or relaying, with additions, deletions, analysis, prejudices etc., creeping in. Even written messages can be distorted because of differences in interpretation, meanings and translation. Secondly, messages may not be retained in the memory of the receivers. It applies more to oral messages, as in the case of written messages, the document would be available for later reference. However, even written messages fail to make an impact if there is lack of trust between the parties. This can be overcome if the messages are drafted properly, keeping in view the purpose of the message and the interest of the receiver.

> *It is said that people remember 10 % of what they read 20 % of what they hear 30 % of what they see 50 % of what they see and hear 70 % of what they say 90 % of what they say as they perform the task.*

1.3.6 Role of the Organisation

When an organisation does not establish clear communication policies and define roles, and fails to provide communicating materials and systems or provide training for better communications, it is in effect creating several barriers to effective communication.

Role of the organisation in maintaining a communication environment:

(i) Organisational policies should stress or support its strategy and facilitate its implementation to permit a smooth flow of information in all directions, both external and internal.

(ii) Organisational rules and regulations should be such that they facilitate effective communication at all levels. Care should be taken to ensure provision of proper channels of communication.

(iii) Review of status and position of the employees, such that *differences in the level or status of the functionaries* do not restrict the flow of information.

(iv) The structure of the organisation is also an important aspect. If the relationships are complicated and there are too many levels, messages can get delayed or distorted.

(v) Organisational facilities, like well-maintained communication system and infrastructure, facilities like meeting rooms, conference halls, suggestion schemes, social, cultural and sport activities etc., contribute to better flow of information at both formal and informal levels.

Every member of the organisation must take specific steps to improve conditions and eliminate roadblocks to effective communication.

> The American Management Association has formulated the following commandments for effective communication:
> - Clarifying ideas before communication,
> - Knowing the purpose of communication,
> - Understanding the physical and human environments of communication,
> - Consulting others in planning communication,
> - Determining the contents and overtones of communication,
> - Value of communication to the receiver,
> - Follow up action congruent with communication,
> - Good listening.

Organisations need to orchestrate and implement communication policies and systems that involve persons from many different levels, locations, disciplines and organisations. To help them function effectively as members of *long-term decision making and problem-solving teams*, they need to communicate effectively and continuously. New strategies to promote growth and excellence in the organisation may involve expanded and new communication challenges. These may be associated with exploring new markets, new products, partnerships, collaborations, and knowledge management. The changing nature of organisational boundaries and strategies and the growing need to establish and manage diverse, geographically dispersed units, partnerships and collaborations, suggests intervention at three levels, viz., (1) *development of understanding and improvement of communication skills,* (2) *identification and deployment of communication technology and* (3) *training to use it effectively.*

- Undertake continuous study of areas of communication deficits or barriers in interpersonal, organisational, and inter-organisational relationships and provide for skill enhancement.
- Identify, deploy and, perhaps, help develop more effective interpersonal, organisational, and inter-organisational communication systems and technologies.
- Improve the methodologies and skills associated with that to ensure their success.

The fact that organisational communication is highly specialised, and may be scientific and technical in nature, presents additional communication challenges, particularly communicating effectively across disciplines.

1.3.7 Challenges for Organisations

Communication is not always easy, smooth and effective. No matter how good the communication system in an organisation is, unfortunately barriers can and do often occur. They are always going to be there because humans are complex beings and in that lay the challenges to effective communication. By the time a message gets from a sender to a receiver, there are multitudes of potential sources of error. In a work setting, interactions involve people who often do not have years of experience communicating with each other. These interactions are further complicated by the complex relationships that exist at work. Attempts may be made to simplify the communication processes to a great extent in an organisation, but *barriers come up that can sabotage the message and render it ineffective by the time it gets to those who must act on it.* When the barriers come in the way, communication becomes difficult and frustrating. It is critical to understand and be aware of the potential sources of communication barriers and constantly avoid them by making conscientious efforts to ensure minimal loss of meaning in the message communicated.

Barriers that exist in the workplace can distract, distort or restrict communication. The first step in addressing this problem is to identify workplace communication barriers. Recognising and understanding them help in improving the communication process. It is the responsibility of every individual in an organisation to take personal responsibility and ensure that he/she works in complete effectiveness with his or her co-workers. No matter how many barriers come in the way, a responsible employee will always know how to overcome them.

The following are a few of the most commonly-found barriers in communication in an organisation:

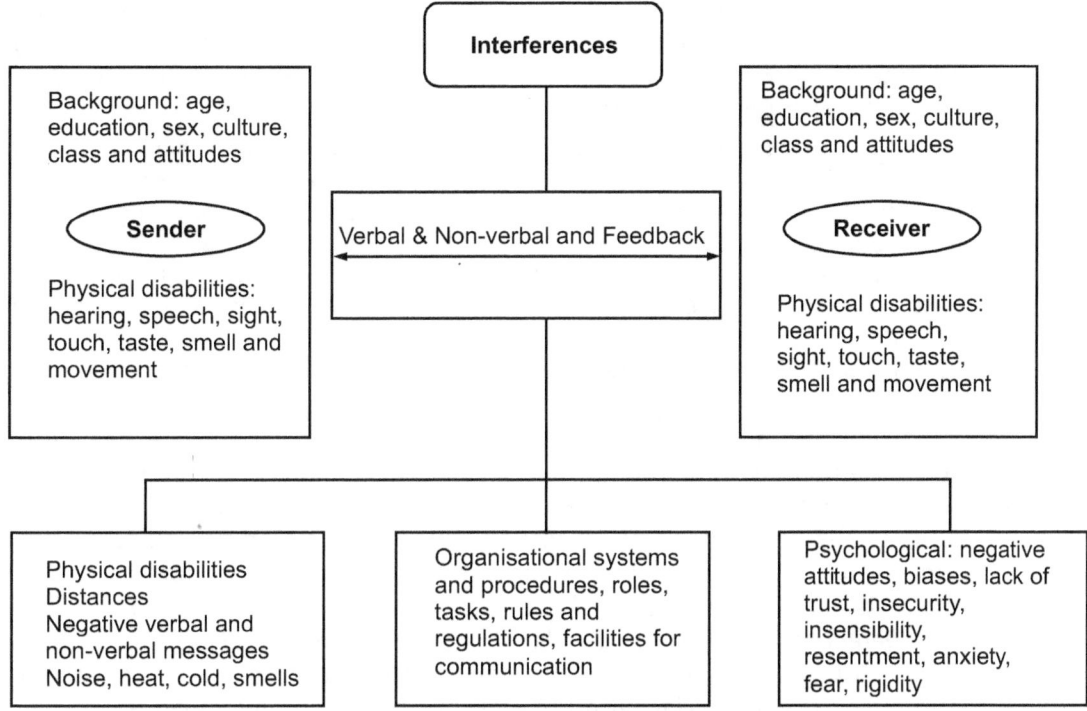

Fig. 1.6: Barriers to Communication

A closer look at the communication cycle and the barriers at various stages:

(a) Encoding Barriers

They include both perceptual barriers, emotional barriers, language barriers and cultural barriers.

- **Perceptual Barriers:** This could be the most common problem faced these days in organisations. It is very natural that there is a lot difference of opinion among people. This is because of difference in their perceptions arising out of the many socio-cultural influences working among them. Everyone sees and understands the world differently. A task may be given to a team of employees and each employee may pursue the objective very differently. For instance, a team leader may ask the team members to complete the task allotted by the end of the day. Some team members may accept this as the usual practice of a superior, but some others may perceive that the leader doesn't trust them to be good workers and the superior is always in the habit of issuing orders. They may perceive it as an affront. A third set of workers in that situation might perceive that the leader is taking care of their best interest.

  The process of selecting and organising symbols to represent a message requires skill and knowledge. It is ironic that even to iron out these perceptional differences, skilful and effective communication among individuals in an organisation is essential.

- **Emotional Barriers:** Another main barrier is emotions like fear and mistrust that inhibit effective communication. Such negative feelings prevent individuals from communicating effectively with others in the organisation. An emotional individual may not be able to communicate well. The receiver on the other hand may be angry, hostile, resentful, joyful, or fearful. Such a person may be too preoccupied with his/her emotions to receive the intended message.

If you don't like someone, for example, you may have trouble "hearing" them.

Lack of Sensitivity to the Receiver can cause a breakdown in communication. Recognising the receiver's needs, status, knowledge of the subject, language skills and emotional status assists the sender in preparing a successful message. For example if a customer is angry, it is natural for him to give vent to his feelings. The response from the receiver depends on how sensitive he/she is to the sender's frustrations.

- **Language and Cultural Barriers:** The world is made up of diverse cultures. Age, education, gender, social status, economic position, cultural background, temperament, health, beauty, popularity, religion, political belief, ethics, values, motives, assumptions, aspirations, rules/regulations, standards, priorities etc., can separate one person from another and create barriers in understanding and interpreting messages. These differences form the basis for attitudes and beliefs as they come from the personal environment, background and experience of the individual. *As such, two people could get the same message but interpret it in two entirely different ways simply because their frames of reference and language differ.*

Different languages, vocabulary, accent and dialect represent national/ regional barriers. Words having similar pronunciation may have multiple meanings, resulting in semantic gap. Badly expressed messages, unqualified assumptions and wrong interpretation are the most common language linked barriers. The use of difficult or inappropriate words/ poorly explained or misunderstood messages can result in confusion.

In an organisation, cultural barriers arise when individuals belonging to different religions, states or countries come together to work towards a common goal. Hence, it is the responsibility of the sender of the message to:

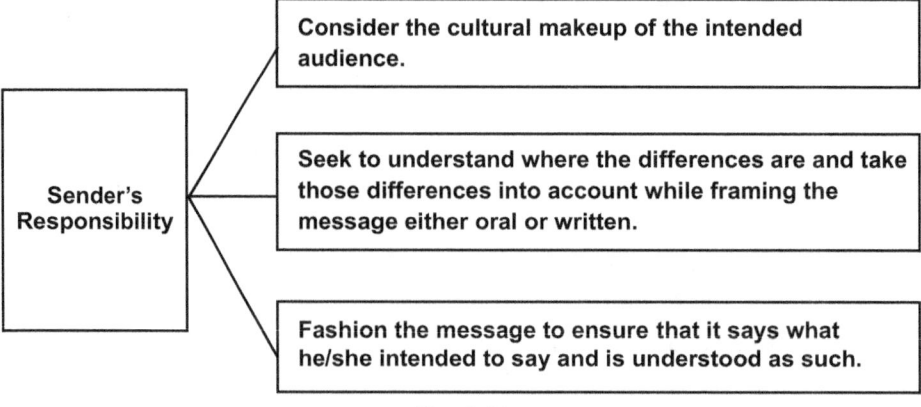

Fig. 1.7

Language is a symbol used to describe what the encoder would want to express and communicate to the others. There could be differences in the language spoken by individuals or groups who send the message and those who receive it. The nature of language and the way it is used often lead to misunderstandings.

In the English language, there are about 500 basic words that are used every day. These 500 words have over 10,000 different meanings. Because language is a symbolic representation of a phenomenon, there is ample room for interpretation and even distortion of the meaning. Here is an example: The Scandinavian company Electrolux had, in its advertisement campaign for its vacuum cleaner in Europe, claimed: *"Nothing Sucks like an Electrolux"* and used the same punch line for its advertisement in the USA without realising that the word "sucks" has a negative meaning in American slang. Needless to say, marketing of the product in the USA got a serious setback.

Differences in language make it difficult for people to communicate freely and effectively. At the outset, *the sender has to appreciate that such differences are there and make all efforts to overcome them. This is extremely important in today's global scenario.* The best compliment we can pay to another person is by speaking and effectively communicating to them in their local language.

Many a times, even when the language spoken by the two parties to communication may be the same, usage of certain words would differ.

> **It is a myth that words transport meanings from the speaker to the listener in the same way that a truck carries goods from one location to another. On the other hand, words may not carry precisely the same meaning from the mind of the encoder to the mind of the decoder.**

Frequently observed causes for this discrepancy are:

1. Lack of common experience between the sender and the receiver is probably the greatest single barrier to effective communication. Words, whether spoken or written, are merely stimuli used to trigger a response. The sender and the receiver should have had the some experience with the objects or concepts to which these words refer, so that they can associate the series of words with the message.

Lack of common experience creates individual barriers depending on an individual's perceptual and personal discomfort. Even when two persons have experienced the same event, their mental perception may/may not be identical which acts as a barrier. This could be accentuated by differences in (1) style, (2) selective perception, (3) halo effect, (4) poor attention and retention, (5) defensiveness, (6) close mindedness, (6) insufficient filtration. These are the individual or psychological barriers.

The sender and the receiver should be able to speak the same language and understand it in more or less similar manner. For instance, the superior has to send the instructions to the subordinates using a terminology understood by the latter. The words chosen should reflect the concern the sender has for the receiver's environment and mental make-up.

Secondly, each discipline or area of study has specific terminology to covey a certain meaning and this should form the link between the sender and the receiver. In short, both the parties should share a common experience with respect to the language and terminology used.

2. Confusion between the Symbol and the Symbolised Object: In all languages, there are words that mean different things to different people. This creates confusion between the symbol and the symbolised object results when a word gives a totally different meaning to the receiver. People often fail to understand this. To communicate effectively, the sender should be aware of the background of the receiver and choose words which convey the most appropriate meaning to the receiver.

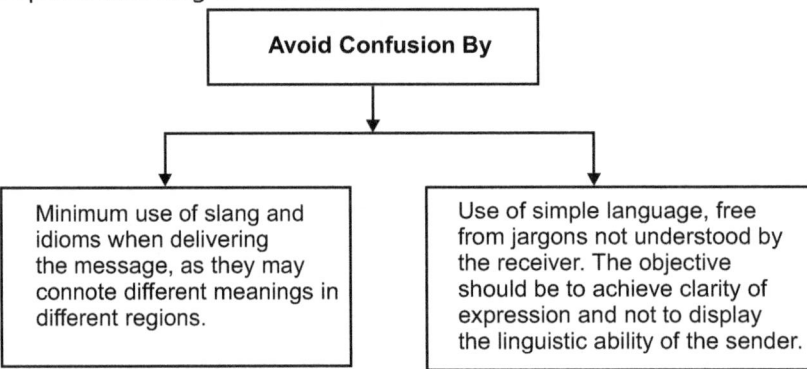

Fig. 1.8

3. Over-use of Abstractions: Abstractions are words that are general rather than specific. Words chosen should specify an idea that can be perceived or a thing that can be visualised. Abstract words stand for ideas that cannot be directly experienced. They do not create exact mental images in the minds of the receivers. The danger of abstractions is that they will not evoke the same specific items of experience in the minds of the receivers that the sender intends. Abstractions should be avoided in most cases, but there are times when abstractions are necessary and useful, especially while explaining some concepts. When such terms are used, they should be linked with specific experiences through examples and illustrations. Here again, as far as possible the level of abstraction should be kept to a minimum by using concrete, specific terms.

4. Lack of Basic Language and Communication Skills: The receiver is less likely to understand the message if the sender has trouble choosing the precise words needed and arranging those words in a grammatically correct sentence. It does not matter whether that audience is of one or one million persons, good sentence structure is essential if a communication is to be 'heard' amongst the various 'noises' of today's business environment. The receivers' past experience with the words and the things to which they refer determines how they respond to what the sender says. Hence *lack of common experience can create a major hurdle to effective communication.*

5. The use of the wrong medium to deliver the communication: The sender may be strong in verbal communication and hence resort to it without considering the circumstances of the receiver. If the message is long and contains a lot of details, a written communication should be preferred, whereas, if the personal involvement of the receiver is important, a one-to-one meeting may be the right approach. In a technical presentation it would be more effective if the details are written and circulated among the participants and are referred to or explained in the speech. The medium chosen should also take into consideration any limitations or disabilities the receiver may have. Similarly, non-verbal communication should complement and not contradict the message.

    6. Insufficient Knowledge of the Subject: If the sender lacks specific information about something, the receiver will likely receive an unclear or mixed message. Lack of knowledge shows up in the form of lack of self-confidence.

    7. Weak Delivery: In business communication, irrespective of the nature of the subject, whether it is a serious one or is light-hearted, a weak delivery fails to impress the audience. Even a shy and reticent person can make an effective communication if the preparation is sound, the information provided is very useful and the message is well structured. It is not the personality of the sender but the nature of delivery that is important.

    8. Poor Structure of the Message: If the message is not properly structured, and there is a lot of back and forth (mix-up) in the issues covered, it can frustrate and confuse the receiver. No matter what the subject is or where it is delivered, a message improperly designed fails to be effective. Structure is critical, because without an introduction, body and close, audiences will have difficulty in retaining, recalling and processing the information. These rules apply to any communication, ranging from emails to public presentations, and to audiences of any size.

    9. Mixed up Messages: A huge barrier to business communication is the ability of to confuse and alienate its audience. It occurs in two ways:

    (i) Using terms and phrases that are 'jargon', the exact meaning of which is possibly recognised but probably not fully understood

    (ii) Trying to 'save time/paper' by including several different communication messages into one. For instance, the communication may suggest cost saving measures and in continuation, talk about new year gifts. A decision arrived at previously may be withheld and soon after, it is upheld due to some pressure.

    10. Bottom of Form Message Sent to Wrong Audience: This can be a complete waste of time and money. It is necessary to choose the audience and choose the medium that will best suit them. There are two basic communication assumptions that can spell disaster for the success of an organisational communication, (a) that all members of the organisation have the same knowledge base as the sender and (b) that information will spread accurately and effectively on its own when it is communicated to a couple of important members. Managements must be proactive and thoughtful while choosing their audience. This can be achieved by giving employees written copies of job descriptions, employee handbooks and other critical company materials and organising strategically scheduled meetings between employees and leaders as well as between different departments.

Meetings can go haywire if, just to get a large number at business meetings, those who are not concerned with the subject also get invited. Out of deference, they may sit through, but will emerge totally bored, feeling that so much of their productive time was wasted.

Similarly, the HR department of an organisation may get a huge brochure printed giving details of its new initiatives and distribute it to everyone in the organisation, whether it has any relevance for them or not.

In conferences, a speaker may, just to gain entry into a conference, give an exciting title to his presentation, but the content may be a total disappointment.

> **Managers Must Be Aware**
>
> In the present day explosion of social media networks, it has become 'cool' or fashionable to post even work related issues on these sites. The employee may not have used the exact names of colleagues or superiors, but the fact remains that instead of discussing the issue at the office level, he has chosen to tell the entire world about his displeasure. The consequence would be a termination letter issued to him without any scope for further explanation. Employees should know what to communicate and when and where to communicate it.
>
> In many companies, while recruiting, the managers run through the applicants' habit regarding usage of social networks and the content posted therein. Any objectionable material posted can be an immediate basis for rejection of the applicant howsoever qualified he/she may be.

11. Distracting Environment: There can be nothing more frustrating than trying to send a message to a group of people who cannot 'hear' the person. The term 'hear' is used in a broad manner to cover a number of situations that can block the communication process such as:

- The sender's voice is not strong enough,
- Too many others are talking at the same time
- Traffic noise outside the venue
- The audience getting too many phone calls at the time of presentation or when the message is being read by them,
- People walking in and out, refreshments being served etc., distracting both the sender and the receiver,
- Incoming emails disturbing the reader while studying the on-line messages,
- The room's air conditioning/heater is not working making the room is uncomfortable,

12. Information Overload: If the receiver gets a message with too much information, or the amount of information given is so fast that it becomes difficult for the receiver to cope with it, he/she may tend to put up a barrier because of difficulty in interpreting that information comfortably. For instance, a sales person may want to inform the prospective buyers (receiver of the message) about a number of features of a product he/she is selling.

Instead of overwhelming the buyer with all the features, it may be better for the sales person to focus on only a few most important aspects and explain them clearly with demonstrations where necessary. This will reduce confusion and make the communication more effective and the salesperson may get the decision from the prospective buyer faster than otherwise.

> In the recent run up to the choice of jet fighters for the Indian Air Force, there was a fierce eight year competition between the Eurofighter 'Typhoon' and the French company Dassault's 'Rafale'. One of the comments reported in newspapers is that the German led bid for the Typhoon was excessively technical and ran to 150 pages, and in contrast, the Rafale bid had only 20 pages of crucial technical details with a lot of glossy display. (Excerpts from newspaper reports)

(b) Physical Barriers

Research shows that one of the key factors in building strong and integrated teams is proximity and approachability. Most offices have closed doors and cabins for those at higher levels while the rest get seating arrangements in large working areas. This may create both physical and mental barriers between the seniors and subordinates and inhibit free communication. Similarly, offices of the same organisation may be located in different buildings, in different parts of the country or the world, creating delays, loss of messages etc.

Likewise, poor or outdated equipment, frequent power cuts, disruptions in transport and communication facilities, failure of management to introduce new communication technology etc., may also cause problems.

Staff shortages are another factor which frequently causes communication difficulties for an organisation.

(c) System Design Faults

These refer to problems with the structures or systems in place in an organisation. The hierarchy must be well-defined and duties and responsibilities at each level should be properly communicated and understood at all levels. Examples of ineffective communication systems might include an unclear organisational structure making it confusing to know who to communicate with. Other examples could be inefficient or inappropriate information systems, including forms to be completed, reporting formats etc. There could also be a lack of supervision or training, and a lack of clarity in roles and responsibilities which can create uncertainties in the minds of the staff about what is expected of them.

(d) Interpersonal Barriers

In an organisation, such barriers could exist at the level of both the superiors and the subordinates.

At the superior's level, the barriers can arise due to (a) Lack of trust in the employees; (b) Lack of knowledge of non-verbal clues like facial expression, body language, gestures, postures, eye contact etc., (d) Different experiences; (d) Shortage of time for the employees; (e) No consideration for employee needs; (f) Wish to capture authority; (g) Fear of losing power of control; and (h) Information overload without understanding the comprehending capacity of the subordinates.

At the subordinate's level they include, (a) Lack of motivation, (b) Lack of cooperation and trust, (c) Fear of penalty and (d) Poor relationship with the superior.

(e) Attitudinal barriers

They arise out of problems with the staff in an organisation and could be a result of such factors as limitation in physical and mental ability, intelligence, understanding, pre-conceived notions, poor management, lack of consultation with the employees, personality conflicts which can result in people delaying or refusing to communicate, the personal attitudes of individual employees which may be due to lack of motivation or dissatisfaction at work etc. All these could be due to insufficient training for carrying out specified tasks, or just resistance to change due to fixed attitudes and ideas.

Attitudinal barriers can take the form of *assumptions* and *biases*.

Biases are shaped by the individual's experiences and their views about *who they are*. It is very natural to have biases, but while working in an organisation, it is necessary to ensure that they do not become an obstacle to effective communication. It is necessary to reach out to even those whose biases do not necessarily align with the sender's. For instance, in an organisation, people from two generations come together, each generation having its own world view and its own challenges. The sender of the message has to be sensitive to such differences. He/she has to take the following care:

- Acknowledge his/her own biases first.
- View the message from the view point of even those who are least likely to agree with their views.
- Listen.
- Frame the message in such a way that everyone can relate to it.

Assumptions can sabotage and defeat the very purpose of communication. The sender may start with the assumption that he knows everything, because of his long experience with the organisation. In an oral communication, the sender may see heads nodding and assume that the audience has understood the message and agrees with the speaker. These may be misleading and the message may lose its effectiveness.

> *"When you assume, you make an ass out of U and Me".*
> **Oscar Wilde**

The sender has to do the following to prevent his/her assumptions from breaking the communication process:
- Start with the consideration that his/her assumptions *could* be baseless or false.
- Discuss these assumptions with others to understand how true they are.
- Anticipate questions and concerns that could be expressed by the receiver/s without any biases and encourage them to discuss them openly.

(f) Transmitting Barriers

Social psychologists estimate that there is usually a 40-60 per cent loss of meaning during the transmission of messages from the sender to the receiver. They also indicate that people in organisations typically spend over 75 per cent of their time in interacting with others. This indicates the stupendous loss to the organisation. It can be said that at the root of a large number of organisational problems is poor communications. *Disturbances that get in the way of message transmission may be due to a variety of circumstances and are sometimes clubbed as "noise."* Noise need not be limited to physical interruptions, but can have many connotations to mean disturbances while transmitting messages, such as:

(i) **Physical Distractions:** A bad phone line or a noisy restaurant can disturb the receiver and block the communication. In written communication either by letter or email, too many spelling and grammatical errors or no proper formatting can distract the reader and instead of understanding the content, the reader may start counting the mistakes! The physical appearance of such a letter or e-mail is sloppy and unprofessional and so gets very poor response.

(ii) **Conflicting Messages:** The sender has to consider the purpose and goal of the message. If for example, the manager wants the subordinate to prepare and submit a report immediately, the receiver is confused whether the emphasis is on speed or accuracy, as, to prepare an accurate report, correct information needs to be gathered, which may take some time. To avoid this problem, the manager could set a reasonable time frame for the submission of the report. Similarly, the use of unfamiliar or irrelevant jargon, mixed messages etc., can result in perceptional difference and so may result in incomplete communication.

Nonverbal signals can either enhance a prepared message or completely contradict it or distort its meaning. Eye contact, proper posture and clothes appropriate to the situation indicate that the message sender is interested, respectful, sincere and credible.

(iii) **Channel Barriers:** If the sender chooses an inappropriate channel of communication, communication may be disturbed. For instance, if a manager gives detailed instructions over the telephone, it may be frustrating for both the sender and the receiver. Sensitive issues like layoffs and terminations are best communicated face-to-face, while other situations like performance reviews and behavioural issues should be documented so they can be reviewed in the future. If the voice mail of call centres do not indicate by a beep when the person has to press the option button, the frustrated customer can direct his/her anger against the organisation in many other ways.

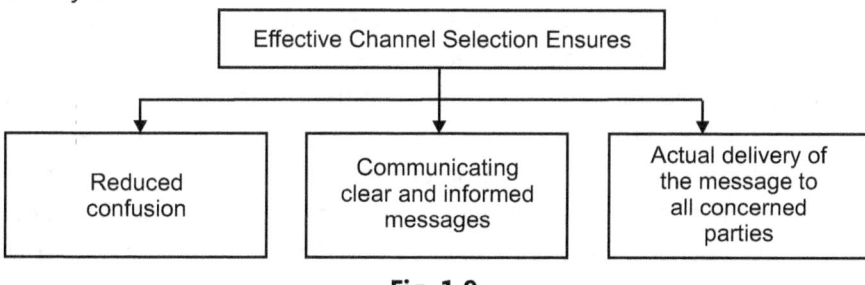

Fig. 1.9

> The following points can be considered while choosing the channel:
> - ✓ The urgency of the message and the time taken to write, edit and produce the communication in the medium chosen.
> - ✓ The percentage of the target audience likely to have access to the medium chosen.
> - ✓ The percentage of target audience that would pay attention to the medium chosen.
> - ✓ Complexity of the message and whether the receiver would comprehend it easily through auditory, tangible or visual (reading or images) methods.
> - ✓ Whether the expected feedback and action is urgent or not.

Organisations must consider carefully what communication channels to use in communicating various messages in given circumstances.

(iv) Long Communication Chain: The longer the communication chain, the greater the chance for error, especially when it is verbal. If a message is passed through too many receivers, the message often becomes distorted, as each receiver could add some unnecessary details or ignore the core parts of the message while concentrating on other details.

(v) Decoding Barriers (At the Receiver's End): The communication cycle may break down at the receiving end for some of the following reasons:

- ➢ **Lack of Interest:** If a message reaches a reader who is not interested in the message, the reader may not pay the required attention. He may read the message hurriedly or listen to the message carelessly. Thus, the receiver will not decode the message as expected by the sender. Hence, the sender has to make sure that the right person is addressed and his/her attention is drawn to the subject.

- ➢ **Lack of Knowledge:** If the receiver is unable to understand a message, communication will break down. This may happen when the receiver has not been briefed about the subject, or is not adequately trained to receive the message. For instance, a technical note about certain features of a product should be sent to only those who are trained in that subject. While sending a message, the sender has to know who the receiver is. The sender should acquaint himself with the educational and training background of the receiver and his/her experience in that field.

- ➢ **Lack of Communication Skills of the Receiver:** Unless the receiver is in a position to understand the subject being addressed, his/her feedback will be ineffective. This depends on his/her listening and reading skills. Those who have weak reading and listening skills make ineffective receivers. On the other hand, those who have a good professional vocabulary and can concentrate on listening or reading, have less trouble interpreting good communication. Such an environment makes communication effective. Many people stop paying attention for various reasons: they may be tired or bored. They may be preoccupied with something else. In some cases, they may be mentally rehearsing their response.

- ➤ **Emotional Distractions:** Emotions interfere with the creation and transmission of a message, disrupting its reception. The receiver may be preoccupied, or feels the pressure of time. It may be a particular dislike for the sender or it may be frustration and anger. For instance, a subordinate may be angry at not getting an overdue promotion, or the superior is unduly checking his work. He may be jealous at the attention someone else is getting. In such cases, a message from the superior may not get the necessary attention. The subordinate may listen to the supervisor or even read the message, but not with the concentration required for effective response.

- ➤ **Physical Distractions:** A receiver of a communication should have an adequately peaceful environment in order to concentrate on the message. If the receiver works in a dimly lit area or an area with bright lights, loud noises, poor ventilation and excessively hot or cold work spaces, or is suffering from physical ailments, such a receiver may have problems while listening to or reading a message. This results in communication breakdowns on a regular basis. The sender will have to find a more suitable way of sending the message. Using a separate conference room, or technological options like the computer intranet and Internet, quick messages on the cell phones etc., are options the supervisor will have to consider.

    There may be other distractions like the cell phones of the receivers may be ringing or vibrating constantly, the internet connection may be slow, there may be distracting activities going on around the place.

- ➤ **Organisational Barriers:** These include poor organisational culture, climate, stringent rules, regulations, status, relationship, complexity, inadequate facilities and opportunities of growth and development etc., result in barriers to communication.

Type of Barrier	Impact on Communication
Language	The communication message might not use vocabulary that is understood by the receiver, such as: too much use of technical or financial jargon or wrong choice of words, spelling and grammar errors etc.
Noise	Various things interfere to prevent the message from reaching the receiver or being heard, such as: poor connection, background noise, distractions, too many people speaking etc.
Overload	Too much information can slow down decision making
Emotion	The emotional status and relationship between the sender and receiver of the communication might adversely affect communication. The message may be ignored or misinterpreted by the receiver.
Gaps	Too many intermediaries, such as too many layers in hierarchy through which message has to be passed, might prevent or distort the message
Inconsistency	If people receive conflicting or inconsistent messages, then they may ignore or block them

(g) Responding (Feedback) Barriers

The communication cycle is complete and effective when the response or feedback is obtained as expected and within the specified time frame. It is broken if the feedback is not received or received late.

> *When you know something, say what you know. When you don't know something, say that you don't know. That is knowledge.* — Kung Fu Tzu (Confucius)

Responding barriers may occur for various reasons, such as:

- **No Provision for Feedback:** Since communication is a two-way process, the sender must be aware of and use proper means of getting a response from the receiver. For instance, proper feedback forms could be designed and used for further analysis. In oral messages, the sender has to make the presentations interesting and informative enough to catch the attention of the receivers. He/she may also permit interaction from the participants to encourage purposeful discussion on the subject. This will ensure that the participants have understood the matter. It is said that face-to-face oral communication is the best type in this respect, as the receivers can send back both verbal and non-verbal feedback without delay. When two communicators are separated, it is the responsibility of the sender to facilitate meaningful feedback.

- **Delayed or Inadequate Feedback:** The response from the receiver may be delayed for various reasons and beat the purpose of the communication. It can be judgemental if the receiver fails to understand the purpose of the message and so does not give importance on all the points on which feedback is sought. For instance, the supervisor may be overbearing and gives instructions in long and wordy messages, without trying to find out if the receiver has understood the message. The receiver may pretend to understand the instructions just get out of the stressful meeting, but his feedback will not be as expected. Employee performance is stunted under such circumstances and the organisation suffers. Similar situations may arise while dealing with other agencies as well.

- **Ignoring the Feedback:** Organisations should use the feedback and act on it, otherwise, they convey the indication that the entire exercise of getting the feedback was of no consequence. When they disregard the information they receive, it can lead to complaints and mistrust and indifference. Companies that are not responsive to employee feedback are in effect stifling effective organisational communication. They risk losing employee loyalty, commitment, satisfaction and engagement.

  Organisations that do not provide for an outlet for employees to voice their issues and concerns would face mounting grievances and a significant breakdown in communication. They must not just be concerned with top-down communication but also from lower level employees to upper management. Processes must be established so that employees can report grievances, cases of sexual, verbal or physical harassment, and also give useful suggestions for improvement.

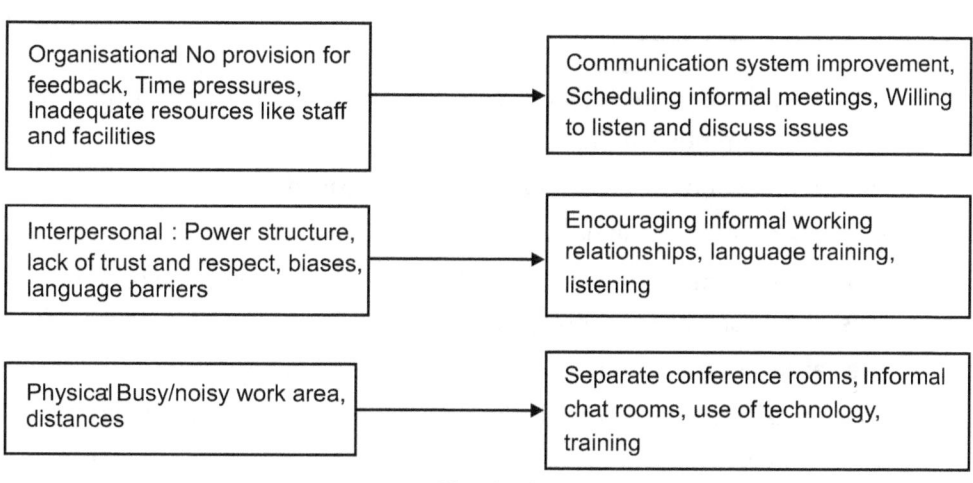

Fig. 1.10

Impediments to Effective Communication can be summed up as follows:

- ✓ Inadequate information, explanations and verification,
- ✓ Language Barriers,
- ✓ Physical arrangements not conducive,
- ✓ Failures to establish on-going informal relationships,
- ✓ Differences in communication styles,
- ✓ Non-verbal cues and body language,
- ✓ Lack of respect for the receiver's sensitivities,

Barriers to communication result in undesirable reaction and unfavourable response.

- ✓ The communication exercise fails because the feedback is absent or falls short of expectation.
- ✓ Barriers to communication are caused by environmental, physical, semantic, attitudinal and varying perceptions of reality.
- ✓ The barriers to effective business communication are many, but with care and attention the majority of them can be overcome. The fewer the barriers, the greater the chance that the communication will be heard and understood and the most desired response or action will take place.

Role of Organisations in Breaking Communication Barriers:

> *"Communication works for those who work at it."*
> — John Powell

- ✓ Organisations should implicitly and explicitly spell out their policies and philosophy with respect to communication.
- ✓ Communication channels should not be one way, top-down.
- ✓ The messages must be meaningful and focused.
- ✓ Create an environment of trust by allowing all employees access to necessary resources, opportunities for self-expression and idea generation.
- ✓ The expectations of the communicating parties should be explicit.
- ✓ Minimum use of absolute words like 'never', 'always', 'forever' etc., which can block all further communication.
- ✓ The practice of attentive listening in the entire organisation.
- ✓ The message should be understood properly, and clarifications obtained if necessary before it is passed on to others.
- ✓ The channel of communication should be short.
- ✓ Special care is needed in choice of words.
- ✓ The background and circumstances of the receiver should be considered. Inculcating the 'you' culture in the entire organisation.
- ✓ Courtesy and Politeness.
- ✓ Oral communication should be clear, well structured and easy to understand.
- ✓ All names should be properly pronounced.
- ✓ Body language should enhance verbal the message and not contradict it.
- ✓ The receiver of verbal communication should ask for clarifications or repetition if necessary.
- ✓ Written communication should be clear, well drafted and edited for correctness, clarity and proper structure.
- ✓ The organisation structure should be more dynamic, flexible, easy to understand and transparent.
- ✓ Proper feedback must be encouraged and information obtained must be acknowledged and be acted upon.
- ✓ Organisational culture should be aimed at congenial relationships.

1.4 Reading Skills

1.4.1 Introduction

Reading skills are specific abilities which enable a reader to:
- Read anything written with independence, comprehension and fluency,
- Mentally interact with the message, i.e., analyse, interpret, integrate it with prior knowledge and experience and in effect, use the knowledge so gained.

It involves a number of skills, such as knowing the words (vocabulary), comprehension or understanding, fluency in reading and critical reading. Critical reading skills help the reader see the connection between and flow of ideas and use these in reading with meaning and fluency. It is the ability to analyse, evaluate, and synthesise what one reads.

Reading skills serve as the foundation for developing effective writing. Regular reading habit gives managers the opportunity to learn new information about the world, people, events, and places, enrich their vocabulary, and improve their comprehension of the subject matter. In the area of business communication, it helps them while preparing impressive application essays, resume, cover letters, review reports etc. Whether the person is employed in an organisation or is self-employed reading a variety of material is essential. One has to develop the capability to read and respond to various written documents like contracts, credit card statements, safety handbooks, reports from subordinates and experts, software manuals, e-mails from the superiors etc.

Reading involves processing of information at two levels, viz., the basic and high level processing.
- Basic or low level of reading is an automatic process as it involves recognising the string of alphabets used, and determining what they mean. This requires very little cognitive or understanding capability.
- The higher level of reading or strategic reading requires conscious awareness of the subject matter presented in the document. This requires:
    o Having prior knowledge about the subject dealt with,
    o Analogical reasoning,
    o Drawing inferences, and
    o Problem solving.

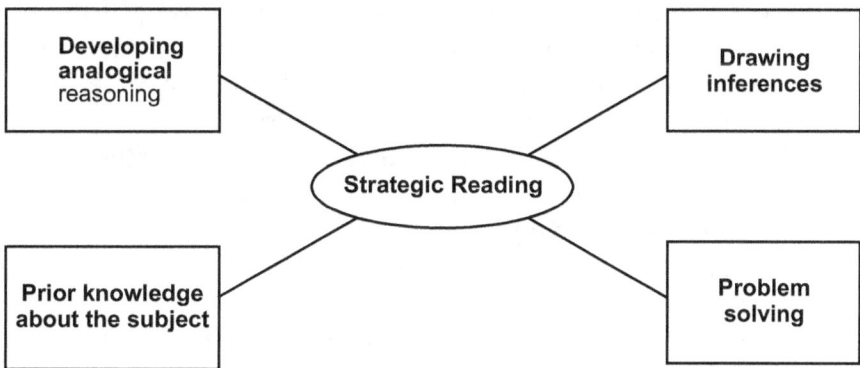

Fig. 1.11: Strategic Reading Activities

1.4.2 Need to Develop Good Reading Skills

Reading habits distinguish a successful manager from the rest. Because of depth and range of information he has, he is able to communicate others with confidence and gain their respect.

- Poor readers will not be able to develop the ability to gain prior knowledge available on the subject and use it with the information being presented. They fail to effectively apply critical reading skills such as analysis, synthesis and evaluation to absorb and utilise the information.
- They may have a small working memory and so lack the capacity to maintain existing information and assimilate new knowledge. Good readers, on the other hand, develop a large working memory and so can integrate existing and new information more effectively.

1.4.3 Reading Techniques

There are many reading techniques, ranging from slow reading to skipping, skimming, scanning and speed reading. Managers can choose it according to the purpose of reading, importance of the document being read and the time available.

1. **Slow Reading:** This technique is adopted when the reader intends to focus on the subject and so needs to study the text in great detail.
2. **Skipping:** The reader skips some sections which are not relevant for the purpose. He can use the Index section to help him select the sections he wants to read.
3. **Skimming:** The reader's eye go over some pre-selected portions of the text to gain an overview. From experience the reader knows which parts of the text generally address the core issues.
4. **Scanning:** The reader goes over the text to find a particular piece of information.
5. **Rapid reading:** This is fast reading and is adopted when the content is not very difficult and the reader is pressed for time.

Seven ways to improve reading skills (VERTIGO)

- **Vocabulary:** Difficulty in understanding some words may slow down the reading process as the reader will have to access a dictionary. The context may provide the necessary clues, but the real connotation and significance of these words are lost. To improve vocabulary, the following methods can be followed:
    - Read widely. It could include newspapers, business and technical magazines and periodicals, books, review reports etc. This increases the familiarity of many words and helps in further reading.
    - Try to know the Latin or Greek roots of certain words and also the manner in which prefixes and suffixes are used.
    - As a habit, make a list of new words and understand their meanings and usage.
    - Prepare a glossary (word list) of technical words in the text and find out their meanings, to improve your mastery over technical words.

- **Eye sight:** If poor vision is affecting proper reading, it is better to consult a specialist and use the prescribed glasses. Do not struggle or use it as an excuse.
- **Regression:** Many readers linger on or go back to some difficult words. This may delay reading. The context and structure of the text may throw light on these words in due course.
- **Talking:** Readers may want to explain vocally some difficult parts of the text for better understanding and retention. One can learn concepts better when they are explaining them to others. But this can slow down the reading process and hence should be avoided if the purpose of the reading can be met without it.
- **Ideas:** The text can be mentally split into units of ideas or concepts. This increases the span of recognition of the words and text. Good readers focus on the content and meaning, whereas poor readers get distracted or confused and look for help at the general structure of the text.
- **Guide:** To be effective, the reader may use the index finger or a pencil or pen or even the computer cursor while reading, to maintain focus and concentration. As it involves vision and touch, it increases better command over what is being read and helps in retention. It avoids regression, talking or vocalising the content and adds rhythm to the reading. The guide may be moved slower or faster depending on the speed required.
- **Operating reading speed:** This involves increasing reading speed. Special attention should be paid to light, sitting comfort, posture, keeping distracting things out of view etc. This will help focus attention on the task of **U**nderstanding, **R**ecalling, **D**etecting errors in your understanding, **E**laborating or **I**ntegrating with previous knowledge and Reviewing the portions that should be remembered. Reviewing is essential for remembering. It is said that a person can forget about 80 per cent of what is read within 24 hours and 100 per cent within a week if the matter is not reviewed.

1.5 Listening

One of the most important factors in removing barriers to effective communication is understanding the message through *Active Listening*. Hearing and listening are not the same. *Hearing* is the involuntary act of perceiving the sound or the reception of aural stimuli. *Listening* on the other hand, is a selective action and involves active participation in the communication process. It is the *reception and interpretation of aural stimuli*, resulting in the decoding of the sound and analysing its meaning. In communication skills, listening is important, as it leads to interpretation and feedback.

Listening can be of two types: Passive and Active.

Passive listening is a little more than hearing and indicates that the receiver does not have the motivation to listen carefully as there is no action indicated. This is when a person is listening to music to relax, or watching television, as in such cases, careful interaction is not expected. Again, when the receiver is being polite, but is not expected to comment or respond, he would be passively listening to the sender (speaker).

Active listening is listening with a purpose, where the receiver has a role in completing the communication process. Generally, people speak at the rate of 100 to 175 words per minute (WPM), but they can listen intelligently at 600 to 800 WPM. This means that in the process of listening, the receiver uses only a part of his/her mind for paying attention to what is being said. The unused listening capacity provides opportunities for the mind to drift. Any small interruption is enough to divert the person's attention while listening to someone. To overcome this distraction, the listener has to become more attentive to what is being said and also take note of the feelings of the sender and the reactions of the others.

The motivational factors that can make the listeners active and careful are:
- Gaining information,
- Obtaining directions,
- Understanding others,
- Solving problems,
- Sharing interests,
- Seeing how the speaker/others feel,
- Showing support, etc.

Active listening *takes the same amount or more energy than speaking*. It requires the receiver to be attentive, fight back distractions and hear the messages with concentration, understand the meaning, and then verify the meaning by offering feedback.

When the listeners are active, they are aware of their responsibility in making the communication process effective. They know that they are equal participants in the communication process and they need to contribute to its success. They show respect for the speaker and do not do anything to distract his/her attention. They try to understand the message before giving the feedback. They give the feedback at the right time. They are attentive, polite and their response is purposeful. The characteristics of active listeners are:
- They spend more time listening than talking.
- They do not dominate the conversation.
- They are paying full attention by not daydreaming or becoming preoccupied with their own thoughts when others talk.
- They are aware of their own biases and the need to control them. They do not jump into conclusions or form judgment before completely understanding what is being said.
- They do not show impatience by finishing the sentences of the speakers.
- They focus on and limit the conversations to what the speaker is saying, and NOT on what interests them.

- They may take brief notes if necessary, so as to concentrate on what is being said and also to plan the response.
- They plan their responses after the speaker has finished speaking, NOT while the person is speaking.
- They do not interrupt in between by giving feedback continuously.
- They do not pose a question in response to a question.
- They analyse the message by looking at all the relevant factors and asking open-ended questions.
- They recapitulate what has been said by summarising. Thus they put the entire speech in the right perspective. The speaker will immediately know if any point is missing.
- They provide feedback at the appropriate time.

1.6 Feedback

Feedback is the response from the receiver to the sender of the message. It is critical for effective communication. It indicates that the receiver has received the original message, understood it in his/her own way and is sending the response. It is a very important phase in the communication process. The sender of the message wants to know if the receiver of the message has understood what is conveyed, as that would help in completing the communication process. He would also be interested in knowing his reactions or impressions about the manner in which it is expressed, and whether it was clear, so that he can improve his communicating skills. *The main idea behind feedback is to motivate behaviour or purpose.*

Feedback can be in verbal or non-verbal form, including written communication or even by way of action.

Example 1: When a superior instructs his subordinate (original message sent), he expects an answer. The response could be as follows:

1. Silence (indicating that the receiver [the subordinate] has chosen to ignore),
2. Action as expected in the original message,
3. Request for further clarifications,
4. Excuses for not following the instruction (based on genuine reasons like lack of adequate time, manpower, supplies, power supply etc.)

Example 2: During the warranty period, a customer sends a complaint letter to the company regarding problems encountered while using their product. The customer (original message) asks the company to either replace the piece or get it repaired. If the company acknowledges the message and sends a service person, this feedback makes the customer comfortable and if the replacement or repair is completed, he is satisfied. On the other hand, if the company ignores the complaint or refuses to accept that the product is defective and argues about it, it is a negative feedback and an unsatisfied customer, which can destroy the goodwill for the company in the market.

Thus the feedback can be **positive** or **negative**. While giving the feedback, the receiver in turn becomes a sender. In the first case above, the superior receives the feedback (message from the subordinate) and in turn, sends his feedback. The superior (receiver of the feedback) can show frustration when his instructions are not acted on. If the feedback he has got is action, he will acknowledge it and support the action. If the feedback falls in the categories 4 or 5, he will initiate suitable action.

In the second case above, the customer has sent his message (complaint). The company's feedback is positive when it acknowledges and acts on it. It is negative when it disputes the complaint. The frustrated customer can spread the message by word of mouth or even in the social network, damaging the reputation of the company, whereas the satisfied customer will help build goodwill for the company.

Thus, for every message, there is a feedback, which completes the process and can start a new communication cycle. *Lack of feedback can lead to frustrated customers, unmotivated employees and a negative corporate culture.*

Feedback is a two way street. A person should know when and how to give feedback and also how to receive it constructively. It is also important to proactively seek feedback from your superiors, colleagues, and customers. *Handled properly, feedback has the potential to make your workplace a much more productive and harmonious place.*

- **Customers** need to be provided with an avenue for expressing their needs, concerns and opinions. When a customer has an issue with a product/service, he needs a proper outlet to provide feedback to the company. That is why many companies use Information technology and services to run help lines. At these help lines, they can even have access to an elevated level if the reply at the initial level is not satisfactory. Many help lines provide for live chat with executives of the company. The only way to know if the customers are happy and satisfied is to gather accurate and honest feedback from them.

- **Employees** who are given the opportunity to provide feedback feel appreciated, important and understood. They will feel empowered. They will not be fearful of sharing their opinions. Generally as they are the hands-on persons and are aware of the ground realities, they can come up with doable solutions to problems. At the same time, they also get feedback about their performance or behaviour from their superiors or peers. Opportunities for upward, downward and horizontal feedback create a committed workforce. People who feel appreciated and respected are more motivated than those who think their efforts go unnoticed. They take more interest in the work they do, and they're more committed to their teams and organisations, because they know that they are making a real difference. And the people involved will improve and become more satisfied because they are being coached to do better. This is especially important if the department is working on tight budgets and so raises and bonuses cannot be offered.

- **Corporate Culture:** At work, it is important to build a culture that values feedback. It is necessary to reinforce the feeling that everyone deserves feedback and that providing feedback is a primary function of a supervisor. With a lack of opportunities for feedback, the corporate culture can become depressing and unmotivated. Every business has a particular culture which can be the result of the communication systems set in place. Feedback allows both customers and employees to voice their opinion, creating a healthy corporate environment which leads to greater productivity and motivation. By making a conscious choice to give and receive feedback, the company can use it as a powerful tool for employee development and customer relationship. Feedback creates a supportive environment built on trust.
- **Profitability:** When the employees are motivated and the customers are satisfied, it gets reflected in the profitability of the company. Customer feedback helps the company to identify problem areas and fix them. It will also help in identifying the strong points on which it can build its future strategies. Hence, in the long run, feedback will create greater productivity and profits.

Tips for Effective Feedback

> *"The leader of the past was a person who knew how to tell. The leader of the future will be the person who knows how to ask."*
>
> *- Peter Drucker, author and consultant.*

- **Try to make it a Positive Process and Experience:** It is necessary to remember the basic purpose of feedback, viz., to improve the situation or performance. Nothing can be accomplished by being harsh, critical, or offensive. *A lot more can be achieved when your approach is positive and focused on improvement.* It is good practice to start with a positive statement.

    For instance, while giving a complaint about a product, the customer can start with the statement that it is a great product, but has developed some problems. It is a great product, otherwise you would not have bought it in the first place. Such a positive beginning takes the edge out of the complaint, but gets better attention.

    While commenting on an employee's behaviour, a positive approach in the beginning and at the end of the meeting will put the other person at ease and make him want to improve and succeed. Very often people do not give enough praise in the workplace. However, it is natural for people, whether they are team members, colleagues, customers, suppliers or even the boss, love to get sincere recognition for a job well done. However care should be taken to make sure that the sweeteners are not too many. Otherwise, it will take away the expected sting in the main message in the feedback.

- **Negativity:** There is a role for negative feedback and even anger if someone is not paying sufficient attention to what is being said. However this should be used sparingly.

- **Be Timely:** The feedback should be as close to the event as possible. For instance, if an employee is not performing satisfactorily, it would be easier to handle if he or the agency he represents gets the notice immediately and not after observing his performance for a whole year. Similarly, the customer should contact the supplier as soon as the defect is noticed. The exception is if the persons involved are emotionally disturbed, in which case, it is better to wait till the situation calms down. There is no point in making a remark for which can cause unnecessary irritations.

- **Make it Regular:** Feedback is a process that requires constant attention. When something needs to be said, it has to be said, so that people know where they stand and there are few surprises and the situation is under control. In an organisation, except in the case of formal feedback, feedback should not be treated as a scheduled, a once-a-year or a once-every-three-month type of event. Depending on the situation informal, simple feedback should be given much more often than this. With frequent informal feedback, there will be no surprises during formal feedback sessions.

- **Prepare Your Comments:** It helps to organise your response, so that there is clarity and smooth flow of points. It may not be written down and read, but a little bit of preparation helps you stay on track and stick to the issues.

- **Be Specific:** The feedback should be based on firsthand experience, without any exaggerations and be aimed at bringing about specific improvements. Tell the person exactly where the improvement is necessary, so that specific facts can be presented and there is total clarity. Vague expectations should not be made.

- **Focus should be Limited:** Only the issues on hand should be discussed. It is advisable to limit feedback to one or two issues, so that the receiver can concentrate on these issues and bring about improvements. If too many issues are taken up, the receiver may feel that he is being attacked and insulted.

- **Discuss Issues that can be changed:** Only behaviour issues that can be changed should form part of the feedback. Otherwise, it becomes a senseless criticism.

- **Do not get Personal:** While giving feedback, it is necessary to be factual and objective and not subjective or personal. It should not be used as an opportunity to settle personal scores.

- **Avoid Absolute Statements:** Usage of words like 'never', 'always', 'all' will put the other party on the defensive. For instance, if the customer says "I'll never buy from your company", he has closed the doors permanently.

- **Use "I" Statements and be direct:** The feedback has to be from the person's perspective, and not include general statements. In an employee review, the suggestions for improvement should be specific, with achievable goals and milestones, giving the feeling that the superior is interested in the development of the subordinate.

- **Criticise in Private:** Public scrutiny or criticism is never appreciated, but public appreciation is always valued. The principle to be followed is based on the saying: "Tell me if you are not satisfied, but tell the world if you are happy with my product or service." Hence, it goes without saying that a negative feedback should be given in a place where no one would interfere or be able to overhear. Especially in these days of social networking, the slightest criticism of a product or the company you are working for can create gigantic ripples with irreparable damages.
- **Listen:** The feedback may bring about some response from the other person, which may be very valid.
- **Document and Monitor:** It may be a good practice to document the entire feedback session so that it can be monitored.

1.7 Principles of Nonverbal Communication
1.7.1 Introduction

'Non-verbal Communication' refers to *'Communication by means of elements and behaviours that are not coded into words'*. It is a medium of communication, which adds another dimension to the spoken word and so it is also known as 'Communication by Implication'. Non-verbal messages express true feelings in a more accurate and accentuated manner than the spoken or written language. Non-verbal Communication is a very powerful means of communicating and hence, it is important to study this as a separate topic. Most people believe that the manner in which you say something is more important than what you say. Words alone are, in many cases, not adequate to express our feelings and reactions. The significance of non-verbal communication can be seen from the fact that the content of a message includes:

- 55% from the visual component
- 38% from the auditory component
- 7% from language

When people communicate, listeners gain information about the speaker's attitudes towards them from visual, tonal, and verbal cues. Similarly, the listeners can send their feedback using these cues. Much depends upon a number of other factors, such as context of the communication, and how well the communicators know each other. It also depends on the cultural background of the communicators.

Nonverbal communication is the process of conveying a message without the use of words. It can include gestures and facial expressions, tone of voice, timing, posture and where and how the speaker stands. It is a significant part of the entire communication process, as it can help or hinder the clear understanding of the message. It does not always reveal what the speaker is really thinking. On the other hand, it can even mask it. Nonverbal communication is extremely complicated. The action flows almost seamlessly from one to the next and hence understanding it is a challenging task.

1.7.2 History

Scientific research on non-verbal communication and behaviour began with the 1872 publication of Charles Darwin's *The Expression of the Emotions in Man and Animals*. Since then, there has been an abundance of research on the types, expressions and effects of unspoken communication behaviour.

Edward T. Hall's (1959) influential book *The Silent Language* placed a heavy emphasis on cultural nuances of non-verbal communication. Hall is generally acknowledged to be the founder of this field of communication studies. The book studies the previously hidden dimensions of human communication, particularly proxemics (how space affects communication) and chronemics (how time affects communication).

In the mid 1960s, Paul Ekman studied emotions and discovered six facial expressions that almost everyone recognises world-wide: happiness, sadness, anger, fear, disgust, and surprise. Although they were controversial at first, they are now widely accepted. Paul Ekman (born February 15, 1934) one of the 100 most eminent psychologists of the twentieth century is a pioneer in the study of emotions and their relation to facial expressions.

1.7.3 Significance

In recent management literature, non-verbal communication has received much attention especially in the areas of business meetings, negotiations, business presentations, sales and marketing, and also in the area of social skills. It is extremely important in general communication as well. *It is estimated that less than ten per cent of interpersonal communication involves words. The remaining 90 per cent is made up of message carriers*, such as voice tone, sounds and a variety of devices such as kinetics (movement), haptics (touch), oculesics (eye-contact), proxemics (space) and chronemics (time) as well as posture, and sound symbols. Even silence can communicate some feeling. In many cases, the communicator may use groups of behaviours to mean the same emotion or feeling, such as combining a frown with crossed arms and unblinking eye gaze to indicate disapproval.

For managers, working in this flat world, where businesses operate from various locations and interfacing with different cultures, the need to understand non-verbal cues gains further importance because of the major differences in the usage and interpretation of these forms based on cultural nuances. Body language, expression, personal space and other non-verbal tools are an integral part of the communication process, irrespective of whether the person giving such messages is the speaker or the receiver.

Nonverbal communication occurs not only between people, but also *internally*. People grimace, stand in certain postures, and show other behavioural stances in order *to reinforce to themselves certain positions, attitudes, and implicit beliefs.* Unconsciously, they suggest to themselves the role they choose to play, such as being submissive or dominant, trusting or wary, controlled or spontaneous.

1.7.4 Characteristics on Non-verbal Communication

- Nonverbal communication is the key in the speaker/audience relationship.
- Nonverbal messages communicate feelings and attitudes. Generally words may not be adequate to express them. People may not want to express their feelings in words. It is said that 93 per cent of the time we communicate our emotions nonverbally, with at least 55 per cent associated with facial gestures. The other ways in which feelings are expressed are vocal cues (tone of voice), body position and movement, and normative space the speaker maintains with the receiver. However, with training, people learn to restrain their immediate responses, especially if the initial response can be a fleeting one.
- Nonverbal communication is fast. Emotional responses are instantaneous. They do not wait for the person to assess his own feelings and thoughts and process them through language or formulate an appropriate response.
- Nonverbal communication can be intentional or unintentional. People see and hear more than what is intended and respond in various ways. Since non-verbal communication happens very fast, the unintentional ones can contradict the spoken words. If the person intends to respond in an appropriate manner by using the right words or gestures, but his unintentional non-verbal expression or gestures do not match it, he is exposing his true feelings and attitudes.
- Nonverbal Communication is by and large universal. However, there are cultural factors that need to be considered.
- Nonverbal communication can be confusing and so contextual clues are necessary to help us understand what a movement, gesture, or lack of display may mean.
- Nonverbal communication is irreversible. In written communication, it is possible to give clarification, correction, or even retraction. In oral communication, it may be possible to restate, explain, clarify, apologise etc., though the original message or its impact cannot be removed. However, non-verbal communication cannot be erased or taken back.
- Words, either written or spoken, can be easily identified and isolated, but not the speaker's gestures, smile, or stance.

1.7.5 Types of Non-verbal Expressions

The manner in which a message is expressed may carry more significance and weight than what is said, i.e., the words themselves. Depending on the situation, the speaker can reinforce his message with a smile or a frown, raise his/her voice, or keep it pleasant, gentle, and easy. In short, depending on the context, the communicating person can frame the message in such a way as to convey the entire meaning. These signals are often so subtle and involuntary that the communicator is not consciously aware of them.

- A gesture can be an ***illustrator*** when it is used to communicate the message effectively and reinforce our point. For instance, a nod can accompany a 'yes'.

- It is a ***regulator*** when used to control, maintain or discourage interaction, such as, raising a hand to tell the speaker to stop as the message is irritating, confusing or irrelevant. For instance, in a sales meeting, the audience may nod their heads in agreement on important points, while maintaining eye contact. Here they are using regulators to encourage the speaker. This is a positive use of a regulator. To convey a negative feeling like boredom, the audience can look the other way, tap their feet, doodle etc.

- Non-verbal communication can be used to express emotions. Then it is known as ***affect display.*** For instance, a smile along with a waving of hand indicates that the person is happy to see the person he is greeting.

- When the communicator does anything by way of gesture or hand movement to help him adapt to the environment he is using nom-verbal communication as an ***adaptor.*** He is trying to feel comfortable and secure in the environment. It could be actions like adjusting or combing his hair. He is adapting something about himself in a purposeful way. Or he can use the objects he has in some other way to indicate lack of interest, like using a pencil to tap on the desk, or chewing its edge and not engaging the speaker with eye contact.

- Nonverbal communication can be used intentionally as well to complement, repeat, replace, mask, or contradict what we say. When a person agrees by saying 'yes' and nods, the nod has the effect of repeating. If a person is bored or not interested, he will raise his hand to ask the speaker to stop. But at the same time, if he shows his watch, he is masking his thoughts and feelings. By showing the watch, he has been diplomatic and has indicated a time constraint though in actual fact he is bored or not interested. Thus, masking involves the substitution of appropriate non-verbal communication for the really intended non-verbal communication. Nonverbal messages that conflict with verbal communication can confuse the listener.

Some Nonverbal Expressions

Term	Definition
Illustrators	Reinforce a verbal message
Affect Displays	Express emotions or feelings
Regulators	Control, encourage or discourage interaction
Adaptors	Help in feeling comfortable or indicate emotions or moods
Self-Adaptors	Adapting something about yourself in a way for no apparent purpose
Object-Adaptors	Using an object for a purpose other than its intended design
Emblems	Gestures that carry a specific meaning, and can replace or reinforce words
• Complementing	Reinforce verbal communication
• Contradicting	Contradicting verbal communication
• Repeating	Repeating verbal communication
• Replacing	Replacing verbal communication
• Masking	Substituting more appropriate displays for less appropriate displays

1.7.6 Forms of Non-verbal Communication

Research has identified several *different forms of non-verbal communication*. The following is a relatively simple classification of non-verbal cues in communication:

Forms of Non-verbal Communication

Kinesics	Body motions, such as shrugs, eye movement, foot-tapping, drumming fingers etc.
Proxemics	Spatial separation (in relation both the social and physical environment)
Haptics	Touch
Oculesics	Eye contact
Chronemics	Use of time, punctuality, waiting, pausing
Olfactics	Smell
Vocalics	Tone of voice, timbre, volume, speed
Sound Symbols	Mumbling and making sounds such as: grunting, mmm, er, ah, uh-huh,
Silence	Absence of sound (muteness, stillness, secrecy)
Adornment	Clothing, jewellery, hairstyle
Posture	Position of the body (characteristic or assumed)
Locomotion	Walking, running, staggering, limping, sudden and jerky movements
Expression	Frowns, grimaces, smirks, smiles, pouting, tears in eyes

1.7.7 Principles of Non-verbal Communication

As can be seen from the above, it is necessary to understand the principles of non-verbal communication, as it accentuates, reinforces or even replaces the verbal message, is visible and can be subject to interpretation by the receiver, either as supporting the verbal communication or not. Hence to use this mode effectively, the communicator has to understand these principles and avoid giving wrong cues. Briefly stated, they stem from the basic propositions that it is necessary to understand the significance of non-verbal communication as the second communication and align it with intent, thought and words. The key characteristics of an effective communicator are openness, connection, passion, and listening. It is necessary to remember that "Actions speak louder than words."

1. It is necessary to **align body language to verbal communication** to make the communication effective. If the two are not aligned, or they give contradictory messages, the receiver will focus more on the non-verbal aspect and believe those cues than what is being said. The receiver will interpret the intent and emotions of the sender through his/her facial expressions, posture, his kinesics etc. These are extremely transparent and it is not easy for the sender to pretend that the situation is otherwise. A speaker may begin his speech with impressive words, but if he is nervous or is not sure of himself, his expressions will betray him easily. That is why, before a speech, effective speakers take some time to take a good look at the audience, focus on the emotions they want to convey and form their words and their body language accordingly. To catch the imagination, interest and attention of the audience, they start with a joke or a story or an anecdote, some statistics etc.

2. Before beginning the speech, it is necessary to **establish an open relationship with the audience**. It is natural for people to start evaluating the person in front of them and developing a relationship even before any words are exchanged. They do it very fast, spontaneously and unconsciously. The two parties to the communication may not be aware of this exchange of non-verbal communication, but even before the speaker utters a single word, his success or failure as a speaker is determined. Hence it is necessary to develop an open relationship with the audience, whether it is a single person or a large group. Only then can he be able to convince the audience and persuade them to think in the way he wants them to. This can happen only when verbal message and body language are in alignment. If you send out mixed messages, your audience will pick up on them unconsciously and resist you because you do not appear honest to them.

3. **Be authentic:** By aligning body language with verbal communication, the speaker conveys authenticity and people will listen to him. People do not trust those who tell lies or pretend in any manner. If there is basic lack of alignment between content and body language, it does not inspire trust and does not get read as authenticity. The door to the audience is closed.

4. ***Decision making process is basically an emotional process and so emotions should be communicated and not hidden.*** Human brain links memories to emotions, depending on how significant the memories are. These emotions are experienced non-verbally. The speaker tries to influence the audience by appealing to their emotions. Thus, the source of non-verbal communication is emotions. When we evaluate the environment and the speaker, it is done non-verbally and unconsciously. We look for signals that indicate comfort level in the environment and try to connect with it. We unconsciously size up the speaker. The conscious part comes in much later.

5. ***Non-verbal communication takes precedence over speech.*** This can be seen from the sequence in a speech: intent (what the speaker wants to communicate), gesture, thought and lastly, speech. But if the speaker consciously thinks about what gestures he will use, it becomes totally unnatural, as the gesture will happen too late. The sequence then will be: thought – speech – gesture. Since people evaluate gestures unconsciously, they will unconsciously notice that the speaker is not authentic or is putting up a false performance, or is foolish. (Students could check this out in front of the mirror and notice the difference.) The fluidity of the speech is lost.

6. ***The speaker should be conscious of his body language and try to master it.*** In an informal meeting where comfort levels all around are very high, such care is not necessary. But if the stakes are high, it is not just about the speaker, but the audience as well. If the speaker's body language conveys tension or fear, the emotions are picked up by the audience as well. While facing the superior or the company board or while negotiating which makes or breaks the company, the speaker has to be mindful of what his body language communicates. As the saying goes, 'see yourself as others see you'.

7. ***It is necessary to be aware of the body language of others***: People use body language to signal their intentions much before they express them verbally. Sometimes, only the body speaks. They speak first and they rarely lie. Words may fail their speakers. An effective speaker does not depend on words alone. Hence it is necessary for a good communicator to consciously learn to read and understand one's own and others' body language and react accordingly.

8. ***It is necessary to have control over one's own emotional intent and the appropriate gestures will follow.*** The speaker should understand the emotions he wants to convey and express it forcefully. This applies to business speakers as well. Emotions are literally infectious. They are picked up from the people around us. While promoting a product, the appeal is not just to the logic but to the emotions of the consumers as well. The enthusiasm, anger, joy or sorrow expressed by the speaker spreads rapidly to the audience as long as the emotion displayed is not a fake. A successful speaker will think of the emotions he wants to convey and rehearses the speech along with gestures, movements, effective pauses etc.

9. **The emotional intent has to be matched by conscious thought and appropriate words.** Very often in the organisational environment, out of respect or as a norm, people may not show their real emotional intent in the words they express. But if the stakes are high and the speaker is being watched by many people, the two need to be properly aligned. It may be a crucial business meeting, where a lot of funding decisions are to be made. It may be a major negotiation process. It may be a meeting with employees to congratulate their team on their significant achievement. There may be many such situations. The speaker will have to focus on his emotional intent and choose appropriate words. The speaker will have to be alert to both emotion and word choice for a longer period. All this takes a lot of practice and distinguishes a man of experience from a novice in this area. Terms like 'charismatic speaker' refer to people who can be passionate, open and capable of influencing the thoughts and behaviour of the others.

10. **An effective speaker shows that he is open, authentic, connected and at the same time passionate about what he is communicating.** *He is a good listener as well.* As has been said in the previous sections, all this comes from effectively aligning the emotional intent, body language and words. In such a person, the emotions and the message are perfectly aligned. He believes in what he is saying. Such a person listens to the other party carefully and responds properly.

1.7.8 Professional Dressing

Objective language is non-verbal message communicated through appearance. As a medium of non-verbal communication, it includes arrangement and display of material things. This method may include intentional or unintentional communication through material things like clothing, make-up, ornaments and other accessories, books, buildings, room furniture, interior decorations etc. These offer signals relating to the context, such as formal and informal settings.

Dress and decoration communicate a great deal about the speaker's rank, status, personality, feelings, emotions, attitudes, opinions etc. What they reveal is something special about the person. For instance, when a professional bathes every day, wears clean clothes and his socks are not stinking, it indicates his outlook and concern for others. On the other hand, if he has body odour and wears clothes and socks which have not been washed for a couple of days, he will be looked down upon right at the outset. First impressions count and whether one likes it or not, people are immediately judged by their appearance.

Professional dressing conveys a non-verbal message as it creates an impression about the person, his background, his tastes and choices. Obviously, the person is instantaneously assessed by the audience. Hence the emphasis is on choice of dress and accessories.

Professional dressing includes dressing appropriately for a job, an interview, an internship, a networking event, etc. Each company and event is different. Secondly, there are many other variables, like time of event, season, the city of residence and work, mode of transport being used, and whether person will be sitting or standing most of the time, dress code announced, what the others are likely to be wearing etc.

Types of Business Attire: There are three types of dress codes viz., Professional Dress, Business Casual and other Casual.

1. Professional Dress: Professional dress is the most conservative type of business wear for most 'white collar', job situations, whether it is accounting, finance, or other conservative industries. For men, professional dress means a business suit or a blazer, dress pants and a tie. For women in the Western societies, this means a business suit, pants suit, or dress and jacket. However, in India, one can see even ladies holding top level jobs wearing saris. At the worker level, viz., 'blue collar' jobs, there are the uniforms, overalls and safety gear.

For those in specialised services like the defence services, police forces etc., there are the Service-Regiment-Seniority-specific uniforms, which instantaneously communicate the status of the person. Religious leaders, political leaders, lawyers, judges, doctors, nurses, sports persons, porters, security persons and other workers have their own way of dressing, which identifies them distinctly.

The professional dress worn by people of different countries varies. What is formal office wear by women in India may be considered informal and dressy in the western countries. Many companies have an established dress code which is binding on the employees.

A professional who does not take the time to maintain a professional appearance presents the image of not being able to perform adequately on the job. If a person looks and behaves like a highly trained and well-groomed professional, he/she will win appreciation, respect and honour. Apart from dress, professional men should take care of various aspects of grooming, such as a fresh haircut, removal of all facial hair, nicely shined shoes and a crisp, nicely pressed suit etc., as they go a long way in establishing a professional demeanour. Cologne and after-shave are optional, but if used, it must not be very strong.

Women professionals as a rule do not wear heavy jewellery, very strong cosmetics and perfumes etc., and they keep their hair neatly organised. Tattoos are discouraged in many companies in America. Those who display them are considered unprofessional, low-class and ignorant.

There are a number web sites where the 'do's & 'don'ts are described.

2. Business Casual: This is a more relaxed but not casual version of the 'Professional Dress'. If the organisation environment is semi-conservative, wearing business casual would be appropriate. Apart from this, some interviews and events may also call for business casual.

Basically, for women, business casual is a shirt with a collar and/or a sweater, khakis or dress pants and nice shoes. They can also sometimes wear a moderate length (knee length or longer) dress or skirt. For men, business casual is a polo shirt or shirt with a collar and/or sweater, khakis or dress pants and dress shoes. No tie is required.

3. Other Casual: This is a type of comfortable outfit a person wears on an everyday basis, or for casual networking events in the organisation, but does not to work. However, It includes jeans, tee shirts, flip flops, sneakers.

4. Adornment and Artifacts: The way in which people carry cigarettes, pipes, canes or glasses also suggests different semiotic meanings. (Semiotics is the science of the emotional or psychological impact of signs, appearances and of how things look). This understanding is gaining a lot of importance, especially in audio-visual communication including advertisements and entertainment, where a lot has to be communicated very effectively in a very short time.

1.8 Body Language

People react to the unspoken, as much (if not more) to how something is said and try to find out the explicit meaning of the words. Failure to identify and understand them can lead to misunderstandings. Hence, to be effective communicators, it is very necessary for managers to learn from reading and through training programmes about how the human body and actions can send signals, both voluntary or intentional, and also about the effects of different methods of non-verbal communication. The following diagram shows the elements of body language.

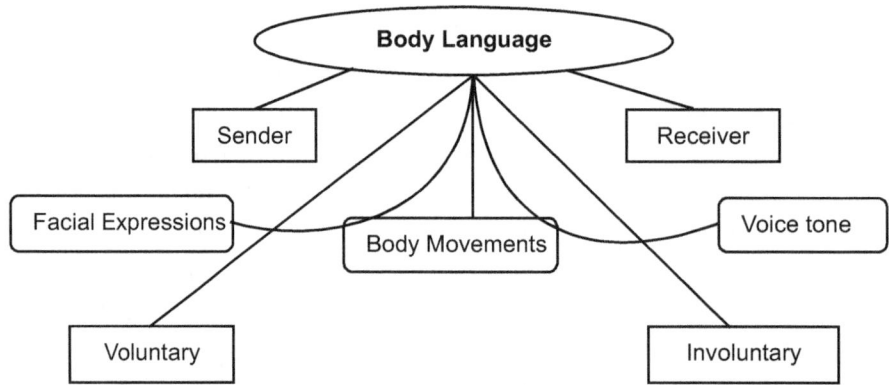

Note: It can be in agreement with or contradict spoken words

Fig. 1.12

Body language is a term used to describe a whole set of non-verbal means of communication, such as body posture, gestures, facial expressions and eye movements.

Human beings possess this unique mental and physical capability to send as well receive such signals and also interpret and respond to them almost entirely subconsciously. They can 'read' others' body language and even mirror them to put the other person at ease. In the 1990s Paul Ekman expanded his list of basic emotions like sorrow, happiness and anger and included a range of positive and negative emotions that the body can communicate effectively. They include:

1. Amusement
2. Contempt
3. Contentment
4. Embarrassment
5. Excitement
6. Guilt
7. Pride in achievement
8. Relief
9. Satisfaction
10. Sensory pleasure
11. Shame

Body language could be involuntary or 'accidental' body language covering all the different types of movements, postures and facial expressions. It could be intentional warm body language, such as empathic movements and touch, postures and facial expressions or intentional abusive body language, such as violent/abusive movements and touch, postures and facial expressions.

Facial Expressions

Of all the types of non-verbal communication, this may be one of the most noticeable. Sometimes, fleeting, involuntary expressions appear on the face which a person is not intending to communicate or even aware of. *People examine each others' faces as they talk, trying to get some information to confirm that the meaning is received in the manner in which it is delivered*. The human face is more highly developed as an organ of expression than that of any other animal.

For instance, *Smiling* is one facial expression that is likely to put other people at ease and make them feel accepted and comfortable. A smile can add happiness and comfort to the conversation. It is a powerful cue that transmits happiness, friendliness, warmth, and liking. The person who maintains a smiling face while talking or delivering a speech will be received warmly by the audience. Such a countenance is indicative of a likable person, pleasant, friendly, warm and approachable. People will react to that person more favourably. It is said that a smile is a universal language. But let us not forget, a person can have a sarcastic smile while talking to someone. A smile with a smirk or grimace can indicate quite the opposite of a pleasant conversation. Scowling, lip chewing, and raising eyebrows can all signal different meanings. A person can express a number of negative feelings such as unhappiness, frustration, anger etc., through facial expressions. So it is important to be aware of how the face looks during a conversation. This is true of both the sender and the receiver.

Here are just a few types of feelings that a human face can express:

pensive	amused	sad	barely tolerant
warning	pouting	anxious	attracted
startled	confused	sleepy	intoxicated

Eye Contact

It is an essential tool in non-verbal communication as it **makes the other person feel heard, respected, and important**. It helps to open and regulate the flow of communication. It signals interest in the other person/persons and increases the speaker's interest, concern, warmth and credibility. Making good, consistent eye contact can elevate a person's status as a great conversationalist. However, it can make the other person feel uncomfortable if it goes on for too long. Modern American business culture values a fair degree of eye contact in interpersonal relations, and looking away is considered as avoidance or even deviousness. In some cultures, it is not appreciated if children look at their elders' face, as it can signify rudeness. For some it may feel too intimate, for others it may feel challenging. When cultures interact, this inhibition of gaze may be misinterpreted as "passive aggressive" or worse.

Gestures

Gestures are another type of non-verbal communication. They can add warmth and personality to a conversation. Hand gesture, nodding appropriately etc., can be an easy way to show that the listener is understanding and is connecting with the speaker. Failing to use gestures while speaking may make the person appear boring and stiff and this perception can hinder the communication process. A lively and animated speaking style captures the listener's attention, makes the conversation more interesting, and facilitates understanding.

There are many kinds of gestures:

clenching fist	shaking a finger	pointing
biting fingernails	tugging at hair	squirming
rubbing chin	smoothing hair	folding arms
raising eyebrows	pursing lips	narrowing eyes
scratching head	looking away	hands on hips
hands behind head	rubbing nose	rocking
sticking out tongue	tugging earlobe	waving

Each of these have many different meanings in different cultures, and what may be friendly in one country or region can be an insult in another (Morris et al, 1979, Maginnis, 1958).

Posture and Body Orientation

The way a person walks, talks, stands, and sits sends numerous messages to others. Standing erect and leaning forward communicates to the listeners that the person is approachable, receptive and friendly. Interpersonal closeness results when the sender and the listener face each other. Not facing the listener or looking at the floor or ceiling should be avoided as it communicates disinterest, or even dishonesty. Posture is always easy to understand. A comfortable and confident person will stand or sit in a relaxed manner, and will have fluid smooth movements. Such a person will face the conversation partner with confidence and engaging conversation skills.

Proximity

Personal space and interpersonal distance, i.e., physical distance between the communicating partners signals their level of intimacy and comfort. If an unknown person stands too close or touches too often, it will make the other person feel uncomfortable. Sitting on the table in the office, standing too close to the superiors etc., may not be appreciated. There are unspoken and invisible rules governing personal distance. People stand too near when they are more intimate. When they are not so close, they should be at a distance.

Edward T. Hall is most associated with proxemics, the study of the human use of space within the context of culture. In *The Hidden Dimension* (1966), he argued that human sensory apparatus is the source of all perceptions of space, and these perceptions operate at the subconscious level and are moulded and patterned by culture. These perceptions can impede communication and understanding in cross-cultural settings. He analysed both the personal spaces that people create around their bodies as well as the macro-level sensibilities that shape cultural expectations about the organisation of streets, neighbourhoods and cities.

Edward Hall's theory of proxemics suggests that people will maintain differing degrees of personal distance depending on the social setting and their cultural backgrounds.

He observes that people want "territories" as their own in any given environment. Such territories include:

(i) Space surrounding one's body artifacts (brief case, books, purses).
(ii) Objects in the environment (chairs, desks, tables).
(iii) Space used by persons such as the area between two persons, as well as larger territories such as houses or offices.

Hall's most famous innovation has to do with the definition of the informal or personal spaces that surround individuals:

- Intimate space – the closest "bubble" of space surrounding a person. Only the closest persons can reach this level.
- Social and consultative spaces – the spaces in which people feel comfortable conducting routine social interactions with acquaintances as well as strangers.
- Public space – the area of space beyond which people will perceive interactions as impersonal and relatively anonymous.

> Hall describes the handling of space during conversations: "A U.S. male...stands 18 to 20 inches away when talking face to face to a man he does not know very well; talking to a woman under similar circumstances, he increases the distance about four inches. A distance of only 8 to 13 inches between males is considered...very aggressive. Yet in many parts of Latin America and the Middle East, distances which are almost sexual in connotation are the only ones at which people can talk comfortably." Hall (1955) concluded: "If you are a Latin American, talking to a North American at the distance he insists on maintaining is like trying to talk across a room."

Hall argues that cultural expectations determine these spaces. Americans travelling to Europe would tend to back away instinctively, as the distance maintained there is almost half of what Americans do.

Every culture has similar internalised expectations about how fixed and semi-fixed features, such as furniture, buildings and cities should be organised. United States cities, for instance, are customarily set out along a network, a preference inherited from the British, but in France and Spain a star pattern is preferred.

In general, distances differ according to culture and the closeness or otherwise of a relationship, such as friends, co-workers, and sales people etc., and very often, this is expressed intuitively. Again it depends on the place of interaction, such as public places like parks, restaurants, or on the street and in private homes. It also depends on the gender of the communicating parties. It is necessary to study the cultural norms and look for signals of discomfort caused by invading the other person's space. It is necessary to be aware of the other persons' body language as well as their attitude and respond accordingly. It is always correct to maintain a dignified distance from the receivers.

Context or Environment – Spatial Language

It is relating to the place or environment in which the actual process of communication takes place. It may be physical or psychological. The necessary requirements of environment are lighting, colour, ventilation, temperature, seating arrangement, display boards, public address system, audio-visual equipment etc., which would help a lot to attract and make listeners more attentive. While this category is not actually a mode of nonverbal communication, the setting up of a room or how one places oneself in that room is a powerfully suggestive action. Where one sits in the group in relation to the others is often useful in understanding that person's status or attitude. Group leaders as well as the participants need to study the way the room is organised, the seating and other arrangements and the manner in which it can affect communication. The variables to be considered in a group setting like a meeting, workshop, consultation or conference are:

- Size of the room
- Colors of the walls, floor, furniture, background etc.
- The source, amount, and direction of light,
- Color of the lighting,

- Obvious props such as the podium, display blackboard, cameras etc.
- The number of people present and seating arrangements,
- The numbers and ratios of high-status and low status people,
- The positioning of the various people in the space,
- Environmental sounds, smells, and temperature

Environment: The observations of *Maslow and Mintz* regarding different types of environment are:

(i) An Ugly Room: would appear as a messy janitor's closet. It gives an impression of monotonous, fatiguing, irritating and unpleasant environment.

(ii) An Average Room: a professor's office.

(iii) A Beautiful Room having carpeting, drapes, nice furniture: a successful business executive's cabin. It indicates pleasure, comfort, importance, enjoyment.

Touch

The manner in which a person touches another communicates a great deal of information. Touch could take a variety of forms, indicating different meanings, such as a gentle grip or a firm one, holding the other person on the back of the upper arm, on the shoulder, or in the middle of the back. It could be a push or a tug. It could be a pat, a rub, or a grab. Each of these indicates different areas of personal intimacy, and this again can be gender- and age-specific. Many adolescents resent any touching that indicates a patronising stance or undue familiarity. Even the angle of one's holding another's hand might suggest a hurrying or coercive implicit attitude, or a respectful, gentle, permission-giving approach (Smith, Clance & Imes, 1998, Jones, 1994).

Locomotion

Physical expressions like waving, pointing, touching and slouching are all forms of non-verbal communication. *This branch of study which covers body movement and expression is known as kinesics.* These movements make communication much easier as they can be used to emphasise a point, or repeat one.

Examples:
- The classic example is *crossing of hands across the chest* to communicate that the person is angry or displeased, is through, and does not want to hear any more, thus putting an unconscious barrier between the communicating parties. If the person is also leaning away from the speaker, it could communicate opposition and if it is accompanied by frown or a harsh expression, it could be outright hostility.
- Eye contact can be interpreted in many ways depending on how it is done. Consistent eye contact may mean that the person has warm feelings and is thinking positively of what the speaker is saying. Interestingly, if the other person does not trust the speaker, his eyes will not wander and stay focused on him/her. On the contrary, lack of eye contact may indicate negative feelings for the other person. If the receiver has

arms crossed across the chest while making eye contact, he may be signaling impatience and may want to talk about something that is bothering him/her. The act of fiddling while making eye contact may indicate that the person is distracted. Looking at the other person by moving from one eye to another eye and then at the forehead may signify an authoritarian posture, while if the focus shifts to the nose, the conversation is between equals. A simple explanation for lack of eye contact could be that the person has anxiety disorder and has problems focusing on the other person.

- Touching the ear or scratching the chin can indicate disbelief. It can also be seen if the person has averted the gaze.
- A tilted head may simply mean neck problem, but as part of non-verbal communication, it means loss of interest in what is being said. The person may engage the speaker in eye contact, but that does not mean anything.

The style of physical movement in space also communicates a great deal, as well as affecting the feelings of the person doing the moving (Morris, 1977). There could be a number of movements, such as:

slither	crawl	totter	walk
stroll	shuffle	hurry	run
jog	spring	tiptoe	march
jump	hop	skip	climb
swing	acrobatics	swim	slink

The pace or the manner in which an action is done can also indicate the mood of the person.

jerky	pressured	nervous	gradual
graceful	fatigued	tense	easy
shaky	deliberate	furtive	clumsy

A related variable to the pace aspect is the time it takes to react to a stimulus, called "latency of response." People can be slower or faster "on the uptake" than others while reacting to questions, or while interacting in conversations. Slow response may indicate that the person is organising his/her thought and is planning a response. It may also mean a superiority attitude almost saying. "How could you put this question to me?"

Silence

The question often arises whether silence is a mode of a communication or not. The answer is that one can communicate silently. Silence sometimes speaks louder than words. For instance, a speaker can stop his speech and remain silent if the audience is getting distracted. This works better than if the speaker appeals to the audience to pay attention. (Of course, silence on the part of the Speaker in a legislative body in India cannot have the same effect! The Speaker has to stand up to signal an unruly set of legislators to calm down and sit.) Silence, combined with an angry look can indicate admonition. Silence could also be in response to sudden shock, excitement, extreme grief etc. In a feedback situation, a written message may be ignored (silence) to indicate that the message had no value to the receiver. The practice of silence is usually taken as assent or approval in a number of personal, business and social transactions, depending on the issue, the participants and the culture they belong to. However, in the law of contract, silence, i.e., failure to respond to an offer is not proof that the offer has been accepted.

Paralinguistics

Sounds are the basis for paralanguage. Paralanguages include tone of voice, power or emphasis, pitch, rhythm, volume, pause or break in sentence, speed or delivery, loudness or softness etc. Speakers can use such non-verbal signals for effective communication. A manager has to learn to vary his/her voice according to the context. For instance, a person who speaks in a monotone voice does not command respect, as the listeners may perceive him/her as dull. A person who has a lively voice can catch the attention of the listeners and ensure that he/she is heard. On the other hand, a person may alter his/her voice quality to indicate something different than the words used in the communication. Then, the paralinguistics become most noticeable. The power of the voice tone over the meaning communicated can never be underestimated.

Paralanguage can be divided into four parts:
1. In-born Voice Qualities : Including such factors as pitch, resonance, volume, rate, and rhythm.
2. Vocal Characterisers : Embarrassing laughter, coughing, throat clearing and sighing.
3. Vocal Qualifiers : Variations in pitch, modulation and volume.
4. Vocal Segregates : Including sounds such as 'ah' and 'er' and pauses. These clues do a lot to influence meaning.

The lesson to be drawn by managers and students of communication studies is clear: Though they have some voice qualities which are in-born, they have to exert some control over the tone and pitch while communicating in the office. Using too many segregates can give the impression that the speaker is not confident about the content and also about how to deliver it. Secondly, they should try to keep the words spoken and the paralinguistics in sync or in agreement with each other. This will help keep the messages clear, understandable, and less likely to be misinterpreted.

Dialect

Related to paralinguistics is a semi-linguistic element, viz., dialect, with all its tonal variations along with difference in grammar and usage. This has deep cultural undertones, suggesting class, age, sophistication, etc., and the resultant prejudices. It affects understanding people from different backgrounds, generations and cultures. For instance, managers seeking to work in rural areas in India should not humiliate them for their appearance, habits, dialect and style of talking. What matters most is the content of the message and how effectively it can be communicated. Managers should understand, accept and respect these nuances and not develop biases based on language and diction.

Sign Language

When in the place of spoken words, numbers or punctuations marks, symbols such as gestures are used, it is known as sign language. For instance, deaf, mute people communicate by making signs with their fingers. These signs are accepted and recognised and standardised. They are trained for this, as also their family members, teachers and care givers. Apart from this set of differently abled persons, under certain circumstances, sign language is used even by those who can speak, such as the sign used by those who cannot hear but see each other due to distance or physical barricades like glass doors or windows, hitch hikers, Morse code, traffic signals, outdoor advertisement hoardings etc. In a work environment, employees can use this mode if they do not want to be heard.

Action Language

It is a language of movements. Action in a particular situation and context can be interpreted to give a meaning. By action, one may knowingly or unknowingly be communicating with others. For instance, anger is generally demonstrated by throwing things around, happiness with clapping etc.

Fig. 1.13: Forms of Non-verbal Language

Demonstration

Demonstration is a process of showing how something works, for instance in a laboratory or a teleshopping show. This can be combined with words for greater effect. Surgeons demonstrate medical procedures either in the operation theatre or through a video-conference. Demonstration can also be used to show feelings, such as a hug to show appreciation or love, and a push or a jab to show extreme displeasure. Demonstration also includes public expression of an opinion by holding meetings and processions and displaying placards. The larger the gathering, the more powerful would be the speaker. Thus it becomes a show of strength for a trade union or a political party or a public campaign. Demonstration is thus a very effective method of nonverbal expression to convey meaning and can be used and dramatised as a means of emphasis on the subject under consideration.

Inaction

Inaction also is one of the non-verbal media of communication. For instance, a manager seeks cooperation from peers from other departments. Such requests may go unheeded to indicate a number of things – the person who has initiated the request is not important, he/she is a threat to the respondent's position in the organisation, the respondent has some old grudge to make up for, or simply that the respondent did not understand the importance. A market research executive may need the statistician's help in analysing the sales figures, but the latter may take no action, for whatever reason he/she has. Such lack of communication may affect the effectiveness of the organisation.

Time

Use of time, also known as chronemics, is an important non-verbal method of communication. *Edward T. Hall* is the first scholar who has investigated this dimension of interpersonal communication and group activities in an organisation.

Punctuality or delay speaks pleasant or unpleasant feelings and attitudes. Tardiness is considered an insult in some cultures. Late arrival for a meeting conveys something about the person – his/her time management skills including respect for others' time, his/her interest in the topic or project, and the importance attached to it. It may simply mean that the person was stuck in some unforeseen traffic jam or there was some compelling reason. A person who is habitually late for office or at meetings gets noticed and that may be the cause of his/her downfall. Hence, a lot of emphasis is given to proper planning and scheduling of activities. Arriving at an appointed place on or before time and completing given tasks well within the schedule clearly indicates the person's sincerity and his/her attitude to work. Similarly, all written communication should be completed keeping the time factor in mind. If a meeting notice goes weeks before the scheduled event, the persons receiving it may forget it and if it is sent too close to the scheduled event, the person may not have adequate time to prepare for it, or may not factor it into his/her busy schedule. The managers have to judge when to send these notices or information and when to make follow-up calls.

New types of non-verbal communication
- Emoticons in emails and text messages are the newest addition to this list.
- FaceBook and other social media offer newer channels wherein people post pictures and comments to provoke a reaction.

1.9 Role Playing

(a) Special features: As a communication technique, role-playing can be used to allow students to experiment with different styles of interaction and investigate complex issues. It is a form of interactive group session where the experience of participating in the role-play is the basis for further discussion.

(b) Uses:
- It can be used to discuss case studies and course material in business schools.
- In actual work situations, valuable inputs can be obtained from various participants on some intriguing issues.
- It can also be used in employee training programmes on proper communication techniques. For instance, in training for customer interaction, it might include making a cold call to a prospective customer to educate him about the product or service the company offers. In a retail store, customers may be requested to role play as an employee suggests a product her.
- The customer service team may need to be trained to deal with difficult customers without ruining the company's reputation. For example, a customer might visit the store complaining about a missing button on a dress she bought recently. The role-playing exercise can show employees that the proper way to handle the issue is to replace the item and provide the customer with a discount card for a future purchase. The objective would be to highlight the need to maintain goodwill that satisfied customers can build for the organisation.
- In employee training for team building and working effectively with co-workers, they can be taught how to positively interact with each other in the workplace. A role playing exercise might include role play to resolve an error found in a report or demonstrating how to work together as a team.
- Conducting interviews is a part of the employee recruiting process. As a role-playing exercise or a mock interview, the human resources staff and managers can be taught about how to conduct effective employee interviews. The feedback will show them which questions are appropriate, how to frame the questions, and how to ask follow-up questions, so that the potential employees share their experience and reveal their personalities.
- Employee evaluations give managers an opportunity to review employee performance and provide employees with new goals for the next quarter or year. Through role play new managers can be helped to learn how to approach tough

topics such as poor performance. A senior manager can act as the employee getting an evaluation, who will then provide the new member with feedback. This is part of employee retention measures.

- Non-verbal cues are an aspect of business communication, which employees can learn from role plays. During meetings with staff and co-workers or with clients, non-verbal cues such as eye contact and posture are major factors. During the role-playing exercise, the employees can demonstrate non-verbal cues, which are then discussed. For instance, an employee can play the role of a person who has lost interest in a meeting, by slouching, crossing his arms, avoid eye contact, doodle etc. The others around the employee can react. Such role plays are useful to demonstrate how negative non-verbal cues can distract other and affect the tone of a meeting.

(c) **Method:** The script for this could be prepared and the actors determined ahead of the workshop, or the tasks can be assigned on the spot where the description of the roles is given to the actors with a time limit specified for preparing their acts. For instance in a workshop on a specific marketing issue or case, a role play can indicate the likely position taken by the prospective client, and the suggested strategy to be adopted. The roles could be that of the CEO wanting to know the situation in detail as it is a tricky but important issue, and heads of relevant departments. The actors suggest and discuss possible strategies in their respective roles. The observers will be making their own notes. The moderator will be assessing the participants and their arguments.

Role plays are generally used in classes dealing with social issues (social sciences, management sciences, etc.) or communication strategies, such as interviewing techniques, conflict management, etc.

(d) **Procedure:**
- Get the scenarios and characters for role-plays.
- Explain the advantages of adopting this group communication technique.
- Describe the background context and the setting for the role-play.
- Assign the roles to the players with a briefing about the characters they are playing, their point of view, characteristics, etc. Based on this, the actors can prepare their acts. Specific time may be allotted to them to prepare their acts.
- Some participants can be assigned the task of observers.
- A time limit for the act could be set, after which the play ends.
- The entire event can be recorded for analysis.

(e) **After the act:** Debriefing and discussion on the role-play. The players' perceptions and observers' notes can be used as the basis for a broader discussion of the case or course material. Special attention will be paid to identify conflicts, ambiguities, supportive arguments placed by the actors and useful suggestions etc.

1.10 Debates

Debate is a method of interactive argument, where one side wins or prevails over the other because of its superior content, context and presentation. More important than the objective facts is the consensus or some formal way of reaching a resolution. In a formal debating contest, there is a broad framework for interaction by the contestants, and within this framework are the rules to be observed by them.

Debates can be formal or informal. Debating is commonly organised in various types of assemblies to discuss matters and to arrive at problem resolution. All deliberative bodies such as parliaments and legislative assemblies in democracies, and meetings of all sorts, engage in formal debates. Political parties engage in debates about their position regarding major issues. TV channels regularly conduct debates on serious issues facing the country.

In educational institutes, debates are organised for competitive, educational and recreational purposes. Children get an opportunity to develop their ability to face audiences and to debate rationally from either position with equal ease. The quality and depth of a debate depends on the knowledge base of the participants and their debating skills. The outcome of the debate may be determined by a panel of judges or by audience vote or a combination of both.

Purpose of debates:
- The basic purpose is to develop critical thinking by the children.
- Children to differentiate between ideas, under the strengths and weaknesses of those ideas and form their opinion, anticipate the questions and accordingly, prepare their points.
- Children learn to verify the evidence before expressing their opinions.
- Children learn to resolve controversies.
- Debates encourage the children to participate in large groups without losing control. In a class room setting, Instructors can plan the debates beforehand, or the activity can emerge spontaneously from the material being taught. They help the students

A formal debate has two teams, one presents a plan or supports the proposition and the other side rebuts it. The team affirming the proposition has to demonstrate the significance, topicality, and viability of the idea. A competitive debate can have the topic announced much in advance or can be on the spot, with very little time allowed for preparation. Sometimes, several topics are written on pieces of paper which are kept folded (fish bowl). The students are asked to pick up one slip randomly and prepare for the debate. Usually there are pre-arranged questions and a time limit is set for each speaker.

Description of the activity: The topic selected is controversial, and the students are asked to place their arguments in an orderly manner, within the time limit stipulated for each stage of argument and rebuttal. The judge or the audience cast their votes to declare the winning team. There could be a follow-up discussion to review the positions taken by the teams and the effectiveness of their arguments.

Prerequisites: The participants should have enough knowledge about the topic being debated. Secondly, they should have adequate time to prepare their case.

Procedure for organising a debate:
- Decide if this will be a formal or an informal debate and determine the format. The formal debate would have clear topics and more rules. Informal debates can be organised to help children explore and understand the subject. In such cases, it would not be possible for the children to take sides. The teacher will then assign roles for the children. He can provide the necessary reading material or let the children find it. Non-participants can be allowed to participate by raising questions. The teacher can give feedback immediately after the debate. Peer review can also be sought.
- Describe the background context, and explain why you are having a debate.
- Set the time for the session.
- Decide on the participating teams.
- Introduce the judges if the panel has been constituted.
- If it is a learning exercise, divide the class into two parts, viz., the proposers and the dissenters and seat them accordingly.
- Establish ground rules for the discussion, such as not using bad words or insulting language, not interrupting the current speaker etc.
- Invite someone from each side to open and present their arguments.
- Expand participation by opening the issue to the audience. In a larger group, the audience can raise their hands to indicate that they want to come in. They can address their questions to specific debater.
- The moderator can ask provocative questions, but should not express judgment on any point of view, as that will appear like a closure to the topic.
- Give each participant time for a closing argument.
- Close the debate at the end of the time period set.

1.10.1 Quiz

A quiz can be an **informal** one such as in a class, to ensure that the children pay attention. It is a non-threatening method for the teacher to get immediate feedback on the student's understanding of what has been taught. The teacher can also use this method to assess the extent of prior knowledge the students possess on a subject before it is taken up for teaching.

In a **formal**, competitive quiz, the participants' knowledge and quick memory are tested. They could be general quizzes or on selected topics like physics, chemistry, geography, movies, sports etc. There could be individual contestants or teams participating depending on the format. Questions may be asked or for each question, or multiple choice answer options provided for the contestant to pick the right answer. Many organisations hold school, district, state and national championships. These days with the proliferation of TV channels, quiz programmes have become extremely popular, with top rated film stars hosting them. Computers are used to select the questions randomly and also provide the answer choices.

1.11 Group

Groups are a part of our life. A basic dictionary definition of a group is *a number of individuals assembled together or having some unifying relationship*. Groups provide an opportunity for people to socialise, work as teams, plan and implement projects together, solve problems etc. A group gives an identity to its members.

1.11.1 Defining 'Group'

Efforts by researchers to define a group have provided various perspectives of the subject. While some have said that working in the presence of others tends to raise the performance levels of all the members, others have focused on the interdependence aspect of a group. Kurt Lewin (1948), for example, found that nearly all groups were based on *interdependence* among their members, whether the group was large or small, formally structured or loose. The purpose of the group formation or the similarity or dissimilarity of the members was not of any significance according to him.

Other researchers have emphasised on various other aspects of group formation, such as purpose, shared identity, structure, face-to-face communication situation, a network of interpersonal relationships etc. Donelson R. Forsyth (2006: 2-3) defines a group as two or more individuals who are connected to one another by social relationships. [emphasis in original]. This definition highlights three elements of a group, viz., the number of individuals involved, connection, and relationship.

Jarlath F. Benson has identified a list of attributes of a group:

- A set of people engaged in frequent interactions
- They identify with one another.
- They are defined by others as a group.
- They share beliefs, values, and norms about areas of common interest.
- They define themselves as a group.
- They come together to work on common tasks and for agreed purposes (Benson 2000: 5)
- Usually, groups come together for a specific purpose or to meet an objective. The basic idea behind this group formation includes. (a) decision-making, (b) problem solving, (c) idea generating, (d) therapy or cure, (e) education or learning.

1.11.2 Characteristics of a Group

- Members interact together
- They become interdependent
- They share norms
- They share values, and
- They have a collective identity

As such, cohesion is expected in a group, which comes from a common purpose understood by all the members, though group dynamics may sometimes work at cross purposes.

Factors that help groups succeed

Positive factors are:

- Valid information. All the members are aware of the main objectives of the group. Without any hierarchical considerations, *all the members have been provided full and authentic information about the issue on hand* and have access to any additional sources they require so as to contribute meaningfully in the group discussion.
- *Free and informed choice of the members to agree* with some proposals put up by the others or to disagree without any pressures from any quarters, and
- *Internal commitment* among the members towards the purpose, duration, and results expected.

Negative Factors are:

If proper care is not taken in the composition of the team some **Negative factors** come into play and hinder smooth functioning of the group activities, such as:

- *Personal conflicts* among the members, which will get reflected in their attitude towards working together. They can project this in their manners, language used etc., dissuading the others from participating in the discussions wholeheartedly. Personal ego, feeling of superiority due to sex, higher education, longer experience, proximity to power sources in the organisation etc., are all detrimental to group functioning.
- *Competitive atmosphere* and a feeling of insecurity among the members, because of which some members may try bullying tactics, manipulate the discussions and the outcome to suit their own agenda. They may even try to claim all credit for the work done in the group in order to secure or promote their own status in the organisation.
- Formation of *cliques or subgroups*, which can hammer down even the most logical suggestions.
- *Unequal member involvement* due to difficulty in understanding the technical and other details, attitudinal problems, time pressures etc.
- *Different level of communication skills*, and
- *Different communicator styles.*

Forces that determine Group Processes and Dynamics

- **Group interaction,** i.e., the way in which people engage with and influence each other. It could be (a) task interaction focussed principally on the group's goals, work, projects etc., and/ (b) relationship interaction, concerned with social and interpersonal aspects of group interaction.
- **Group interdependence,** the realisation that the outcomes of the group depend not only on the actions of individual members, but also on the actions of others in the group. A member's feelings, experiences, actions and decisions can be influenced by the other members.
- **Group structure,** which indicates the roles and patterns of relationship among the members of the group. Size of the group determines the nature of interaction among the members. Generally large groups function differently than smaller groups. They are more likely to include people with a range of skills and this can allow for more specialisation among the members. Members may feel more comfortable, as they can avoid any focus on themselves. However, they may feel irrelevant and hence their morale may be very low. In smaller groups, more number of members are likely to participate.
- *Group norms.* Norms are basically rules of conduct or codes of behaviour that indicate what attitudes and behaviour might be expected or demanded. They are the shared beliefs regarding what is normal, correct, true, moral and good. Group life is dependent upon trust and a certain amount of loyalty and hence, group norms are essential for the group's survival and success. These generally have powerful effects on the thoughts and actions of group members. They also act to reduce uncertainty in difficult situations. They provide a way forward for interaction.
- **Group roles:** Different members play different roles, either assigned or evolved and generally, the evolved roles emerge during the interactions. These roles help to differentiate the members from one another. The leader is expected to be the 'information giver', 'harmonizer', 'recorder' etc.
- **Group goals** are the ends or the aims or the outcomes the group would be working towards and entail some sort of joint vision. Without some commitment towards common goals the group will not survive or be effective. However, a group may in fact have several conflicting goals as well, depending on the personalities of the members and their independent agenda.
- **Group cohesion** which can be described as the forces or bonds that connect the individual members.

Groups develop as the members want to know something about the other members, have to develop a degree of interdependence in order that the group or team may achieve its tasks, group work is satisfying to its members and the members have to learn at some level to deal with conflict to ensure its survival. Bruce W. Tuckman (1965) has developed a model to explain the process of development of a group, including forming, performing, norming, storming and adjourning as a later addition.

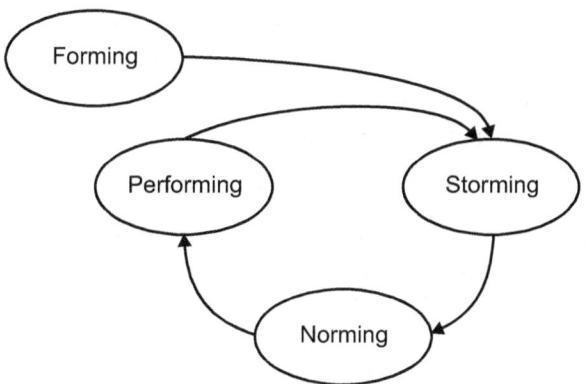

Fig. 1.14

Groups are important in an organisation and it is necessary to strengthen them as they can foster mutual help and organisational well-being.

> *It is said that you may find it difficult to live with groups but you cannot live without them.*

1.11.3 Group Communication

As can be seen from the description of a group and its characteristics, the quality and depth of communication within the group essentially determines its success or otherwise.

Group communication is described as communication between 3 or more individuals. Small group communication includes numbers from 3 to about 20 people, and large group communication includes numbers larger than that, such as lectures, theatrical productions, religious discourses etc. It basically implies a many-to-many communication style in a *group*, going beyond both one-to-one communication and one-to-many communication.

The use of Group Communication for solving problems and for other purposes is as old as our social system. It is only during the twentieth century that group communication got wide acceptance for sociological analysis, decision making and a host of other objectives.

> *"A group is a bunch of persons who are interacting with one another in such a manner that each person influences and is influenced by each other person".*
> – Marvin Shaw

1.11.4 Characteristics of Group Communication

Social psychologist Robert Bales observes the following characteristics of group communication:

- Groups have *tasks* to complete and at the same time, the discussion tends to be influenced by the *relationship* among the members and the members and the task. Conflicts could arise during task discussions and this stress among members must be released through positive relational talk. Thus, there is an implicit attempt to balance the demands of task completion and group cohesion.
- The group discussion shifts from an emphasis on exchange of opinion to *making the decision*.

- Irrespective of the size of the group, the most talkative member tends to dominate, making 40 to 50 percent of the comments and the second most talkative member, between 25 and 30. As a result, large groups tend to be *dominated by one or two members* to the disadvantage of the others.

1.11.5 Purpose of Group Communication

The purposes of Group Communication in an organisation could be many. As most of the senior executives and managers are generally pressed for time, meetings are scheduled much in advance, depending on the time slots available of each manager. The objective could be any of the following:

- To inform the employees about policy decisions, generally formal and structured in nature and called by the top management of the organisation. The leader does all the talking except when he/she asks questions to any individual or the group. Interruptions are not tolerated.
- Routine review of activities. The schedules are known to all participants and are prepared with all information. These are held on a regular, generally weekly basis to review actions, day-to-day problems, progress achieved on tasks identified at the previous meeting etc. In a multi-location organisation like a chemical, petroleum or oil services company, where breakdowns can be extremely devastating, such weekly meetings wherein all locations report about their operations is very crucial. The reporting is done in an order, each at a time, with no interruptions.
- Emergency meetings if there are major breakdowns. The extent of damage, immediate actions to be taken, identification of the causes for the breakdown and assignment of responsibilities.
- To share and exchange information and ideas, brainstorming on important issues.
- To collect information or feedback on any project/policy/scheme, including important milestones achieved, 'go'/'no go' decisions. They cover issues including market diversification, new projects, acquisitions, mergers etc.
- To arrive at a decision on important matters, such as hiring new employees.
- To solve a problem that is of concern to the entire organisation.
- To discuss the issues related to a particular topic in relation to the group itself or for the benefit of a larger audience
- To elaborate upon any work undertaken or research done in order to educate and also elicit feedback.
- At the company level, there are the formal, structured Statutory Meeting after formation of the company, AGMs and Extraordinary General Meetings.

1.11.6 The basic types of Group Communication

- **Standing Meeting:** These are meetings that occur regularly and the agenda is known and well established. They could however be rescheduled in case the superior has other commitments. Such meetings could be regularly scheduled appointments with a superior or a department head. They could also be project meetings convened at regular intervals over the duration of the project.

- **Topical Meeting:** A gathering called to discuss one subject, such as a work issue or a task related to a project.
- **Presentation:** A highly structured meeting where one or more people speak and a moderator leads the proceedings. The purpose is usually to inform. Attendees may have an opportunity to ask questions, but typically their participation is limited. Much depends on the comfort level of the speakers.
- **Conference:** A highly structured, moderated meeting, like a presentation, where the agenda is fixed and various participants contribute according to the time allotted to them.
- **Seminar:** A structured meeting with an educational purpose. Seminars are usually led by people with expertise in the subject matter.
- **Emergency Meeting:** A meeting called to address a crisis, whether internal or external. Such meetings are often arranged with very little notice, but attendance is mandatory. Emergency meetings typically take precedence over all other commitments.

1.11.7 Importance of Group Communication

1. Group communication is much better for producing an acceptable decision than an individual taking all the decisions. It is said that two heads are better than one. It pools together the resources of the organisation, both intellectual and experience.
2. It allows the division of labour according to the expertise available in the organisation.
3. The group communication process prevents occurrence of errors of judgements as opinions expressed are subjected to scrutiny by the others.
4. The group communication process acts as a stimulant by encouraging intellectual competition as each member tries to come up with more superior arguments.
5. The group communication process ensures commitment to the decisions taken jointly by the group.
6. It fosters greater understanding of the members as they come together physically and mentally. They begin to think of themselves as a body of persons.

1.11.8 Facilitation of Group Communication

Groups can have structured facilitation or they can be loosely organised. The extent to which a meeting is structured depends on the issue being discussed, background of the participants and the comfort level of the speaker.

The benefits of using structured facilitation techniques to organise a meeting are:
- Efficiency in generating, organising and prioritising many ideas in a short period of time,
- Minimising the opportunity for any one group member to influence heavily the thinking of the others because of his or her position in the organisation,

- Ensuring that everyone participates and that no one person dominates the discussion,
- As a number of ideas are generated right in the beginning, the members do not focus on one or a few ideas too early in the discussion. All the suggestions are discussed threadbare.
- Ideas/discussion highlights are easily documented for all to see in "real time",
- Participants can see that their contributions are valued.
- Records of the discussions can be maintained, duly signed, for further reference.

1.11.9 Positive Factors for Group Communication

Discussions play an important role in groups. Discussion, as with other forms of communication, takes both time and patience. A positive discussion includes opportunities for each group member to share information, ideas, and feelings (Glencoe, 2005). Discussions allow group members to exchange information, ideas and opinions. The members get an opportunity to ask questions and clarify issues. Hence, the most important positive factor of group communication is a *cooperative atmosphere*. The quality of group discussion is affected by the extent of cohesion within the group. With cohesion, group members share similar values and support one another.

1.11.10 Negative factors for Group Communication

Group facilitators should take the following *negative factors* and take appropriate measures to make group communication effective.
- Competitive atmosphere. Group members in this negative environment are more concerned about forcing their point on the others than sharing and learning new information. A sense of debate is common in a competitive atmosphere.
- Unequal member involvement,
- Formation of cliques or subgroups;
- Different level of communication skills,
- Different communicator styles, and
- Personal conflicts.

1.11.11 Methods for Reaching Group Decisions

Many methods may be used for reaching decisions in a group. They are:
- The most popular method in Western culture is by *majority*. Majority voting speeds up the decision process, and hence it is the most widely used.
- A second method is by *consensus*. Building consensus is time consuming, but it is the most satisfying for all concerned, as it allows everyone to bring forward their opinion.
- A third method is by *averaging*. This method requires all teammates to reach a decision by compromising.

- Reaching decisions through *committees*. This process calls for a subcommittee getting together and reaching decisions without the whole group being involved.
- A final method is by *authority rule*. In this method, the group leader listens to individual group members' ideas, and has the final say on the decision. The members would feel frustrated that they spent so much time discussing the issue, but were being sidelined in this manner. But it helps the management, as they will have understood the perspectives of all the members and hence can rationalise their decision.

1.11.12 Indications of Breakdown of Group Communication in an Organisation

An organisation will have to be on the lookout for signs that indicate overall loss of efficiency and total breakdown of communication leading to displeasure, circulation of rumours and even employee turnover.

1. It is very difficult to get some people to cooperate. They resort to complaining to the management most of the time.
2. Some people are being left out of the communication loop.
3. Replies to messages are being delayed or messages are completely ignored.
4. Groups in the organisation are failing to reach their goals.
5. Mistakes are cropping up more and more often leading to customer dissatisfaction, complaints from vendors and also by investors.
6. People are resorting more to criticism and placing the blame on other people.
7. Morale of the teams is going down.
8. Productivity is dull or at zero level.
9. Moments of conflict result in expressions of anger.
10. There is significant employee turnover.
11. Business is going to the competitors instead of the company.

1.12 Meetings

The literal meaning of the word "meeting" is *"an assembly of two or more persons"*. A company meeting has been defined by Shaw and Smith as *"an assembly of two or more persons connected with the company who have so gathered for the purpose of discussing matters related to it"*.

A meeting can be defined as coming together of two or more persons (by previous notice or by mutual agreement) for discussion and transaction of some lawful business. *Every meeting is an event to plan, schedule, evaluate and accelerate the company's work.*

In their day-to-day working, managers have crowded schedules with one meeting after another – staff meetings, project meetings, tactical meetings, strategic meetings, budget meetings, operations reviews and so on.

Meetings can be informal or formal.

Informal purposes:
- To communicate important or sensitive information
- To explore new ideas and concepts
- To provide feedback
- To present a report
- To gain support for an idea, or project

Formal Decision Making purposes:
- To reach a decision
- To solve a problem
- To reconcile a conflict
- To negotiate an agreement. This refers to a meeting to settle an argument or issue or close a deal in such a way as to benefit all the parties.
- To win acceptance for a new idea, plan or system.
- Conference, Seminar etc. A conference is a getting together for a discussion or an exchange of views. A seminar is a discussion group before whom the findings of some research or advanced study are placed in the form of oral or written reports and then discussed in detail.

One-on-one meetings

Such meetings allow the manager to make a *real connection* with each and every member of the team. This will make him/her a problem solver, a coach, an advisor, an influencer, or even an enabler. These meetings give the manager the necessary updates on group status, delegated tasks etc. Generally one-on-one meetings are focused on performance and/or goal review discussions. They also focus on what the subordinates want to communicate.

Need for one-on-one meetings are:
1. They provide an opportunity to connect individually to all the team members.
2. They should be used as an opportunity to build rapport, gauge morale, identify potential fatigue points, discuss key issues, etc.
3. They improve the morale of the employees and hence should be held as frequently as possible.
4. For the management, they can be a great forum to ask probing questions and get feedback on any management initiative. They also help build consensus on strategies on key issues.
5. They should be scheduled in advance, so that the members can participate meaningfully.
6. They should have mutual benefit. It would be beneficial for the participants to spend some time to discuss the subject matter set for the meetings.

Managing Meetings

Managing meetings effectively is *a core skill every manager should develop*. Even in these days of emails and social networking, meetings either in person or by way of conference calls, are important to clarify many issues. Tasks, like bringing in and weighing alternatives and generating ideas are best achieved in groups. However, there may be times, when a committee or a subcommittee needs to be formed to assess the situation and find solutions, which can then be presented to the group.

He/she should know when and why to call a meeting. The following situations may warrant meetings:

- **Project Management:** Projects tend to require meetings at various stages: at the beginning, as the project plan is coming together, and at regular intervals while the work is in progress. The frequency of the meetings is determined according to urgency felt. For instance, towards the end of the project, depending on its size, the number of people whose work needs to be coordinated and its complexity, daily meetings could be necessary.
- **People Management:** Many managers have periodic one-on-one meetings with the staff apart from weekly review meetings. These meetings give an opportunity for the manager to review the work accomplished in the previous week and look ahead to what will be accomplished in the coming week. Periodic one-on-one meetings add inputs to the weekly review meetings.
- **Client Management:** Ongoing relationships typically involve periodic meetings with the clients. Apart from these, many companies, especially professional services firms, make presentations to clients for various purposes such as sales presentations, commencement meetings, interim status meetings, and final presentations.
- **Problem Solving:** The manager may face many problem situations such as: the project is getting off course, there are interpersonal conflicts or there is some emergency situation.

The purpose of the meeting should help determine the appropriate format. If the matter is simple, and an off-hand suggestion is sufficient, the manager would walk across to the concerned person's office and talk the matter over in an informal manner. However, larger companies tend to have many formal meetings with established protocol. The length and formality of the meeting will vary depending on how many people are invited, how much notice is given, the size of the company and who is leading the meeting.

Advantages of Meetings

In an organisation, frequent meetings are held at various levels for its proper functioning, as it fosters team work and a cooperative environment. Collective thinking is applied to crucial issues facing the organisation.

1. Decisions are taken in the most democratic manner.
2. Meeting provides a sound platform to the members to express their views freely.

3. Through meetings, the members exercise their control over the functioning of the company.
4. Through meetings, members get the opportunity to vote on important matters relating to the company and so feel empowered.
5. The decisions taken in the meeting have a wider acceptability.
6. The actions and policies of the management are governed by the resolutions passed in the meetings.

Disadvantages of Meetings
1. Meetings (both formal and informal) are time consuming and expensive. Too many meetings may result in a fatigue factor that may blunt the enthusiasm of the managers. Managers may feel that it is a waste of time and infringement of their valuable productive time.
2. A great deal of money and time has to be spent on making preparations for the meeting and on the actual conduct of the meeting.
3. Meetings may not provide any useful outcome if some members take it lightly and attend them without any preparation, just for the sake of spending some time away from their work place.
4. Even with all genuine efforts, a meeting may end without any useful conclusion.

A manager learning the skills of managing a meeting effectively will have to plan for the meeting meticulously. The activities before a meeting include decisions on agenda, list of participants, time, duration, venue and the supplies, presentation tools and equipment required at the venue. He will have to issue meeting invitations/notifications to the participants well in time, neither too early, nor too late, such that the participants remember the event and make time for it in their schedule. The data sheets or information required by the participants should be dispatched to them so that they can come prepared.

The manager has to be a keen observer and should learn to pay attention to details and should practice excellent listening skills.

Components of a Meeting
   (a) **Authority to hold a Meeting:** Every meeting must be properly convened and duly constituted which means the meeting must be convened by a proper authority. At the topmost level, the proper authority to hold a company meeting is always the Board of Directors except in the case of extraordinary general meetings. Within the organisation, meetings can be called by the Chief of Operations, and various department heads to arrive at decisions for smooth operation of the company/department.
   (b) **Notice:** A notice is a written communication or intimation of the date, time and place and the business to be transacted at the meeting to all persons who are entitled to get it. Sending a notice is the first step. It can be hand delivered or sent by email for internal meetings, and for company meetings, it can be sent by post or inserted in

the newspapers in the form of an advertisement. In the case of company meetings, the notice must be sent at least 21 days prior to the meeting. For other meetings, a reasonable period should be given for the participants to prepare for the meeting.

(c) **Agenda:** Agenda is a statement of items to be discussed at the meeting and is intended to enable the members to study the subjects and come prepared for the discussion. The items should be arranged in a logical order and should be within the scope of the business to be transacted at the meeting. The agenda is usually sent to members along with the notice. The main purpose of the agenda is to provide advance information to the members regarding the matters to be discussed at the meeting.

(d) **Quorum:** Required quorum must be present for the meeting. The term 'Quorum' denotes the minimum number of members necessary to initiate and conduct the business of the meeting. In company meetings, this is spelt out in the company formation documents.

(e) **Chairman:** There should be a proper person in the chair. He/she would be responsible for moderating the meeting and get the records of the proceedings prepared.

(f) **Proxy:** Proxy is a person who is mphasized to attend a meeting instead of a member. Proxy can be a member or a non member. In the case of company meetings, all rules and regulations regarding proxies are spelt out in the company formation documents. In other meetings, proxies or representatives could be sent if the invited member feels that the proxy would add to the depth of understanding or that the subject is not too significant to warrant his/her presence.

(g) **Motion:** A motion is a proposal placed before a meeting for discussion and decision. It indicates the type of decision or line of action that the meeting may adopt with or without modifications. A meeting discusses the motion placed before it. A motion adopted by a meeting becomes a resolution. Thus a resolution is an adopted motion.

(h) **Resolution:** A resolution means a formal expression of the opinion of a meeting. It is a motion carried and passed by a meeting. It is a collective decision taken at the meeting with the required majority. The resolutions are recorded in the minutes book.

(i) **Ascertaining of Sense of Meeting:** The sense of the meeting should be ascertained by the person in chair, through any of the following methods of voting:

(i) Acclamation   (ii) Show of hands   (iii) Ballot
(iv) Voice vote   (v) Division   (vi) Poll

(j) **Minutes:** Minutes can be defined as a written record of the business transacted, resolutions passed and decisions taken at a meeting. Minutes are a concise, accurate, factual and official record of the proceedings of a meeting. They constitute legal evidence of the proceedings conducted in a meeting. Minutes are prepared by the

Secretary on the basis of the notes taken down by him during the course of a meeting. The objective is to preserve a written record of the business done at a meeting. The minutes are signed by the chairman.

Purposes of a Meeting

1. **Statutory Requirement:** The Companies Act has made it compulsory for companies to prepare and maintain the minutes of company meetings. Hence, the main objective of keeping minutes is to fulfil this statutory requirement.
2. **Record:** The minutes preserve the historical record of the business transacted, decisions taken and resolutions passed at each meeting. They are useful for future reference. They help in recalling the decisions taken at previous meetings.
3. **Evidence:** In a court of law, minutes can be produced as legal evidence of the proceedings of a meeting.
4. **Proof of Attendance:** Minutes furnish the complete list of members present at the meeting. Thus, the members' attendance once listed in the minutes cannot be questioned or challenged.
5. **Authenticity:** The individual opinions and views of the members taking part in the discussions are authentically available in the minutes and the document is signed by the chairman.
6. **Source of Authority:** They contain resolutions mphasized the executives to implement the decisions taken at the meetings. Therefore, the implementation of the decisions taken at the meeting cannot be challenged.
7. **Check on the Participants:** As the members are aware of the fact that the proceedings are being recorded for drafting the minutes later, they remain careful while participating in the discussion.
8. **Continuity:** Minutes provide the link between meetings, thus ensuring that the questions which were not discussed in one meeting can be taken up in the next.
9. **Aid to Proper Understanding:** Sometimes the details and intricacies in oral discussions at the meetings may not be fully understood in the right sense. But when the minutes are mphasize and ready, one can go through the same carefully and understand the implications of the decisions taken.

Characteristics of an Effective Meeting

There are two important ways to evaluate the success of a meeting. The first is to review the results of the meeting, whether the group was able to accomplish the objective. The second way is to find out how worthwhile the meeting was the manner in which the meeting was conducted and the decisions arrived at. A good indication is if the participants got along very well in the group and viewed the time spent as worthwhile.

Characteristics of an effective meeting are:

1. They achieve the objective set for the meeting.
2. The meeting takes up a minimum amount of time. This is important because the participants will have to adjust the meetings in their busy schedules.

3. The participants feel that they were part of a sensible process and so will go out with the satisfaction of having contributed something meaningful. This will enhance the stature of the manager.

A poorly managed meeting is remembered forever, affecting the credibility of the manager. Such a meeting goes on purposelessly, and the manager or the team will not benefit from it. The participants will leave wondering why they were even present there and wasted their time. On the other hand, an effective meeting makes the manager feel that he/she has achieved something. The manager will get energy from such a meeting.

Planning a Meeting

The manager has to apply himself/herself to the following aspects of a meeting, viz., proper planning, preparation, execution, and follow up. That will ensure an effective meeting.

1. Objective of the Meeting

Right at the outset the manager has to be clear about the desired outcome of the meeting and should not digress or get confused or create confusion in the minds of the participants. Some examples are:

- Arriving at a decision,
- Generating ideas,
- Getting status reports,
- Informing or communicating something, or
- Making plans.

The objective or the expected outcome will help the manager plan the other details, such as the contents of the meeting, and the participants.

2. Agenda

Time is a precious resource, and no one wants their time wasted. This calls for a well chalked out agenda. To prepare an agenda, the manager should consider how the points can be mphasized d and time that should be allotted for each. The following list can help the manager chalk out the agenda:

- Results to be accomplished at the meeting,
- Priorities: the points that have to be covered, in their order of importance, or sequence,
- Time to be allotted for each point,
- Participants who can contribute meaningfully for the success of the meeting. The criteria for attendance should be established and shared with them.
- Plan the meeting venue and physical environment. Consider parking, access, room arrangement, room temperature, noise, lighting, food, etc. Pay attention to special needs if there people with physical or vision challenges.
- Date and Time for the meeting, taking into consideration the availability of the participants and the urgency of the meeting. In these days of Computerised

scheduling of meetings, the available time slots of each participant can be ascertained first and then the person can be approached. It helps if the meetings can be scheduled in advance so that the participants can prepare their calendars.

- The meetings should be tightly planned and streamlined. Everything that happens in the meeting should contribute towards fulfilling the objective. Nothing superfluous should be included. *Time wasted in a meeting is time wasted and activity lost for all those who are present.* The agenda should be circulated among the participants and their feedback obtained. If necessary, it should be communicated clearly and multiple times.

(A template for an agenda sheet is presented at the end of sub point 1.8.9)

3. **Planning the Contents**

The manager then will have to pay attention to collecting and collating the information that should be prepared beforehand. He/she should dwell on what the participants would need to know in order to make the most of the meeting time. For example, if it is a problem solving session, the participants may be asked to study the problem and come with a possible solution. If it is a discussion on an ongoing project, each participant could be asked to make a summary report on the progress achieved by him/her so far. It is optional for the manager to circulate these reports among the members.

If others are expected to lead some discussion, this should be mentioned in the agenda. This will ensure that there is participation from all present. They should be given adequate time and access to all necessary information. The participants will then come prepared to take over at the expected time slot.

4. **Time Management**

In an effective meeting everyone respects the time that is allotted. The meeting should start on time and it should be finished according to the agenda. Activities like distribution of information sheets or reports, formation of smaller groups etc. should be done prior to the meeting. Testing of the audiovisual equipment, seating arrangements etc. should be attended to before the commencement of the meeting. Latecomers can wait till after the meeting to get inputs about what has transpired.

The agenda should be the reference point to keep the meeting running on target and on time. In case of digression, the manager has to politely bring the discussion back on track, assuring those who have raised any new issue, that it would be taken up in a subsequent meeting or referred to a sub-committee.

5. **Conducting the Meeting: Role of the meeting facilitator**

Meetings can be tiring and quite a brain drain for the members. This could be the result of poor meeting preparation and leadership. Preparation for meetings would include describing the problem to be addressed, careful selection of members and circulating their profile notes to all the members, giving adequate information (circulation of hard copies or by email, so that the members have sufficient time to prepare for the meetings) etc. The facilitator has to ensure that there is no shortcoming of any sort.

Points to Remember
- Arrive at the meeting room early enough to ensure that the room set-up is consistent with the expectations and will support, rather than inhibit, achievement of the meeting objectives.
- Start the meeting on time. He/she should state the purpose, objectives, and desired outcomes clearly. The meeting agenda can be reviewed to gain consensus on it.
- The agenda should include the beginning and ending times for the meeting, the objectives and the desired outcome for each session and each agenda item. The dates and timings should be such that the members can conveniently take time off to attend and participate in the meetings.
- The physical environment should be pleasant and without disturbances. If there is too much noise on the outside, the members may find it difficult to concentrate on the group proceedings.
- The seating arrangements should be planned properly. If the members are sitting too close, it may distract them and if they are too far apart, some may feel like outsiders to the group.
- Care should be taken to ensure that the required audiovisual equipment is available. This equipment should be placed such that all members should be able to see it comfortably.
- If the proceedings are to be recorded, make all necessary arrangements, check the working of the equipment and place them at appropriate locations.
- The roles of the participants should be in writing: Who speaks? Who facilitates? Who records? Who prepares summaries? If the manager is busy keeping the meeting in order, another person should be available to record the discussions.
- A pleasant greeting to welcome, acknowledging the value of the participants' time and effort and making them comfortable will set the right trend for the meeting. All the participants should be introduced, so they know one another.
- Encourage everyone to say something during the opening session of the meeting.
- All members should be treated on an equal footing without fear or favour.
- If certain people are dominating the conversation, the others should be asked for their ideas.
- During the course of the discussions, make sure each person participates, but not all at the same time. Prevent or stop people from talking over each other, or form sub-groups with their own agenda. The main agenda should be the focus.
- Unequal member involvement may be corrected by allowing the group to create its own goals. When members help in deciding the direction of the group communication, their involvement would increase.
- Cliques and subgroups form when some members of the group continue interacting outside group meetings. This is common as employees meet and interact with each other at various levels and for a variety of reasons. To avoid rumours to circulate because of this, it is important to be proactive and consider the type and extent of information that should be shared with all the group members.

- Different levels of communication skills for group members can impact group discussions. Allowing group members to have an opportunity to participate in the discussion is important. Accepting the fact that levels of communication skills vary, it is necessary to convince the members that what they say may be more important than how they say it. At the same time, at the broader level, the top management should provide opportunities for enhancing communication skills for all employees appropriate to their level of group interaction required.
- Dealing with different communication styles is a part of life. This is because the cultural background of the employees differs. Members should be mphasized to accept and respect these differences and develop warm relationships.
- Personal conflicts can derail group discussions. The members may be encouraged to indicate the areas of conflict and also give suggestions for overcoming them in the interest of the group's success. Once such conflicts are resolved, the discussions can become more meaningful.
- Relationship among members is another area which determines the success or failure of groups. These were addressed by Hirokawa, DeGooyer and Valde (2000). They have identified seven factors, viz., relationships, group structure, group process, member emotions, group communication, member attributes and external forces. They have particularly mphasized on the quality of relationships, emotions felt before and after group action, and attributes of group members. For example, if the quality of the relationships among group members is poor, that may be an area that needs to be addressed. With better relationships, participation and discussion levels may be higher.
- The manager has to ensure the meeting stays on topic. Any digression should be stopped politely.
- The manager should have good listening skills, as also conflict management skills to keep the meeting under control. He/she should join in if necessary to keep the meeting moving forward.
- A quick summary of each agenda point discussed would help in confirming the points made and actions suggested. Managers with a busy schedule summarise only the *action points and follow-up needed*. They also make a list of the *persons responsible for each action*. If some further discussions are needed on some points at subsequent meetings, such points are noted separately.
- The body language of the participants indicates how the participants are taking the entire thing. If there are signs of fatigue, a break may be indicated or the speaker needs to be stopped.
- The manager should develop a decision making process. It could be Voting, Consensus or Majority rules. He/she should know when to "sleep on the subject" or put it aside.

- Acknowledge all contributions even if the opinions put forth are not acceptable.
- In conclusion, recapitulate the main accomplishments of the meeting, give an opportunity for each member to ask questions, thank them all for their contribution and if a follow-up meeting is required, offer a tentative date and time, to be confirmed in writing.
- After the meeting, prepare and send to all the participants, a meeting summary, Tasks identified to be accomplished, contact information for all participants, debrief with the meeting planning team, and file the documents properly.
- All these activities should be completed on time.

Meeting Summary

The manager should take some time to meticulously prepare the summary of the meeting and circulate it to all the participants along with a covering note thanking them for participating. It is a record of what was accomplished and who is responsible for what as the team moves forward. A written record of the proceedings, along with a list of actions and individuals who have agreed to perform them becomes a reminder for them.

Conclusion

Managers should remember that running an effective meeting does not begin and end with sending the notice and making necessary physical arrangements. *An effective meeting needs a structure and an order.*

The manager should look back on the meeting and how it was run to determine (a) whether the purpose was achieved, (b) what went well, and (c) what could have been done better. This evaluation will help the manager improve his/her group communication skills.

AGENDA TEMPLATE			
Date:			
Time:			
Duration:			
Place:			
Meeting Purpose:			
Topic/Item	**Time Allocated (in minutes)**	**Topic Leader**	**Objective (Choose one)**
1.			
2.			
3			

1.13 Techniques for Facilitating Discussions

In a structured meeting, the facilitator can adopt useful techniques for encouraging participation by all the members.

- **Round Robin method:**
  (a) Silent Generation of Ideas before any discussions have really started, and Round Robin Recording to quickly record a large number of top-of-mind ideas that reflect creative thinking. The members are requested to refrain from passing their opinions or judgements.
  (b) Posing a question to the group, making certain that it is written on the board for all to see, and allowing four to five minutes for each person silently to generate a list of responses to the question,
  (c) Asking each person to share one item on his/her list, and writing them on the board so that ideas are not repeated.
- **Brain writing Pool:** This method is valuable for having a small group to obtain responses to a single question or problem from several perspectives. The technique also quickly provides rich feedback to each individual in the group, perhaps sparking new ideas about how to respond to the stimulus question. This technique can also be particularly effective for developing a plan of action by using multiple questions, such as (a) What are we trying to accomplish? (b) Who is responsible? (c) How? (d) How to assess the outcome?

  The steps are:
  - Each participant writes his/her name and a response to a stimulus question written at the top of a piece of paper,
  - The participants pass that sheet to the next person who briefly responds to what is on the paper by adding comments, qualifying, adding suggestions, or pointing out strengths or weaknesses,
  - Once the pieces of paper have been passed full circle and are back to the originator, each participant reads or summarises aloud the content to the group.
  - The facilitator records the content highlights and leads the subsequent discussion.

Managing Open Discussions: It should be noted that each of these techniques will lead to open discussions and managing them is not easy. The facilitator can develop suitable techniques for monitoring open discussions, such as:

- Asking open-ended questions, the response to which will be more complex.
- The questions are leading in nature, more general and objective, and are aimed toward decision-making, such as: opinion on a project or a person, facts, emotions, interpretation and decisions.

1.14 Brainstorming

Introduction

Brainstorming is a systematic process which encourages participants to actively contribute ideas in a non critical or non evaluative environment.

The simplest reason to hold a brainstorming meeting is to increase the volume of possible ideas. A brainstorming meeting taps into the collective knowledge and subconscious of a group to discover or reveal ideas and connections around a particular topic. The idea is to get a rapid interchange of ideas. In these sessions, the creativity of the members is given full opportunity to flow, or in effect, *create a storm or explosion of new ideas*. Hence the term *'brainstorm'* is used, and not 'brain-calm.' Momentum is the key. When people are thinking quickly, they are not self-conscious. When the discussion is animated, people feel free to express their true thoughts and opinions and the manager is able to find new connections between ideas from others. The key to the success of a brainstorming is in understanding how the brainstorming session fits into the larger decision making process the team has. Even with the best run brainstorming session, if the manager cannot migrate the new ideas into the decision making process for the project, the entire exercise goes to waste.

It is generally a structured process. Structured brainstorming sessions are undertaken by organisations to find solutions to problems that arise in a work environment. It is used as a key tool when it comes to decision making. The participants are given guidelines and rules to follow, the discussions are conducted according to a set pattern so that there is no chaos. The input from the sessions is obtained in an orderly manner and is constructive. If it is unstructured, there are many ideas put forth by participants, but the entire session may become a fruitless exercise as it may not lead towards any specific goal.

Brainstorming can take place one-on-one, in small groups, or done for just 5 minutes as a small part of some other meeting. Common examples where it can be used are names for products, product features, possible solutions to a difficult situation, goals for the team etc. Each and every participant gets to participate. No one person can dominate. The manager gets the feedback in a very orderly manner. The contours of the problem are given to the team either in advance or at the meeting and each participant is asked to suggest possible solutions. Thus it is a collaboration of ideas.

The Mechanics of Brainstorming

The very best way to run a brainstorming meeting is with a projector, transparencies, and fine-tipped markers. It is easy to switch rapidly between transparencies and also go back to any previous transparencies if necessary. Now a number of software packages that can support brainstorming are available. The disadvantage of these is that the members would be typing while everyone is watching them. Instead, a whiteboard could be used and each sketch or point made could be filmed. Animated participation brings forth the energy of the members

Use of mind maps, bubbles for ideas etc., is more interesting than making a list of ideas. The central idea could be in a bubble and the others can be depicted as branches. New ideas can be put in between ideas. Related ideas should be connected by a line. Any digression should be prevented and the members should be informed that their stray ideas could be taken up at some other meeting. If a new worthwhile idea is to be discussed, it could be indicated as a sub-storm. The meeting should not be bogged down with too many detailed discussions on any point. The objective should be to get maximum number of ideas within the time set for the meeting.

Reasons for its Popularity

It is popular in organisations for the following reasons:

1. All the participants feel that they are contributing to what they will be working on in the future. It can be a bonding experience and, typically and more importantly, it can get people thinking and communicating with each other about topics relevant to their work. They have some shared questions and ideas to discuss informally as well. This perhaps is more important than the end result of it.

2. It is a convenient way for bad managers to pretend that the entire team is involved in the direction of the project. If the manager does not know how to apply the technique for best results, decisions will be taken much the same way as before. In worst cases, the manager may use it to deliberately manipulate his team and forestall any complaints that his team was not involved in the decision making process.

Steps in Brainstorming

A badly structured brainstorming session will cost the organisation money, energy, and time as it will fail to meet the purpose. Raw lists of poorly formed and highly divergent suggestions are a nightmare to work with. To ensure meaningful participation and constructive results, the facilitator should be very capable of conducting group communication. Good facilitation requires good listening skills, very sharp group awareness, and the ability to help people express their ideas. The facilitator should manage the whiteboard, writing down ideas as people come up with them, preventing people from interrupting each other, and giving the floor to quieter people who would otherwise not participate. He/she should not dominate by offering too many ideas. To make it effective, the following steps can be followed:

- The purpose of the meeting should be clearly stated. This will save time and energy of the team.
- The ground rules should be established, whether it will be a free for all, or one-by-one by raising their hand or the issue is passed round the gathering according to the seating order. Whether and at what point interruptions are allowed should be stated. The rules should not be arbitrary, but flexible, practical and positive in approach. *Brainstorming should be about communicating, not competing.*

- It should be clearly communicated to the members that they are not allowed to criticise one another's opinion or idea. This will make the members participate without any inhibition.
- Focus is crucial. Some exercises can be used at the beginning of the session to sharpen the concentration levels of the participants.
- Each team member should get a chance to demonstrate or voice his/her idea. This is repeated until such time that the team members do not have any more ideas or solutions.
- The discussions should cover all the causes for the problem at hand and all the possible solutions. Never miss an idea. Have someone recording the brainstorming session.
- The participants should be informed that there is no constraint regarding cost or time while thinking out new ideas.
- After the meeting is over, the entire feedback is reviewed. This analysis has to be done immediately after the session so as not to lose any point made. Duplicate inputs discarded. Irrelevant ideas are discarded. Similar views are clubbed together. Priorities are established. The most interesting ideas can be used for further discussions.
- The team members can be given a chance to offer their comments if any.
- The members can be informed that the summary would be sent to them later.

The most important and interesting part of a brainstorming session is the analysis of the inputs after the session is over.

Benefits of Brainstorming

Brainstorming is roughly defined as any group activity involving the quest of new ideas. The benefits gained from structured brainstorming are as follows:

- The manager gets inputs from all participants. Thus, he/she gets a collection of ideas with regards to the particular issue and hence it will prove to be more successful.
- It fosters the culture of team work, where members are free to voice their ideas. It promotes synergy among the team members.
- It prevents dominant team members from taking the lead and forcing a decision.
- It can be used to think through small issues, or to take on big strategic themes. Big formal brainstorming meetings can help insecure or unfamiliar teams to become more comfortable and skilled at working with ideas. Sometimes a brainstorming meeting can be used to retrain people in how to approach problem solving or creative thinking. The teams that get the most out of brainstorming sessions are the ones that have the best team culture around ideas, and the process for going about finding, refining and harvesting ideas.

Tools for Structured Brainstorming

SWOT Analysis & PEST Analysis are very effective tools for structured brainstorming.

Brainstorming sessions often use SWOT as an analysis tool for reviewing strategies. Some examples where SWOT (Strengths, Weaknesses, Opportunities and Threats) analysis can be used are:

- Sales distribution methods
- A new brand or a product
- A new business idea
- A new strategy e.g. entering new markets

PEST analysis refers to Political, Economical, Social and Technology approach. PEST analysis is often used in brainstorming sessions to understand the market position of an organisation. Some areas where PEST can be used are:

- Market analysis
- Assessing a particular brand in relation to its market
- A new business venture or an investment opportunity, including acquisition, diversification
- New strategies for entering a market

Conclusion:

Structured brainstorming is a technique used to generate ideas which can help to solve a problem. Structured brainstorming helps to encourage creative thinking and enthusiasm between team members.

1.15 Negotiations

Meaning

The term 'Negotiation' refers to attempts to settle an argument or issue to the benefit all the parties. The word "negotiation" originates from the Latin expression, "negotiatus", which means "to carry on business".

Negotiations take place in businesses, non-profit organisations, government departments, legal proceedings, among nations, in international fora as well as in domestic issues like marriage, divorce, settlement of property matters, etc. In the corporate world, negotiations take place for a variety of purposes, such as sale, purchase, borrowings, hiring of people, dealing with unions, outsourcing of services, appointment of dealers and distributors, mergers, acquisitions etc. In various fields, there are specialised professional negotiators, like financial negotiators, legal negotiators etc.

A Negotiation takes place in the form of a dialogue among two or more people or parties, with the objective of directing the outcomes in such a way as to satisfy the interests of the parties involved. It could be aimed at reaching an understanding, settle a point of difference, to arrive at an agreement regarding the future course of action, to bargain for individual or collective advantage etc. The parties come to the table with the intention of gaining an advantageous position for themselves throughout the process. The discussions are intended to bring the parties to a compromise position and find an amicable solution.

Traditional negotiating is sometimes called *win-lose* i.e., one party gains at the cost of the other. This is true if the 'pie' is fixed or in other words, the discussions cover only one point. For instance, in a sales negotiation, price could be the only consideration for the negotiation. However, when a whole package is under discussion, there would be mutual shifting of positions or an environment of 'give and take'.

There are two opposite types of negotiations:

Distributive Negotiation

The term distributive negotiation means that there are only a few limited issues for distribution or division among the people involved, or the 'pie' size is fixed. The proportion that can go to each party is also more or less fixed, with very little room for review. For instance, when a buyer negotiates with the seller of a house or a vehicle, he is aware of the extent to which he/she can go. The issue being discussed is such that the two parties will have come together to the negotiation table perhaps for the first time and the chances of their coming together again in the near future for such discussions would be very few.

Integrative negotiation

As the word integrative means joining several parts into a whole, integrative negotiation means that the parties are aware that to achieve something together, they have to cooperate. It is a creative way to solving problems. Both the parties want to close the discussion with the feeling that they have achieved something. Hence, they agree to some form of value concessions. It is often described as the 'win-win' scenario. This sort of negotiation takes place when the parties have a wide range of issues on the table and want to build long term relationships. As a result, they display a higher degree of trust. This is a problem solving approach.

However, if one of the parties pretends to negotiate, but secretly has no intention of compromising, that party is considered to be negotiating in bad faith.

A negotiation can be following a principled method if the parties are able to:
- Separate the people from the problem,
- Focus on interests and not on positions,
- Consider a variety of possibilities before deciding what to do, and
- Arrive at a result that is based on some objective standard.

Process of Negotiation

Negotiation involves three basic elements:
- *Process*, or how the parties negotiate: the context of the negotiations, the parties to the negotiations, the tactics used by the parties, and the sequence and stages in which all of these play out.

- *Behaviour* refers to the relationships among these parties, the communication between them and the styles they adopt.
- *Substance* refers to what the parties negotiate over: the agenda, the issues, the options, and the agreement(s) reached at the end.

Negotiations are characterised by:

- Strategy, comprising the top level goals, including the relationship of the parties and the final outcome.
- Process and Tools include the steps that the parties will take and the roles they play in both preparing for the discussions and negotiation, and
- Tactics: these are the more detailed statements and actions and responses of one party to those of the other. This would also include *persuasion and influence*, as they are integral to modern day negotiation.

  The tactics may range from simple straight forward accurate statement of facts and the preconditions or expectations, to intimidation and negotiation hypnosis. The negotiating party can consist of two persons balancing each other, one playing the role of the bad person, trying to block the deal and the other playing the role of the good person wanting to close the deal, while trying to get some concessions.

Role of Emotion in Negotiation

As the parties come with their arguments, positions and attitudes, emotions play an important role in the negotiation process. The decision regarding whether to settle or not, rests to a great extent on emotional factors. It is not just what one party's emotional status is, but what the other party feels might be just as important. Very often the parties display their emotions with the intention of influencing the outcome of the negotiation. Emotions like anger, pride, guilt, regret, worry, disappointment and how they are expressed influence the expectations of one party, concessions offered by the other and the final outcome.

Negative emotions and irrational behaviour on the part of one party can cause tension and conflicts and result in any one of the following outcomes: (a) the negotiations may break down, or (b) may help the party to get a lot of concessions.

Positive emotions can also lead to two different types of outcomes: (a) facilitate reaching an agreement and maximise gains for both parties, or (b) may help one party in attaining a lot more concessions.

Barriers to negotiations

- If any one party is a diehard bargainer.
- There is lack of trust.
- Adequate information has not been made available,
- There are structural impediments like constitution of the team if it is not empowered to close the deal etc.
- Cultural and gender differences.
- Communication problems.

Care to be taken at Negotiations:

(i) Do the background homework: Before any negotiation begins, the party should understand the interests and positions of the other party in relation to its own. It is a good idea to look at the position from the other party's perspective.

(ii) Always keep the negotiation under control.

(iii) Try to remain flexible in the negotiation process.

(iv) Always keep in mind your limits and the other party's needs while negotiation.

(v) Do not jump to early conclusions at the negotiation process. Do not negotiate against yourself. Understanding the position of the other side will help. During the discussion, insights can be gained about the other party's stand. Explain the rationale for your stand and stay firm on your initial set of positions. Wait to understand the points which are more important to the other side.

(vi) Try to remain patient during the negotiation process. Discussions may enter a stage of stalemate with apparently no room for compromise. In an emotionally charged environment, the parties might have lost sight of logic. The approach would then be to accede to any significant point of the other side, while drawing concessions on an unrelated point that is relatively more important to you.

(vii) The party might be in a dilemma, whether to close or not to close. The golden rule of negotiation is to let the other party break the negotiation and walk away. This can be achieved by being logical, rigid, honest and straightforward on key terms, and explaining your position clearly.

(viii) It is necessary that all the parties to negotiation should gain something.

(ix) Do not exploit the other party at the negotiation process.

Negotiations in the Global Environment

Globalisation and growing business trends have brought to focus team negotiations. Teams can effectively work together to understand and follow a complex negotiation process, as they come with varied skills. To be successful in the global negotiating environment, negotiating teams should have superior communication skills, such as writing, listening, and talking. This will reduce chances of making mistakes, increase familiarity and understanding and lead to better negotiating positions.

1.16 Group Discussion

'Group Discussion' is one type of formal meeting. It can be a very stimulating and useful activity in an organisation. It helps in understanding a situation, in exploring possibilities and in solving problems as it generates multiple viewpoints. It gives a sense of participation to all those who participate in it. Such meetings can be based on a topic or on a case study.

Group discussions are widely used in many organisations for decision making and problem solving. Organisational group discussions are: Brainstorming, Nominal Group Technique and Delphi Technique.

It is used as a tool for selecting candidates by observing their behaviour and abilities in taking part in it.

Characteristics of Group Discussion
- Evaluation Components
- Knowledge
- Communication skills
- Active Listening
- Clarity of Thought and Expression
- Apt Language
- Appropriateness of Body Language
- Group Behaviour
- Leadership Skills

Group Discussion for Selection Process

Normally a group consists of 8 to 10 students. The normal time duration for any GD is about 10 to 15 minutes. For a GD relating to any particular topic, 2-3 minutes thinking time may be given. For GDs relating to case studies, 15 minutes time should be given for studying the case. The valuation of the participants is normally done by experts (usually professors from business schools). All these experts possess vast experience and expertise in their respective fields.

Essential Requirements for participating Effectively in GDs

1. Give proper respect to the views expressed by other speakers.
2. Maintain courtesy while speaking.
3. Do not use very insulting, harsh and aggressive language.
4. Speak clearly and pleasantly to all the members of the group.
5. Stick to the main point of the GD. Do not speak irrelevant matter in the discussion.
7. Do not use loud and angry tone while speaking.
8. Do not interrupt other members of the group while they are speaking.
9. Learn to disagree politely.
10. Use positive body language while speaking.

Note on GD for Candidate Selection

There are no fixed rules for a GD held for candidate selection. The participants are generally eager to be the first to speak. The first speaker should mention the topic and state the issues. He should not give any opinion at this point. Later, the person may offer clarifications. This should be in the form of a statement, and not a question. Care should be taken to address the entire group. The candidates should maintain calm even if there are opposing arguments. The candidate should acknowledge others' viewpoints.

Situations may arise, when one's point of view has already been expressed by someone else. The best approach would be to acknowledge the contribution of the other person and add to it and thus become the centre of attention.

If there is an interruption from someone else, the approach should be to request the person to allow you to complete your statement and offer the field to that person.

The group should move towards a consensus but due to the all round anxiety to make one's point, this may not happen at all. The idea is to exhibit some leadership qualities in steering the group while making one's contribution. A person with leadership qualities will look at the clock and when it is almost nearing closing time, may start summing up. If the group is too noisy, the facilitator may allot one minute to each candidate to sum up the discussion. This is an opportunity to put on one's best effort. Without criticising the group, one can sum up and give one's own views. The candidates should not stray from the topic.

The candidates are evaluated on how they speak. Fluency, meaningful contribution, depth of knowledge on various topical issues, and leadership qualities are what the selectors would be looking for. Whatever personal views one may have, it is important to know both sides of the argument. One must be able to defend one's viewpoints convincingly and therefore the need for acquiring wide knowledge. Candidates should select topics, prepare and talk in front of the mirror, family members and friends to understand where they need to strengthen their arguments or presentation skills. They can also record their speech to know where they falter, and this will indicate the areas for further improvement. The voice quality, body language etc., can also be assessed during this process. The practice sessions can be used for ensuring that the thought process is well organised. One way to practice this is to write down the points and keep it in front of you. By periodically looking at it, you can arrange your thoughts mentally.

1.17 Other Aspects of Communication

1.17.1 Cross Cultural Dimensions of Business Communication

Cross-cultural communication is also frequently referred to as intercultural communication. It is a field of study that looks at how people from differing cultural backgrounds communicate across cultures.

It is defined by Gotland University of Sweden as *"a process of exchanging, negotiating, and mediating one's cultural differences through language, non-verbal gestures, and space relationships."* In particular, intercultural communication occurs when the communicating parties come from cultures with different communication norms, practices and expectations.

Generally, in communication, we seek to reduce uncertainty by predicting or anticipating the responses to our messages. Communication with strangers involves relatively greater degrees of uncertainty with regard to their attitudes, feelings and beliefs, and hence their responses. Anyone could be considered a stranger, given a sufficiently foreign context. Both the local and the stranger have limited knowledge of each other's beliefs, interests and habits. When communicating with someone familiar we are usually confident about their beliefs and expectations and can more or less predict his/her responses. In contrast, when we communicate with strangers, there is a lot of uncertainty about how they will receive our messages and respond.

Hence, it is necessary to understand the stranger's culture, his group interactions and the individual's characteristics. However, while understanding these, it is necessary to avoid stereotyping these people, but try to focus on their unique, individual features. Apart from this, effective communications with strangers requires an increased awareness of our own communication behaviours and modify them accordingly.

1.17.2 Cross-cultural Business Communication

Business communication is the exchange of messages related to companies through symbols, action and verbal words. In the business world, cross-cultural or intercultural communication occurs when business associates from different cultures must participate in business exchanges, negotiations or partnerships.

As the business world becomes increasingly global, the need for effective cross cultural communication becomes essential, as it plays a vital role in building international customers, employee relations and business partnerships. It plays a vital role in successfully establishing a product, concept or service in a different area of the globe. To make the communication effective, it should be designed appropriately to meet the cultural norms and expectations in the receiving culture, thus resulting in its acceptance. Ineffective communication cross culturally can offend, confuse or send a misunderstood message which could lead to broken relations with customers, investors, employees and authorities.

Thus, cross cultural communication in business requires effort and technique to address the different barriers that may occur. Following appropriate codes of behaviour and etiquette, which take into consideration each other's cultural sensitivities, is crucial to securing business deals.

Over the last three to four decades, there have been vast changes in economic relationships, political systems, and technological options across the globe began. There has been tremendous advancements in product, service and communication technologies, which have made huge dents in old cultural barriers. As the markets in the developed world became saturated, multi-nationals started reaching out to new markets and business transformed from individual-country capitalism to global capitalism. It is no wonder then that the study of cross-cultural communication was originally found within businesses and the government both seeking to expand globally. As they entered new markets, businesses began to realise that their employees were ill-equipped to meet these challenges. Initially, they focused on language training and then, taught them how to act when abroad. The next logical step was to introduce global comparative research into various cultural aspects and the term 'world view' was added to their research and training programmes. The universities across the world started to feel the pressure and incorporated intercultural and international understanding and knowledge into the education of their students.

Changing workplace: In the changing workplace brought about by globalisation and international cooperation, people of different national and ethnic origins play regular and important roles, each bringing different skills and points of view. At the same time, it is imperative that everyone in the organisation adjusts. A diverse workplace means different communication styles, expectations of behaviour and approaches as well as incorporation of new talent.

Changes in Demographics: Globalisation has meant movement of people across geographic, political and cultural boundaries. As people relocate to newer environments, the urban space in these cultures becomes diversified. As the demographics change, changes become necessary in sales and marketing communications to the various populations that make up the country. Many companies recognise that varying demographics in different cities, regions and even neighbourhoods require different communication approaches.

Entering new markets: Companies have to understand the economic, historical, social and cultural issues of a country they propose to enter. It is a misconception that selling their products in foreign markets involves mere changing of slogans and branding strategies to meet the tastes of a new target demographic entity. Such an approach can lead to failures. For example, in many developing countries, fast-food restaurants serving low cost-high value products could be actually expensive to the local population. In such a setting, fast food becomes a premium product. Similarly, in many traditional cultures, selling of products that accompany sexually suggestive themes may be considered offensive to the sensitivities of the population and hence require a different approach.

When **conducting business internationally**, entrepreneurs learn that cultures have different expectations and protocols when it comes to meetings and interpersonal discussions. Cultures such as those of Japan and China have strong power distance values (superior-subordinate relationships), and much of the speaking and interaction is done by the most senior member of a group. They also expect a similar protocol, where superiors talk to their counterparts and not a subordinate level person sent to speak to a superior in their organisation. Middle Eastern and Southeast Asian cultures consider socialisation and getting to know one another a very important part of interpersonal meetings. Building trust between parties is essential to the business process. Therefore, the American standard approach of "getting down to business" may not be appreciated in these cultures.

Dimensions of Cross-cultural Business Communication

The key to effective cross-cultural communication is knowledge. Knowledge can be acquired by passive observation, from friends of the strangers or by reading. The foreigner may also be approached directly by asking relevant questions. The stranger can also volunteer a lot of information ahead of the meetings. Conflicts can arise if the parties approach each other with inadequate understanding of their respective background. To ensure better business relationships, these conflicts can be avoided by using appropriate words and adopting a policy of 'stop, listen, think, and withdraw temporarily from the situation if necessary'. Active listening, repeating what one thinks he or she has heard and confirming that the message has been understood accurately can go a long way in establishing a healthy communication environment.

Sometimes intermediaries may be helpful in creating a better understanding of each other. However, these intermediaries may tone down the communication process unnecessarily. Secondly, they may appear to be biased.

- **Language** poses the largest impediment in business communication. Even if the two parties speak the same language, some words may have different meanings in different cultures. When the two parties speak different languages, they have to rely on translations. The effectiveness then would depend on the translator and his ability to understand and interpret messages effectively. To reduce the risk of misunderstanding, it is necessary to ask and answer questions patiently.
- A country's **customs** play a large role in business. This can be reflected in many ways like food, dress, tone of speaking, eye contact and many aspects on non-verbal communication. For instance, in China, people slurp loudly indicating that they respect the generosity of the host and are really enjoying the food. Eating quietly can suggest quite the opposite to them.
- International communication scholar Geert Hofstede identifies five other areas, or dimensions, in which these differences manifest themselves, making communication complicated. Geert's model, when introduced in 1980, came at a time when understanding cultural differences between societies had become increasingly relevant for both economic and political reasons. His concepts however became popular after the publication of his 1991 book, "Cultures and Organisations: Software of the Mind." His model emphasises the following dimensions:
    o Power distance,
    o Long Term orientation,
    o Masculinity,
    o Uncertainty avoidance and
    o Individualism.

One of the main ways that cultures can differ is in their **power distance index (PDI) rating**. It focuses on the degree of equality, or inequality, between people in the society. A High Power Distance ranking indicates inequalities of power and wealth, which is accepted and expected and significant upward mobility is not possible. A Low Power Distance ranking indicates that in these societies equality and opportunity for everyone is stressed. This is seen within the organisations as well and is seen in the extent of respect the subordinates pay to their superiors. In most traditional cultures, this distance index is higher than in the developed Western world. Individuals in the Western organisations expect more equal treatment and within the power structure, there is increased vertical mobility.

Masculinity (MAS) focuses on the degree of emphasis on male achievement, control, and power or gender differences. A High Masculinity ranking indicates a high degree of male domination.

Long-Term Orientation (LTO): High Long-Term Orientation ranking indicates that the society respects the values of long-term commitments and tradition. This supports a strong work ethic where individuals believe that today's hard work will be rewarded over the long term. In such cultures, businesses take a long time to develop, particularly for an "outsider". In a Low Long-Term Orientation ranking culture, changes can occur more rapidly.

Uncertainty Avoidance Index (UAI) focuses on the level of tolerance for uncertainty and ambiguity within the society, or how the society can adopt to unstructured situations. A High Uncertainty Avoidance ranking indicates the country has a low tolerance for uncertainty and ambiguity. This creates a rule-oriented society, where laws, rules, regulations, and controls become important. A Low Uncertainty Avoidance ranking indicates that the society has more tolerance for a variety of opinions and readily accepts change, and the people are more willing to take risks.

Individualism (IDV) focuses on the degree to which the society supports or reinforces individual achievement and interpersonal relationships. For example, the Chinese culture ranks low on the individualism scale, as they emphasise more on the collective good. The American approach on the other hand is to emphasise more on individual success. Such differences affect the way messages are communicated and hence are critical in designing effective business-related communication.

- **A High Individualism ranking** indicates that individuality and individual rights are very important. There is a higher emphasis on the importance and welfare of the individual, like personal success and promotions. The individual is seen as the end and improvements to communal arrangements as the means to achieve it. The process of decision making in individualistic cultures is usually very short, and the decisions are taken by a lonely individualist. This helps in quick decisions, but implementation problems may arise. Individuals in these societies may tend to form a larger number of looser relationships.

- **A Low Individualism ranking** describes a more collectivist nature with close ties between individuals. These cultures reinforce extended families and collectives where everyone takes responsibility for fellow members of their group. On the other hand, in collectivist societies, the group and its success takes precedence over individual success. This should be understood while communicating with business partners in these countries. In these cultures, decisions are taken after prolonged deliberations and consensus will be achieved, because of pressures to agree on collective goals. However, this team approach very often is aimed at supporting individuals.

Seven Dimensions of Cross-culture Communication: Fons Trompenaars is a Dutch author and consultant in the field of cross-cultural communication. His books include: Riding the Waves of Culture, Seven Cultures of Capitalism, Building Cross-Cultural Competence, 21 Leaders for the 21st Century and Innovating in a Global Crisis. They are based on the insights he gained firsthand at home, where he grew up speaking both French and Dutch, and then later at work with Shell in nine countries. In their 1997 book, *'Riding the Waves of Culture',*

Trompenaars and Charles Hampden-Turner have developed a model of communication with seven dimensions. According to them, differences in culture are not random, but very specific and even predictable. This is because each culture has its own way of thinking, its own values and beliefs, and different preferences placed on a variety of different factors. (*For details, read The Seven Dimensions of Culture - Communication Skills Training ... www.mindtools.com*)

The various dimensions of cross-cultural business communication according to them are:

1. Universalism vs. particularism (What is more important, rules or relationships?)
2. Individualism vs. collectivism (communitarianism) (Do we function in a group or as individuals?)
3. Neutral vs. emotional (Do we display our emotions?)
4. Specific vs. diffuse (How separate we keep our private and working lives). This dimension is sometimes referred to as "concern-/commitment-dimension", which is expressed at the level of an individual affected by a particular situation or action.
5. Achievement vs. ascription (Do we have to prove ourselves to receive status or is it given to us?) – power distance.
6. Sequential vs. synchronic (Do we do things one at a time in a planned manner according to a strict schedule or several things at once?)
7. Internal vs. external control (Do we control our environment or are we controlled by it?)

1.18 Technology and Communication

The development of technology has considerably improved our lifestyles. Its impact is felt on each and every aspect of life, including communication techniques. From the symbols of long time ago to the latest classy computers and mobile phones, communication systems, modes and styles have changed a lot. Each century has seen a new addition to the ever-growing list of means of communication. The invention of the telephone by Alexander Graham Bell in the year 1875 was the first technological invention that impacted communication in humans to a massive extent. Other subsequent inventions like that of the computer, the Internet, cell phones with newer applications like 2G, 3G, 4G and now even 5G (generation) services have further eased and changed the communication process.

Every new development comes with both positive and negative influences, and this applies to the impact of technology on the communication process as well. Technological elements like telephones, cell phones, emails etc., have become the most popular means of communication. In fact, mobile phones and the Internet are literally the basic necessities these days. The social networking sites are a world in themselves, like a virtual world! In businesses as well, all these have made the process of communication quick and easy. Emails, teleconferencing, video conferencing, networking sites, etc. are among the favourite tools. In businesses, there has been a movement away from face-to-face meetings and communication. Instead, people and businesses use video conferencing, (incorporates chat and presentation conferencing facilities) and virtual conferencing (Second Life). These are effective globalisation forces. It is estimated that in 2010, around 30% of the world's population was online, and by 2016, around 15 billion devices will be networked, which twice the world population. The amount of information available on the Net is also increasing exponentially. Global monthly information flows are expected to exceed 10 exabytes (1 followed by 19 zeroes!) by 2016. According to a McKinsey report, the impact of the Net on India's GDP is likely to touch Rs. 5 lakh crore by 2015. By that year, the number of Internet users will touch half a billion. That is the power of the Net.

Positive Impact

Information Technology has transformed the vast world into a tiny global village, where anyone can connect with others in any part of the world. A number of potential benefits of computer-mediated communication have been studied by researchers and these include increased interaction, the provision of non-hierarchical communication environments, the negation of gender and racial imbalance, a focus on the content and not context of communication, and the breakdown of power and allied knowledge structures (Boshier, 1990; Edmonds, 1998; Hiltz, 1986; Kayne, 1987; McCreary, 1990).

Advantages of Technology in Communication

- **Speed:** Time and money can be saved because it is much quicker to move information around. In case of situations when something has to be conveyed urgently to someone, telephones, fax, mobile phones and emails come in handy.
- **Cost:** Messages or data transfer on the Net is very cheap compared to other media like telephone. Videoconferences and teleconferences save on travel expenses.
- It is available 24/7. People can do shopping / banking / chat / work at any time they like, irrespective of time zones.
- Online communication brings people together across distances.
- Technology is more portable and people have and expect constant access to the internet wherever they are.
- Communication is virtually instantaneous as compared to snail mail (post).
- Communication is less rigid and less inclined to conform to traditional standards and rules. It's less formal. Mistakes are common. Acronyms are also common.
- **Better solutions:** Technology has brought the world closer and hence exchange of thoughts is faster. People and businesses can discuss and find better solutions to any problem without loss of time.

The specific advantages in various fields are:

- Education: Services like video-conferencing has made it possible to give best education to students via online peer group discussions an expert faculty on the web. Even technical and medical education has made good use of this because of extensive data transfer facilities, both written as well as audio-visual. This facilitates a lot of cooperative and collaborative modes of learning. Students can opt for on-line degrees and study at their pace. This flexibility has opened up innumerable opportunities for the youth to improve their academic qualifications and career prospects. There is a clear shift in emphasis from teaching to learning. An astounding fund of knowledge is available through various web sites.

Administration function of educational institutions and universities has been streamlined with the help of improved communication systems. Admissions, payment of fees, examination notifications etc., have all migrated from the old world paper work to web-based activities. As university information brochures from all over the world are available in their respective web sites, students find it convenient to know about the specialties offered by each of them and decide which course and which university to select.

- Employees benefit, as it permits flexi-time and working from distance. Their efficiency improves.
- Benefits for organisations: Using technology in communication has become a necessity to an extent that many people and businesses cannot survive without it. The days of writing memos are gone in most modern companies. This is because managers are able to organise and maintain the company's activities online. It means that even when the manager is away nothing comes to a standstill. Organisations can advertise their products and services online such that people are able to read their brochures online instead of contacting them. Also, recruitment of employees can be done online. This saves time and energy of both the applicant and the organisation. As the information is gathered according to a standard template, the employer saves on the time required to manually going through the papers of the applicant. In other words, professionally, technology has become cost effective to everyone.

  Employees located in different parts of the world can come on the same page in 'virtual meetings', share their computer screens as they continue to talk to each other on their VOIP (voice over Internet phone) devices and so save a lot of travel time, exchange of documents in physical form etc., and hence, these organisations save on costs and also achieve reduced carbon footprints. In many organisations in the developed countries, physical office space is used only for crucial face-to-face meetings. Organisations can improve their bottom line by outsourcing various operations.
- Linking of hospitals and primary health care units through telemedicine helps to take expert medical advice to remote places on a real time basis.
- Trade, both within country boundaries and across can be done by the click of a mouse and the products are delivered at the consumers' homes. Attractive advertisements on the entertainment media and the Internet and social networking sites reach the consumers very fast. Financial transactions have been facilitated across branches of the same bank and among banks as well. The share markets all over the world have gained in volume and spread because of this and the transactions are

immediate and transparent. Similarly, activists can mobilise millions of voices within a very short time and use it to make their pitch.
- News and Entertainment: The entertainment industry has benefited tremendously by the developments in communication technology. There is a blurring of lines between the traditional entertainment and news channels and the social networking sites.
- Quick communication in cases of disasters help save hundreds of lives and the relief and rehabilitation efforts and funds reach the sites without much delay.
- Interpersonal relations: Technology is the power behind the success of long distance relationships. Video chats and social networking sites have played a big role in keeping people in touch. Thus technology has made it easy to keep in touch with old contacts, develop newer ones and maintain them on a continuous basis.
- Functioning of the Government: Most government departments and even the Supreme Court have their web sites with a lot of information and news about the latest developments in these areas. For instance, when a parcel is dispatched by courier or the postal service in India can be tracked right up to its delivery at the receiver's doorsteps.
- Development: It has promoted faster decision-making, and led to the development and progress of the world. Most of the businesses today depend on technology for communication.

Negative Impact
- The charm of the good old world is missing, where interesting letters and lengthy and warm face-to-face conversations used to make communication fascinating. They have been replaced by telephone, texting or chatting.
- **Impact on interpersonal communication:** Communication using technology deprives people of essential interpersonal skills, or the ability to express the ideas and thoughts to others in writing or in face-to-face meetings. Online education deprives students the advantages of peer group meetings and exchange of views. It promotes individualism as against communities learning and working together. The various beneficial aspects of group dynamics, team working, leadership development are lost.
- **Effect on non-verbal communication:** Technological means have also affected non-verbal communication. Lack of face-to-face interaction has reduced the resourcefulness, sensitivity and ability of people to understand and react to non-verbal communication.
- **Maintaining relationships:** Those who are hooked to communication gadgets and social networking sites are more close to online friends, but find very little time to interact with their parents and other near and dear ones. This gap widens if the parents are not comfortable with these new age modes of communication. This disrupts relationships within the family and reduces social interactions. This is not a healthy trend for the parents and the children, who have to face the world on its terms and as they want. They may feel lonely and isolated, especially when they are faced with adverse situations.

- **Education:** Face-to-face communication provides for more personal modes of learning and spontaneous and immediate feedback than could be offered by an on-line course or discussion forum. The ambience of an educational institution and lively interaction with the teachers and the peer group can be more human, motivating and enjoyable, resulting in better learning outcomes. On the other hand, online discussion forums are far less immediate and interactive (disjointed), more isolating and time consuming and for many it may be least motivating.
- The current trend in the type of spelling and language used in Internet and text messages can adversely affect the writing skills of people. As people rely on technology, which provides spell check and grammar check, they do not bother to learn proper spellings or applying the principles of grammar.
- **Malicious motives:** Though communication has become fast and efficient, the other side of the coin cannot be ignored. Since money transactions are done with credit and debit cards, if they are stolen, within seconds, the owner can lose thousands of Rupees. Secondly, unsuspecting persons can be lured into fraudulent Internet transactions perpetrated by people with malicious intent.
- In the virtual world, there are risks attached to the unknown / hidden elements on the Internet (you do not necessarily know who you are talking to). When people air their personal details, views and feelings to unknown persons, they expose themselves for exploitation by unscrupulous individuals. This can be dangerous physically and emotionally.
- A variety of cyber crimes have become very common, requiring a different approach to investigating and solving them. They are related to hacking, introduction of viruses, identity thefts, frauds etc.
- Critical financial services and government information etc., contained in the web sites is dependent on other technologies which provide connectivity, such as power supply. Any failures in the electrical grid, even minor ones, can set off disruptions across various sectors.

1.19 Ethical and Legal Issues in Business Communication

'There is no such thing as business ethics – there is only ethics'
— Peter Drucker

Ethics means different things to different people, but it generally narrows down to a basic sense of societal right and wrong. Within the business context, it involves making decisions that align with that sense of right and wrong, as well as with the law. Business ethics is a subject that can vary greatly from one business to the other its interpretation and implementation. What may seem ethical to one business may not be so to the other and the same goes for employees as well. That is why it is important to clearly communicate the ethical stance of the business to all employees. They should fully understand the ethical stance of the business and function accordingly.

Ethical and Legal Issues in Communication considers a range of ethical, regulatory and legal issues surrounding communication within the organisation, such as with employees at various levels and also communication with the other stakeholders including the public at large - whether local or global, regulatory bodies and concerned government departments. It also covers the 'new media' and the 'old media' and telecommunications and the internet. In an age of convergence, globalisation and deregulation, ethical and legal issues have gained great significance. These issues also concern with laws related to media ownership rules, defamation, concern for sensitivities of various population segments, reputation management and protection, copyright and other aspects of intellectual property, deceptive conduct and false representation, privacy protection, censorship, whistleblower protection etc.

Ethics Policy

In the complex global business environment of the 21st century, companies of every size face a multitude of ethical issues. In order to ensure that employees understand the difference between ethical and non-ethical practices, organisations should chalk out a sound ethics policy and communicate it effectively throughout the organisation. Fundamental ethical issues include not only such traditionally understood concepts as integrity, fair play and trust, but also more complex issues such as social awareness, accommodating diversity etc. The ethics policy should cover all areas of decision-making, compliance and governance.

Every business should have a written ethics policy that details what is expected of employees within the business and how the organisation communicates with the outside world. It should communicate the basic ethical standards expected in all aspects of communications dealing with other employees as well as customers fairly. The policy should also outline the consequences of acting unethically. There should be a system for reporting any violations to this code that the employees witness. This policy should be signed by new employees following their recruitment to indicate their acceptance of the code. It should also be reviewed and signed on an annual basis for reinforcement. Awareness of the policy should be reinforced by way of praise for following it and reprimand or punishment for violating it.

Every business needs to impress upon its employees the importance of communicating ethically, whether the communication is between company employees or between company representatives and the outside world. Employees must be honest, fair, sensitive and respectful in communicating with one another and in communicating with customers, vendors and the public.

It is necessary that the ethical issues of business should be reflected in their communication as well, whether it is within the organisation or with other organisations and the public. This applies to marketing communications through PR, advertisement and so on.

Ethical Issues

1. **Fundamental or essential ethical issues:** The most fundamental or essential ethical issues that businesses must face are integrity and trust. A basic understanding of integrity includes the idea of conducting your business affairs with honesty and a

commitment to treating every customer fairly. When customers perceive that a company is exhibiting an unwavering commitment to ethical business practices, a high level of trust can develop between the business and the people it seeks to serve. Such a relationship may be key to the company's success.

Dishonesty, using exaggeration or making manipulative statements seems to be common in business, both in internal and external communication. This can lead to loss of credibility and respect both for the individuals and the organisation.

Favouritism refers to unfairly rewarding, assisting someone in order to promote his career, or punishing someone without any justification. It can be hurtful and create an environment of frustration. Favouritism can reflect itself in inappropriate communication. Employees and organisations need to practice communication practices that are free of favouritism.

Entering into side deals without proper sanctions or authorisation is unethical and can even be a breach of contract. For instance, if a manager has signed an employment contract with the organisation, but in course of time, perceives that he can make an extra amount by diverting a part of the business elsewhere. Such an act can attract severe punishment as it is a breach of both contractual (legal) and ethical duties. Similarly, in partnerships, it is the duty of the more active partner to communicate the status of the business to the other partners.

In a business, if the concerned authority fails to take due care while performing his duties, he could be accused of gross negligence. A senior manager may have been tasked to investigate a wrong doing within the organisation. It would be his duty to conduct a fair enquiry and communicate his findings to the appropriate authority in the prescribed manner.

2. **Diversity Issues:** According to the HSBC Group, "the world is a rich and diverse place full of interesting cultures and people, who should be treated with respect and from whom there is a great deal to learn." The expanding global economy and mobility of labour mean that many workplaces include members from diverse backgrounds, including different national origins. These workers bring new perspectives and ideas to the businesses they work for, but they also raise issues about communication when workers speak multiple languages on the job.

Secondly, with access to better education, women enter the workforce in a big way. It is necessary to ensure that they are not victims of inappropriate words or behaviour. Sensitivity training and providing equal opportunities can keep the environment healthy. Secondly, any complaints about indecent behaviour at the work place should be addressed without delay, and in such a manner that it is not hurtful to the person complaining. Treating female employee differently based on her gender or in response to a harassment complaint may be considered discriminatory and unethical conduct. It is important to remember that problems can arise not only from words that people use but also from non-verbal communication.

Workplace language discrimination can take many different forms, ranging from understated to open. Language discrimination can involve accents, languages, or national or regional dialects, which means that even when a supervisor or manager speaks the same language as a subordinate, that leader's attitude can indicate language discrimination.

A person should keep his religious beliefs to himself while communicating with others unless he is answering someone's inquiry about religion. An employee should be cautious about displaying religious symbols. Similarly, the organisation should treat people of all religions on an equal footing.

Cultural and lifestyle differences among the workforce can be as simple as a person's degree of formality while communicating with others or the style of dress. They can also reflect a complex blend of social customs and personal values. There could be differing perspectives on the importance of work and the role of communication in the workplace. Even something as simple as how close you stand to a person with whom you are talking, can create problems in business communication.

These diversity issues can influence and complicate how people approach business communication. Everything from conducting a meeting to reaching an agreement or addressing a conflict can be challenging. For example, an Indian leading a discussion or brainstorming session may be more informal, allowing the participants to intervene and talk freely, so that they are able to express their top-of-mind impressions without any time to consider the consequences. This may appear chaotic and a madhouse to those who consider discipline and order as extremely important. A similar meeting conducted by someone from a developed country may be more structured, each person waiting for his turn to speak. Other complications with business communication can result from differing values regarding verbal skills, dissimilar approaches to non-verbal communication and varying attitudes toward disclosure and candor.

The starting point is recruiting a diverse workforce, which will bring in a variety of talents and skills. The organisation should assure equal opportunity for all in training programmes and promotion avenues. There should opportunities for exchange of each other's traditional values and cultural ways. No discrimination on the basis of country of origin, gender, religion, language, accent etc., should be permitted. Only then can the employees enjoy a respectful workplace environment that values their contributions.

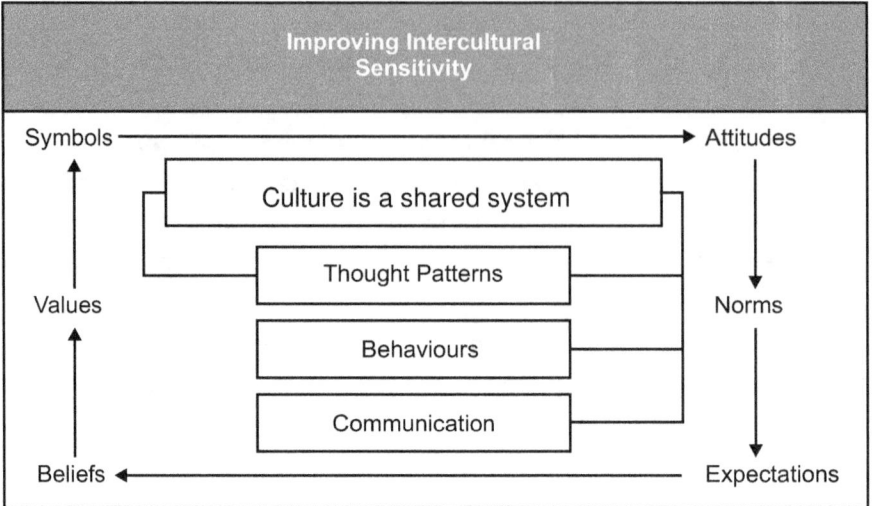

Fig. 1.15

3. **Decision-Making Issues:** Ethical decision making processes should emphasise on (a) protecting the rights of the employees and the customers, (b) ensuring justice and fairness in all business operations, (c) protecting the common good and (d) making sure individual values and beliefs of workers are protected.

4. **Legal Issues:** Businesses are expected to fully comply with all civil rights laws, corporate laws, environmental laws, central and state safety regulations, regulations regarding reporting of financial status, etc. No employee at any level should be instructed to break any law or go against the values, policies and procedures of the organisation.

The Ethical issues are represented in the **THEIRS** principles:
Truthfulness
Honesty
Equity
Integrity
Rationality
Sustainability

Organisations have to be watchful to identify any breach in the framework of ethical policy and principles laid down by them. Breaches can happen due to the following reasons:
- There could be conflict of interests, favouritism and nepotism, which effectively silences criticism.
- The subordinates may keep silent even when they see any irregularity due to fear of punishment from the superiors.
- The organisation may be under pressure to maintain the figures the market is expecting of them.

- The CEO may surround himself with yes-men, who will willingly support him.
- The management may be arrogant and argue that their market performance is adequate to cover up irregularities in accounting and for not following other principles of good governance.
- The management may be under the wrong notion that taking measures to showcase its corporate social responsibility would make up for unethical practices.
- The board of directors consists of weak and inexperienced person, who do not know what questions to ask.

Characteristics of Ethical Communication

Communication is essential and continuous, especially in the information age. Knowledgeable professionals know how to communicate quickly, effectively and ethically.

Business communication consists of internal company communication and external communication to the market. When companies and employees communicate for business objectives, there are ethical considerations they must take into account.

Internal Communication: Communication within the organisation fosters good working relationships and teamwork. Leaders use it to inform and motivate. Professionalism, understanding, respect and tact are important to ensure effective, ethical internal communication. Effective, consistent and ethical internal business communication among employees at all levels is essential for a professional work environment.

External Communication: External communication coordinates the organisation's plans with business partners and suppliers, and markets a company and its services through advertising, promotions and public relations. Key ethical elements include concern, honesty, integrity, credibility and consistency. Consistently honest and reliable external communication with partners and the marketplace establishes the credibility of the organisation in its industry and market.

The term "ethical communication" has different meanings depending on the context. For instance, a shampoo advertiser using a child model may have different notions about child labour than an agency which is crusading against this practice. Communication guidelines are only applicable to certain situations, such as cigarette smoking, while others could be understood as ethical in one situation and unethical in another. Every aspect of ethical communication should be considered within the boundaries of the issue at hand.

Communication is ethical when it is open, forthright and honest and shows concern for the welfare of the parties concerned. Communication that is intended to conceal the truth or harm another person cannot be described as ethical. While ethics are not the same as morals, there is a strong relationship between the two: morals are ideas of what is right and wrong, while ethics are behavioural principles influenced by moral beliefs. The ethics of communication are therefore strongly influenced by moral principles.

- **Honesty:** In general, ethical communication is honest communication. While there are cases where it would be ethical to tell a lie, (such as to a prospective murderer about the whereabouts of a potential victim), these cases are the exception rather than the rule. Also, honesty is more than just not lying; it means being open, and volunteering whatever information is available, even if it puts your own short-term interests at risk. Trust is closely related to the track record of people for their honesty. Encouraging an environment of trust can go a long way in promoting ethical communication in a business or organisational setting.

    When they are young, most people learn not to tell lies. However, this simple idea can get lost in the world of business and mass communication. For instance, advertising is especially known for making exaggerated claims by stretching the truth and omitting the facts. The products being advertised may not be in the best interest of the consumers, but the message may be so appealing that the consumers would get convinced to buy the product. It must be remembered that ethical communication need not to be exceedingly truthful, but it should protect the interest of the public, consumers and stakeholders and prevent any harm to them. Consistent honest communication results in public trust and the organisation which follows this policy is held in great respect by all the stakeholders.

- **Openness to Others' Views:** Openness is one of the key pillars of ethical communication. In communication, openness means being open to diverse ideas and opinions, as well as being ready to offer one's own opinions whether it will be acceptable to others or not. A business environment where people are not free to express unpopular opinions is not an ethical one, because intolerance of divergent opinions means intolerance of differences. In an organisation, free flow of information is essential to the organisation's long-term well-being and is in the interest of the public.

- **Commitment to free flow of information:** In the context of business communications, commitment indicates that the organisation is open to discussions and permits free flow of information in all directions. It is willing to allocate the necessary time and resources for discussions on concerned issues fully. In such an organisation, there are adequate systems and procedures for people at all levels to offer their feedback, with the assurance that their voices will be heard without fear or favour.

- **Goal-orientation:** Ethical communication is goal-oriented rather than status-oriented. The members of the organisation do not form self-serving groups opposed to each other primarily on the basis of political and status-seeking interests. Such an organisation will not accomplish things for the good of the organisation as a whole. The organisation should consciously encourage a style of communication which promotes consensus building. The members should focus on doing what they can for the company rather than aiming at professional advancement to positions they are not suited to. Consensus building should be the goal which guides the ethical style of communication far as it helps the organisation and is morally essential.

- **Workplace diversity** can enhance business communication, but issues surrounding it can also complicate and obscure the communication process. Employees might work with colleagues who have ethnic, cultural and social backgrounds different from their own. These differences can impact everything from passing on instructions, one-on-one interviews, conducting interdepartmental meetings and giving internal memos to external news releases. Understanding the issues of diversity can help the organisation in developing a positive impact on workplace communication.

- **Proper understanding and interpretation – audience centered approach:** Communication is a two-way process, and communicators both receive and transmit messages. Ethical communicators take time to fully interpret the message they receive, so that they can respond with understanding. Ethical communicators ensure that they cut through 'noise' on both the receiving and transmitting side of their message. The most ethical messages are characterised by the communicators understanding the needs of the recipients and responding accordingly.

- **Concern for others:** Concern for the well-being of others and the community at large form the fundamental principles of every organisation. In legal terms, this is also known as "duty to care". It is the responsibility of the communicators to ensure that their messages take into consideration the welfare of all concerned and pass the test of common good. Such communications are free from prejudice or deceit. They are not hurtful. They do not use intolerant language. They also aim to promote ideals such as justice and freedom. Such communicators are held in great respect by the organisation and the society they belong to. For instance, some corporate communications publicly support concepts like equal employment, social justice, social welfare, environmental protection etc., and sponsor organisations and activities that serve and/or further these causes. Similarly, judges, while delivering their judgments, take a lot of care to ensure to uphold justice, fairness and concern for the society.

- **Maintenance of Confidentiality:** Ethical communicators do not indulge in spreading rumours or giving away confidential information of others as that could be hurtful. They double check all their messages to make sure that they violate the principles of confidentiality. They respect the privacy of others. As a policy, many organisations require that employees desist from communicating sensitive information. This may at times be against the policy of honesty. In such cases, ethical communicators should weigh such factors as social and business consequences of their actions. For instance, when an employee commits an irregular act, the management may consider it to be in his interest to keep his offense confidential, but if it follows this approach, the organisation may appear to be weak and give rise to a belief that all such irregularities will be ignored. In the best interest of the organisation, the HR department may take necessary action and communicate within the organisation the circumstances under which the punitive action has been taken.
- **Avoiding plagiarism or Copying:** Plagiarism is defined as "wrongful appropriation," "close imitation," or "purloining and publication," of another author's "language, thoughts, ideas, or expressions," and representing the stolen information or knowledge as one's own original work, without giving due credit to the original author. This is more an ethical issue than a legal one. Such unethical practices are seen more in academic and scientific work, and may result in sanctions, ban, termination of any contact etc. It results in loss of credibility of the organisation which permits it. There are software packages which can alert people about such unethical practices.
- **Awareness about Consequences:** Ethical communicators consider the consequences of their messages before they deliver them. Messages can have different consequences for different groups of people. Ethical communicators may consider the consequences for: employees, investors, consumers or the community. Thinking through consequences can clear up some ethical and legal communication dilemmas, such as honestly versus confidentiality.
- **Security of information:** Organisations should protect sensitive information falling in to unwanted persons. A lot of private data is transmitted through voice mails, emails, phone calls, faxes and company intranets. A lot of information is stored in back-up on servers. The frequency of creating back-up can be set as required. There are many ways in which to build fire walls and protect digital, such as login identification, limiting access to certain levels or individuals etc. As the use of technology in the workplace expands, so do the legal and ethical complications that can result. Reliance on technology increases the risk posed by system failure and malicious attacks. Information security management deals with maintaining the

integrity and availability of organisational information and knowledge. This covers protection of digital data, the records maintained in physical forms and also knowledge management issues.

> **The Ten Basics of Ethical Communication are:**
> 1. Try to get the best from the communications and interactions with other group members.
> 2. Listen when others speak.
> 3. Make sure that everyone has time to speak.
> 4. Avoid interrupting or engage in side conversations when others are speaking.
> 5. Speak non-judgmentally.
> 6. Speak from your own experience and perspective, expressing your own thoughts, needs, and feelings.
> 7. Do not communicate what you hear from others, unless adequate evidence is available. Check and understand the facts. One should avoid generalising his/her opinions, beliefs, values, and conclusions by putting a label on the person, which can be damaging.
> 8. Seek to understand others. Do not approach any issue with the arrogance that you know best.
> 9. Manage your own personal boundaries regarding what you are comfortable sharing with others.
> 10. Respect the personal boundaries of others.

Responsibilities of the Employers: Employers have the right to monitor their employees' business communications to ensure work is being conducted properly. However, employers are prohibited from monitoring personal telephone conversations or voice mail messages. Employers must not violate the privacy rights of their employees and must take steps to keep employees' personal information confidential.

Role of the Management: Management's role in ethical communication practices covers (a) Always demonstrating ethical behaviour in verbal and non-verbal form. If they expect employees to act in a certain way, they must also act in the same way and lead by example. (b) Management should reinforce ethical behaviour in others by conducting training programmes frequently. (c) The management should praise or reward those who follow these practices.

Ethics Training: Because the concept of ethics can differ from individual to individual and from group to group, it is important that organisations conduct ethics training for all employees. For instance, for some employees, taking office stationery home may appear to be unethical, while others may consider it as 'no big deal'. The business should educate the employees about its own ethical standards through office notes, role play, discussions on hypothetical scenarios, stories from news etc.

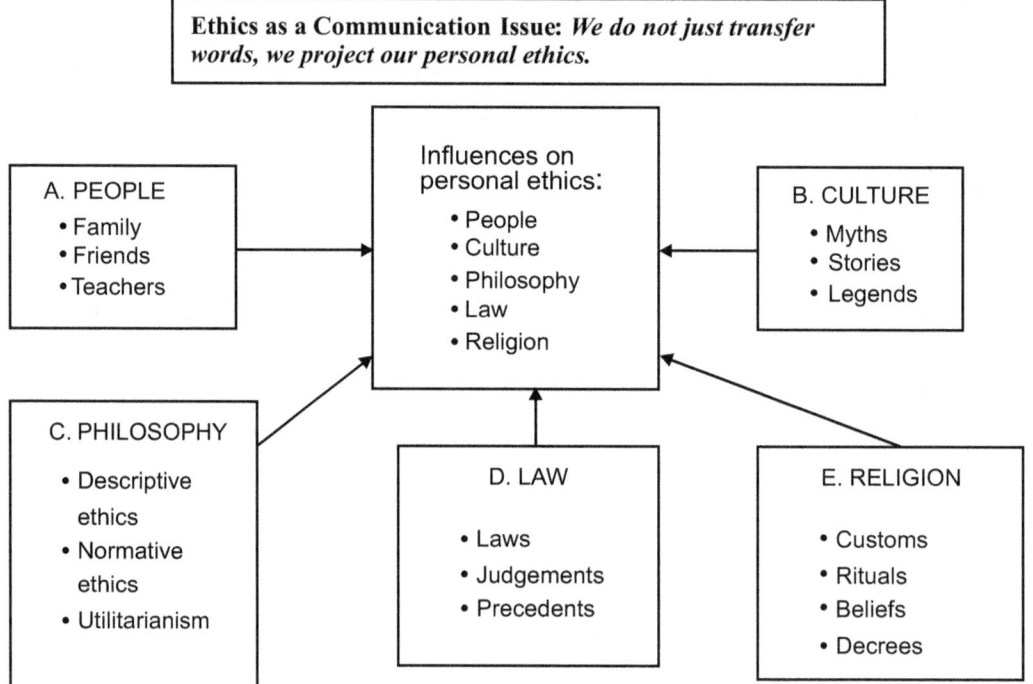

Fig. 1.16

Example: Ethical Issues in Marketing Communication: No marketing communication is inherently good or bad. It is its persuasive power, methods adopted and its impact that differentiates a good marketing communication from an unethical one. *Since it is public by its very nature (business to people or B2C), it is constantly scrutinised for false promises, misleading statements, or the undermining of social values.* In delivering the brand messages, there is constant tension between marketers on the one hand, who want to adopt every possible method to persuade people to buy their products and on the other hand, the many regulations and social norms in this regard. The social norms may not be spelt out or written in clear terms. Responsible companies know that if they push beyond acceptable limits, they can spoil their image and risk penalty as well as public humiliation. Advertisers should understand that these standards and norms are different for different communities. They have to be constantly aware of these issues while they strive to stay ahead of competition. They should maintain a balance between attention grabbing and exciting, and being truthful. Marketing communicators must have a basic understanding of what is and is not socially acceptable, what is legal and illegal, and what is ethical and unethical. Some unethical practices in marketing communication are:

- It adds to the cost of the product unnecessarily,
- Indulges in puffery and fraudulent practices, like offering unnecessary or unwelcome incentives, coaxing consumers to accept unwanted upgrades etc.
- Creates a barrier for new and smaller entrants,
- Making exaggerated claims by using glamorous models,
- Creates unhealthy expectations about the product by misleading statements, misquoting research reports or misrepresenting facts,
- Done in bad taste, offensive, imposes an alien culture on the society and creates visual pollution,
- Sells inferior, unhealthy and dangerous products,
- Targets vulnerable sections of society like children, women, minorities, differently abled persons, developing countries etc.,
- Violates the moral values of the society and acts crudely as behavioral guidelines for a society.

Considering the power of the advertisers, self-regulation is not often the remedy. Censorships, public scrutiny and strong public voice, action by concerned non-governmental agencies etc., can regulate and tone down the unethical practices in marketing communication.

Points to Remember

- **Scott and Sprige** underline the importance of communication in an organisation by saying that *"Communication is the process involving the transmission and accurate replication of ideas reinforced by feedback purporting to stimulate actions to accomplish organisational goals."*
- **Chester Barnard**, *"In an exhaustive theory of organisation, communication would occupy a central place because the structure, extensiveness and scope of organisations are almost entirely determined by communication techniques."*
- **Simon**, *"The question to be asked of any administrative process is: How does it influence the decisions of the individuals without communication, the answer must always be: It does not influence them at all."*
- **Communication Process:**
  o The Encoder
  o Symbols Used
  o Channel
  o Decoding
  o Receiver
  o Feedback

- **Characteristics of Effective Business Communication:**
    - Clarity about the Purpose of Communication
    - Systematic Arrangement of the Message
    - Understanding the Needs of the Receiver
    - Selection of Proper Media
    - Selection of Appropriate Time
    - Feedback and Prompt Action on Receiving Response
- **Principles of Communication:**
    - Principle of Completeness and Adequacy
    - Principle of Consistency
    - Medium of Communication
    - Principle of Timeliness
    - Principle of Information
    - Principle of Channel or Media Adaptation
    - Principle of Appropriate Time Element
    - Principle of Integration
    - Principle of Flexibility
    - Principle of Informality
    - Principle of Feedback
    - Conciseness
    - Attractiveness
    - Correctness
    - Consideration
    - Courtesy
    - Careful use of Body Language
- **7C's of Effective Business Communication:**
    - Correctness
    - Clarity
    - Conciseness
    - Completeness
    - Consideration
    - Concreteness
    - Courtesy
- **Other Variations of Principles of Effective Business Communication:**
    - The Eight Cs of Communication:
    - Credibility
    - Context
    - Content
    - Clarity
    - Continuity
    - Consistency
    - Channels
    - Capability of Audience

- **The three corners of the barriers to communication are:**
  - The thought of the sender and the receiver
  - Their speech or delivery of the message, and
  - Their action
- **Frequently observed causes for this discrepancy are:**
  - Lack of common experience
  - Confusion between the Symbol and the Symbolised Object
  - Over-use of Abstractions
  - Lack of Basic Language and Communication Skills
  - The use of the wrong medium to deliver the communication
  - Insufficient Knowledge of the Subject
  - Weak Delivery
  - Poor Structure of the Message
  - Mixed up Messages
  - Bottom of Form Message Sent to Wrong Audience
  - Distracting Environment
  - Information Overload
- **Reading Techniques**
  - Slow Reading
  - Skipping
  - Skimming
  - Scanning
  - Rapid reading
- **Principles of Non-verbal Communication:**
  - Align body language to verbal communication
  - Establish an open relationship with the audience
  - Be authentic
  - Decision making process is basically an emotional process and so emotions should be communicated and not hidden
  - Non-verbal communication takes precedence over speech
  - The speaker should be conscious of his body language and try to master it.
  - It is necessary to be aware of the body language of others
  - It is necessary to have control over one's own emotional intent and the Appropriate gestures will follow.
  - The emotional intent has to be matched by conscious thought and appropriate Words.
  - An effective speaker shows that he is open, authentic, connected and at the same time passionate about what he is communicating.
- **Forces that determine Group Processes and Dynamics:**
  - Group interaction
  - Group interdependence
  - Group structure
  - Group norms
  - Group roles
  - Group goals
  - Group cohesion

- **The basic types of Group Communication:**
  - Standing Meeting
  - Topical Meeting
  - Presentation
  - Conference
  - Seminar
  - Emergency Meeting
- **Purposes of a Meeting:**
  - Statutory Requirement:
  - Record
  - Evidence
  - Proof of Attendance
  - Authenticity
  - Source of Authority
  - Check on the Participants
  - Continuity
  - Aid to Proper Understanding
- **The ethics of communication are therefore strongly influenced by moral principles:**
  - Honesty
  - Openness to Others' Views
  - Commitment to free flow of information
  - Goal-orientation
  - Workplace diversity
  - Proper understanding and interpretation – audience centered approach
  - Concern for others
  - Maintenance of Confidentiality
  - Avoiding plagiarism or Copying
  - Awareness about Consequences
  - Security of information

Questions for Discussion

1. Explain the importance of meetings in an organisation. What is the procedure for conducting a meeting?
2. Give an example of a cola drink marketing communication and list the messages they could be sending and to whom. What ethical concerns do they raise? Examples may be from commercials as well as in entertainment programmes.
3. Find an example of a social marketing campaign and analyse how it relates to various stakeholder groups.
4. What is brainstorming? What are the barriers to effective brainstorming?
5. Explain the significance of negotiation in business communication. What are the conditions for a successful negotiation?

■■■

Chapter 2...

Managerial Writing

Contents ...

- 2.1 Introduction
- 2.2 Types of Written Communication
- 2.3 Media for Despatch of Written Communication
- 2.4 A Process of Effective Written Communication
- 2.5 Writing Skills
- 2.6 Business Letters
    - 2.6.1 Importance of a Business Letter
    - 2.6.2 Essential Qualities of a Good Business Letter
    - 2.6.3 Physical Appearance of a Business Letter
    - 2.6.4 Layout of a Business Letter
- 2.7 Résumé / CV / Biodata
- 2.8 Memorandum
- 2.9 Minutes
- 2.10 Circulars and Notices
- 2.11 Executive Summary of Documents
- 2.12 Preparing Press Release and Press Notes
- 2.13 Creative Writing
- 2.14 Poster Making
- 2.15 Framing Advertisements, Slogans and Captions
- 2.16 Maintaining a Diary
    - Points to Remember
    - Questions for Discussion

Learning Objectives ...

- ➤ To equip the students with the various types of written communication
- ➤ To understand the process of effective written communication
- ➤ To learn and get acquainted with the different writing skills
- ➤ To know about press release and press notes
- ➤ To understand what is Creative Writing, Poster Making, Framing Advertisement, Slogans and Captions

2.1 Introduction

The success of any business depends upon sound relationships within the organisation and with other stakeholders and the public. Written correspondence means exchange of letters, which is the best and cheapest means of communication. In modern days, trade and industries have expanded to national and international borders. Business activities are diversified. The businessperson has to maintain contacts with the suppliers, the customers, the media and the government in carrying out daily transactions. In other words, written communication is at the root of a successful commercial and industrial activity.

Speech came before writing. Humans like to see and hear the people they communicate with. Yet, verbal communication is not always the most effective method of communication. Many times the message is not clearly understood because of other factors such as environmental distractions, body language, tone of voice and emotions. The message is lost because the audience is distracted by other factors. Even in staff meetings or training sessions, the way in which the content is delivered can cause misunderstanding or loss of interest in the message and so written communication is used as a back-up.

Writing is more unique and formal than speech. Effective writing involves careful planning of the ideas to be communicated, choice of right words, their organisation in correct order, in cohesive sentences, and in paragraphs. While verbal communication can be spontaneous and fast, writing is more valid and reliable than speech. But it can cause delay as feedback is not immediate.

Objectives of Written Communication: Written communications have a goal or are intended to achieve or "do" something. The goals may be to:
- Inform
- Respond
- Request
- Report
- Develop goodwill

Managers move through the workforce in stages. Each stage has its own set of characteristics and requirements. This includes good written communication skills. A manager's communication skills indicate his level of professionalism. In a professional environment, the clearer the manager is in written and verbal communication, the more proficient he will seem. *If a manager's letter is badly worded or his presentation is badly planned and disjoint, it might appear that the person has not taken the matter seriously, or lacks the skills required for his position. Such a manager is termed as unprofessional.* The effectiveness of a manager is judged by his ability to get across his points or views clearly in as few words as possible. Such a manager will demonstrate the capabilities of a good communicator who knows his subject well.

Written communication usually requires more thought and effort. Writing must be concise, informative and easy to read as both an informative and instructional tool. The importance of written communication in business is evident by the plethora of forms, manuals and materials that companies publish each day.

It should be noted, however, that the reader's reaction to a written communication can be coloured by his knowledge, biases, values etc. A written communication will fail to convince if the reader has had an earlier bad experience with that person or organisation or has developed a prejudice through hearsay. Just like oral communication, written communication can also encounter barriers.

Advantages of Written Communication

- Written communication can be well thought out and organised to convey the message in a more precise and explicit manner.
- It can be erased, revised, rewritten and edited before it is dispatched. Hence it is possible to take away emotions, biases and negative inputs.
- It is effective as a standalone medium.
- It can be targeted to reach specific individuals or parties.
- Written communication helps in laying down the principles, policies and rules for running of an organisation.
- It can be stored and reproduced.
- It is a permanent record of communication. Thus, it is useful where record maintenance is required. It is accepted as evidence in the courts of law.
- It assists in proper delegation of responsibilities. In the case of oral communication, it is impossible to fix and delegate responsibilities as the speaker can take back the words or deny having said anything. Spoken words can be forgotten and cannot be retrieved. Hence, oral communication is not valid for taking decisions or instructing subordinates.
- Effective written communication develops and enhances an organisation's image.
- It can be cost effective, as it can be reproduced using appropriate technology and distributed to a large number of parties. With the Internet, it is faster and cheaper to communicate with a large number of parties and get feedback.

Disadvantages of Written Communication

- Written communication adds to the time and costs in terms of stationery and the manpower employed in writing/typing and delivering letters.
- Without the help of body language and vocal intonation to guide the reader, written communication is open to his/her interpretation, which can lead to huge misunderstandings. There is lack of personalisation in letters, emails, text messages and instant messenger tools. This lack of personalisation means there is greater need to think carefully about how these messages will be perceived. Poor written or verbal communication can lead not only to a distortion of the facts, but also of the writer's thoughts and intentions.

- Perhaps the biggest problem with written communication is that once it is in the hands of the reader, it does not provide a second chance to make your point in a different way. Once the reader is lost, it is difficult to get him back. This is why you need to pick and choose your words carefully, and present your points in a style, manner and sequence that best suit the message you are sending.
- If the receivers of the written message are separated by distance, and if they need to clear their doubts, they will have to wait.
- Feedback is not immediate. The encoding and sending of message takes time.
- Effective written communication requires great skills and competencies in language and vocabulary use. Poor writing skills and quality have a negative impact on organisation's reputation and can create confusion and even disputes.
- Too much paper work and e-mails burden is involved.

2.2 Types of Written Communication

The different forms of written communication and their methods of delivery are described below. Each form has a use and, in some cases, a phraseology of its own. Only black or blue ink will be used in communications. A small margin of about one inch will be left on all sides (left, right, top and bottom) of each page of communications to ensure filing and better preservations of records as at times the paper gets torn from the edges, making reading of the documents difficult.

1. **Letter:** This form is used for corresponding with individuals, various authorities, organisations and the public. A letter begins with an appropriate salutation. A letter can be informal, formal or in government parlance, semi formal or 'demi-official.'
2. **Office Memorandum:** This form is generally used for corresponding with other departments or in calling for information from or conveying information to its employees. It is written in the third person and bears no salutation or supersession except the name and designation of the officer signing it.
3. **Circular:** This form is used when an important and urgent piece of information or decision taken internally has to be circulated within a department for information and compliance by a large number of employees.
4. **Inter-departmental note:** This form is generally employed for obtaining the advice, views, concurrence or comments of other departments on a proposal or in seeking clarification of the existing rules, instructions and so on. It may also be used by a department when consulting its attached and subordinate offices and *vice versa*.
5. **Office order:** This form is normally used for issuing instructions meant for internal administration, e.g., grant of regular leave, distribution of work among officers and sections, instructions, financial sanctions, disciplinary actions appointments and transfers etc.

6. **Notification:** This form is mostly used in notifying the promulgation of statutory rules and orders. The government notifications of certain types are contained in publications in the Gazette of India.
7. **Report:** This is detailed document describing an event, the current status of a project, marketing information etc. This is a time consuming activity and requires a lot of planning, so as to include all necessary information in a logical manner. For instance, a marketing survey report will contain information about market expectations, market size and shares of competitors, qualitative information regarding the activities, strategy and future plans of the competitors, government policy implications and the future outlook for the client party. The report will also give specific recommendations based on the study.
8. **Resolution:** These are policy decisions taken at company level meetings and are recorded as 'resolutions'. These are communicated to the shareholders and the executing authorities base their actions on these resolutions. In the functioning of the government, important matters of policy, e.g., the industrial licensing policy, appointment of committees or commissions of enquiry etc., are passed as resolutions by the concerned legislature or at cabinet meetings. These are published in the Gazette of India.
9. **Press communiqué/note:** The purpose of this is to give wide publicity to any matter of significance to the issuing organisation and the public. A press communiqué is more formal in nature than a press note and is expected to be reproduced in exact words by the press. A press note, on the other hand, is intended to serve as a hand-out to the press. It contains information which may be edited, compressed or enlarged by the media according to the importance that is attached to the matter.
10. **Endorsement or expression of support:** This form is used when a paper has to be returned in original to the sender, or the paper in original or its copy is sent to another department or office, along with approval, for information or for action. It is also used when a copy of a communication is forwarded to other parties.
11. **Advertisement:** This form is used for communicating with the general public to create awareness and may take the form of audio-visual or written communication.

2.3 Media for Despatch of Written Communication

Written communication can be sent by the following media:
- **Telegram:** This form is used for communicating with out-station parties in matters demanding prompt attention. The text of the telegram should be as brief as possible. With the increasing popularity of email, telegrams are not common.
- **Fax facility:** In urgent and important matters (including legal and financial messages), managers may use fax facilities to send messages, wherever available.
- **Registered Post, Speed Post:** This method of delivery is used in sending written communication when receipt of despatch is required. With the advent of IT enabled services, movement of the document till it reaches the addressee can be tracked on line.

- **E-mail:** This is a paperless form of communication to be used by managers having computer facilities supported by internet or intranet connectivity and can be widely used for subjects where legal or financial implications are not involved.

Various media of mass communication, such as press, hoardings, audio-visual communication, Internet based publicity.

2.4 Process of Effective Written Communication

The business world is replete with various types of business writing, such as business letters, circular messages, printed pamphlets, brochures etc. Any organisation will have some amount of business communication, whether handwritten, typed or printed.

The process of making a written communication involves the following steps:
- Planning
- Organising
- Drafting
- Revising or editing
- Proof reading to eliminate errors.

Planning: This stage involves the following:
- Identifying the purpose. This is two-fold: the main reason for writing the message, and the need to build goodwill. The main reasons could be: (1) Informational, (2) Invitational, (3) Negotiator, (4) Order or (5) Request. The relational purpose is to maintain goodwill.
- Analysing the audience: (1) Their needs, interests, attitudes and culture, (2) Whether they are being contacted for the first time, (3) If possible, visualising them as individuals, (4) Their names correctly spelt and appropriate salutation (5) Their level of knowledge regarding the subject and the information they need in this communication, (6) Their likely response, whether positive or negative.

For instance, managers read technical and scientific documents for a variety of purposes:
- to aid in making decisions
- to assess current situations
- to maintain their general level of expertise
- to evaluate projects and employees

In general, managers read for the *bottomline*, a concise summary of the present situation and specific recommendations for action.

It should be remembered that the readers do not have: (1) the same vocabulary or knowledge of the subject, (2) the same mentality or ability to understand. Hence it is necessary to adapt to individual situations. However, while addressing a group, it is necessary to visualise those with least level of education, knowledge and understanding, so that no one is left out.

- Choosing the ideas to be communicated depend on the type of message, situation and cultural context. If it is a spontaneous letter, it is a good idea to list the ideas, brainstorm, pick and prioritise the ideas. If the message is a response, it is a good strategy to keep the letter in front, highlight the main points to be discussed, write down the responses on the margin and then plan the message.
- **Collecting supporting data:** This includes: (1) all concerned names, dates, addresses, information and statistics, (2) Company policy, procedure, details of product or service offered or is being discussed, and (3) Any legal issues that may arise.
- **Organising the message.** It could be done as: (1) Direct or deductive request plan, when the audience is expected to be receptive to the message, and so all necessary explanatory details for decision taking are included with an appropriately friendly closing; (2) Good news plan (for instance confirming job appointment/granting a request etc. and offering further help); (3) Bad news plan; and (4) Persuasive request plan. Plans 3 and 4 can result in audience resistance. Hence, the writer will have to deliberate on the subject and be careful while preparing.

The Golden Rule for written communication is to take care of the big "W"s:
- WHO... Who is the primary reader? Who should get the copies?
- WHAT... What are you trying to get accomplished? Action? Inform? Apologise? Refuse? or Propose?
- WHY... Why are you writing now? Why is this important or interesting to the reader?
- WHEN... When will things happen? When is the deadline? When will additional information follow?
- WHERE... Where will it happen? Are directions needed? Where can additional information be obtained?

2.5 Writing Skills

It is a business adage that the time wasted because of insufficient or inaccurate information being passed between colleagues, employees and organisations translates into loss of money. For example, while preparing a project proposal, a lack of detail in the brief could mean that the proposal is not accepted or at best, it will have to be rewritten and resubmitted. In this process, the organisation could incur additional cost for the rework, or in the worst case, because of the resultant delay, even lose the business opportunity. This indicates the need to develop good writing skills.

A brief list of points that need to be addressed while preparing written communication is given below. These can be seen as general guidelines, the specific contents being determined by the subject, the purpose and the recipient.

1. **Avoid being verbose:** One of the most common problems is wordiness. It dilutes the message and confuses the reader. The main point is lost. The objective is not to impress but to communicate. Hence, choose shorter words and sentences. For instance, a notice for cancellation of a meeting could read, "I write to bring to your

notice that the meeting has been cancelled". This has ten words. The same message could be shortened to seven words: "Please note that the meeting has been cancelled". Another common mistake is the use of negative words and phrases that warn the reader immediately and usually it generates a negative response. Improper use of grammar is another common problem. The reader's attention will get diverted to the mistakes and the intended message is lost. It is a wrong notion that the computer has spellchecker and grammar check facilities which will take care of all mistakes.

2. **Subject lines:** The subject of the memo / letter / e-mail should be stated in an objective manner and should reflect the content of the message. For instance, if the letter is intended to communicate a contract terminate notice, it should be clearly stated: "Notice for Termination of Contract" to convey to the reader that the message content will be related to a particular contract which is not running satisfactorily.

3. **Decide your audience:** If the communication has to reach different reader segments, it is advisable to write to each segment separately, as the language or terminology to be used would be different. While addressing the general public, a simpler language and tone need to be adopted, as highly technical work may not be understood by them. The author may have to write at levels lower than theirs. On the other hand, while addressing a highly educated and knowledgeable person or group, the manager has to ponder and try to maintain a standard which will earn him/her respect. The author has to adapt to the readers' levels.

4. **Prepare an outline of the document:** Identify the main theme and then start working. This is essential whether it is a brief email or a lengthy report. It will help the writer break the task up into manageable pieces of information, organise his/her thoughts, prioritise the points to be included and thus provide the basic guideline for the document. The writer will not forget any point. The document becomes complete in all respects, well organised and professional in approach. If your document has to motivate action: use the *Attention-Interest-Desire-Action (AIDA)* formula. These four steps can help guide the entire writing process.

5. **Purpose statement:** The purpose or the action expected from the reader should be clearly stated. Never leave the reader guessing "what do I do with this piece of information? What next?" The reader should know what is expected out of him / her. For instance, while announcing company-wide decisions: Do not overload employees with a lot of wordy or text-heavy mails. The message has to be appropriately divided and organised. For instance, if a company proposes a training programme for writing skills, the message to the employees contains four parts: (1) announcement that the training programme has been organised along with venue, date and time, (2) credentials of the faculty (2) the levels of employees for whom it is intended, and (4) how to apply and register for the programme.

6. **Format:** The first step to writing clearly is choosing the appropriate format. It depends on the type of document being created, such as a quick email, a detailed report, an advertising copy or a formal letter. The format, as well as the audience, will define the "writing voice" – that is, how formal or relaxed the tone should be. For instance, an email to a prospective client should be quite formal. It is necessary to identify who will read your message. That will define the tone as well as other aspects of the content. The writer should know who the target reader is. Is it targeted at senior managers, the entire production or marketing team, or a small group of engineers?

7. **Organise the contents in paragraphs:** There should be a logical connection between various paragraphs included in the document. The overall content in the message should be consistently conveyed through the document. There should be no confusion or contradiction anywhere.

8. **Pay attention to the Structure of the document:** Make sure it is reader-friendly. Use headings, subheadings, bullet points, and numbering whenever possible, to demarcate various points. It is not comfortable to read a page full of text presented in long paragraphs. A document that is easy to look at will get read more often than a document with a long text. The title or the header should catch the attention of the reader. In some cases, like advertisements, using questions will make the reader pay attention. In emails and proposals, use short, factual headings and subheadings. Adding graphs and charts help in breaking the monotony. Through such visuals, it is possible to communicate important information more quickly. Readers tend to remember facts presented in this manner.

9. **Be effective and persuasive:** If you're trying to persuade someone to do something, make sure that you communicate why people should listen to you. Present your message information rationally and coherently in such a way that it engages your audience. The

10. **Address one reader rather than many:** It increases the focus and also creates accountability of the reader. For instance, if a reminder notice has to be sent to defaulters, the communication should be specifically addressed to the defaulters identified through a thorough check of payments received thus far. It should not go to all the members, whether they have paid or have not. It will irritate those who are prompt.

11. **Engage the reader's attention:** The flow of language should be interesting and engaging, as if the writer is talking to the audience. For instance, while writing a sales letter, a little bit of empathy is required. Tell the reader how the product or service will help the reader. Audience's needs should be kept in view all the time. The Rhetorical Triangle is a useful way of formulating your thoughts and presenting your position. A note on Rhetorical Triangle is presented in Appendix 1.

12. **Take care of spelling and grammar:** There is a tendency to use SMS style spelling and grammar in written documents. The reader may construe this as trivialisation of the subject matter or lack of respect for the reader. The writer has to make sure that the words are properly used to convey the right meaning. There is a lot of confusion regarding the usage of definite and indefinite articles. Mistakes do get noticed.

    Some examples of commonly misused words:
    - Affect/effect
    - There/Their
    - Then/than
    - Your/you're
    - Its/it's
    - Company's/companies
    - Confirm/Conform
    - Coma/Comma

13. **Check before sending (Proofing):** This aspect can never be over emphasised. It is always better to be sure than to be sorry. Always proofread the document that is to be sent. The enemy of good proofreading is speed. Many people rush through their documents, as they are confident of what they have written. But this is how mistakes are overlooked. Follow these guidelines to check the written document:
    - **Proof your headers and sub-headers:** People often skip these and focus on the text alone. Just because headers are big and bold does not mean that they are written or typed correctly.
    - **Read the document out loud** – This forces you to go more slowly, so that you are more likely to catch mistakes.
    - **Use your finger to follow text as you read** – This is another trick that helps you slow down.
    - **Start at the end of your document and** go backwards.
    - Proofread one sentence at a time. This helps in focusing on errors and not on the content.
    - **Third party assessment:** If time permits, get someone else to proof the document.

    Proofing includes all aspects such as content, word choice, grammar, formatting, subject lines, audience salutations, and reference to attachments if any. Make sure all attachments are numbered and put together in the order in which they are mentioned in the text.

14. **Communicate with confidence:** In any organisation, written communication is essential and no manager can escape it. Hence through proper drafting and finalising after the required reviews, the manager should have no hesitation in sending the document to the intended person or party. Even if the subject matter is unpleasant or negative in nature, the manager will fail in his duty if he 'sleeps' over the matter.

Key Points:

(a) More than ever, it is important to know how to communicate your points professionally.
(b) Identify your audience before you start creating your document.
(c) Create an outline to help organise your thoughts.
(d) Determine how much information you want to include.
(e) Learn grammatical and stylistic techniques. This will help you write more clearly; and
(f) Be sure to proof the final document. Like most things, 'practice makes perfect!'

2.6 Business Letters

Routine letters, Bad news and persuasion letters, sales letters, collection letters, Maintaining a Diary, Résumé/CV, job application letters, proposals.

2.6.1 Importance of a Business Letter

The following are some of the situations where business letters are important:

1. **Permanent Record:** A business letter serves as a permanent record which can be referred to when needed. It can also be produced in the court of law as evidence in case of disputes.

2. **Promotion or Business:** In an organisation, letters are written for facilitating production, administration and distribution. The letter may be internal or external. For instance, after a review of the inventory position, the purchase department writes to the vendor placing an order with details of item, quality expected, order quantity, expected date of delivery etc., and sends copies to the quality assurance, finance and production departments. Similarly, after inspection, the quality control department writes to the vendors with copy to all concerned. When a new product is to be introduced in the market, product brochures, sales literature etc., are prepared and sent to dealers with covering letters, contacts are established with the media and so on. It would be almost impossible to prepare a list of situations in an organisation requiring business letters.

3. **Creates Goodwill:** A good letter can open up new channels of business, get better performance from employees, better results from the customers, reduce bad debts etc. This can be done by writing letters in a courteous tone and language, which can enhance the reputation of the organisation and its products/services.

4. **Useful in finding out the Creditworthiness of a Customer or vendor:** In order to promote business, the manager has to place orders from vendors and also deal with customers. It becomes essential for the manager to assess the credibility of the agencies with which the organisation is dealing. This will necessitate writing to the prospective vendors/customers requesting for all the necessary back-up information.

5. **Collection of Overdue Payments:** The initial contract specifies the credit period and mode of payment. If reminders have to be sent after the expiry of the credit period, it would be in the long term interest of the organisation to do so in a polite but firm manner without hurting the ego of the customer.

Letters reflect the personality of the sender and the organisation he/she represents. An outgoing letter carries a message which helps build the reputation of the firm. The reader should feel that he is talking directly to the other person. Hence, business letters have to be warm, friendly and lively.

A good business letter helps in removing misunderstandings. A good letter writer should be able to convert bitterness into a smile. He should explain his case and present the facts in a frank manner. The point of view of the reader should be considered while writing business letters.

Thus, every letter should have a personality and be a messenger of goodwill. It should act as a silent ambassador of the organisation, whether the intention of the writer is just to gather information from or to do business with.

2.6.2 Essential Qualities of a Good Business Letter

Introduction

The success of a good business letter depends upon effective communication of the message and the motivation it provides to the reader to take the expected course of action. These letters must be drafted very carefully. In order to make the letter effective, the writer should be equipped with certain basic requirements like logical thinking and a good command over the language, knowledge of certain standard technical terms, knowledge about the character and position of the recipient etc. The following are the essentials of a good business letter.

1. **Completeness:** A business letter should be complete in all respects. It should contain all the information required by the receiver, so as to avoid the irritations associated with back and forth communication, misunderstandings and delays. The letter should have the necessary references to the numbers and dates of earlier letters on the subject, so that the meaning becomes absolutely clear. All important and relevant matter should be covered. Incomplete letters do not produce the desired results. A business letter should be comprehensive and should cover all aspects of the subject matter.

2. **Clarity:** A business letter should convey the message clearly. Nothing should be left for the assumptions and imagination of the reader. The writer should take into account the level of understanding of the reader as well as his/her limitations. This helps in bringing out clarity in the letter. To achieve clarity, the words and sentences should be arranged to convey the exact meaning. Words and phrases should be chosen carefully and used in the exact sense. Long complex sentences should be avoided. The writer should have clarity of thought and expressions.

The writer should know the language well and use the words that can effectively create a concrete picture about the subject matter in the mind of the reader. Clarity should find expression in the following aspects of a good business letter:

- Proper appearance of the letter
- Correct facts and figures.
- Appropriate language used in the letter.

3. Accuracy: The statements in a business letter should be accurate. It is fundamental to an effective business letter. All facts and figures should be checked and verified. If necessary, proper references to earlier correspondence should be made to establish the veracity of the facts. Documents like bill of exchange, invoices, statement of accounts etc., should be carefully prepared and checked. Legal action may be taken against the organisation and damages may be claimed if there is any misrepresentation of the facts.

4. Brevity or Conciseness: Brevity is the soul of business correspondence. A business letter should be concise. The content should be communicated using the least possible number of words. A businessman's time is precious and he/she cannot waste it in trying to consume unnecessary and irrelevant statements. Every sentence should convey the intended meaning. All the words which are essential to convey the meaning should be used and superfluous and unnecessary words should be avoided. Business letters should be written in a way that the reader will be able to understand the communication properly. The other side of this statement is that when a person tries to write an unnecessarily long letter, there is every possibility that he will make errors and confuse the reader.

5. Courtesy: Courtesy means politeness on the part of the writer towards the reader. It is a sincere attempt to be polite and effective. The general tone of the letter should be pleasant unless it is intended as a strict warning. Courtesy is absolutely essential to *maintain good business relations*. Failure to reply a letter is considered as an act of rudeness. A polite and courteous letter rarely fails to receive reply. Curt and rude letters have no place in the business world.

A calm, reasonable person writes letters that presents all the facts politely and courteously, as that will get better results and can win over even an offended customer. One should be very tactful while writing letters. Some examples are:

(i) **Instead of saying,** "*You are wrong*".

   A tactful businessman will say, "*We are afraid that what you have stated does not conform to the facts as understood by us*".

(ii) **Instead of saying,** "*You have failed to pay our bill for six months*".

   A tactful businessman will say, "*Perhaps due to an oversight our bill has remained unpaid*".

(iii) **Instead of saying,** "*We shall file a suit against you*".

   A tactful businessman will say, "*We have been compelled to hand over the matter to our legal advisor for suitable action.*".

6. Sincerity: A business letter should convey sincerity. The manager should be sincere in giving information and making statement of facts. He should desist from making false claims or providing deceptive information. A letter should show that the writer has genuine interest in the reader and means what he has written. It will help prevent misunderstandings and create healthy relations between the parties.

7. Simplicity: A business letter should be simple, clear and easily understood. The use of high sounding words and phrases should be avoided. The following points should be noted for making a business letter simple:

(i) Make proper use of clear, simple and easily understandable language.
(ii) Use simple words, short sentences and short paragraphs.
(iii) It should be written in a natural manner. The extent of formality depends on the status of the organisation and the receiver.
(iv) It should be written to convey a clear message. Ambiguity should be avoided.

8. Style: The words used in a business letter express the writer's personality and gives the letter what is called its style. Style is determined by the background, training, and experience of the writer. The style of a writer is reflected in the clarity and conciseness of the writing, its appropriateness by content, salutation and language use, and the way it is organised. For instance, some managers develop the habit of writing most parts of the letter in capital letters, assuming that it emphasises the argument being made. This can be very annoying. It appears as though the person is screaming. On the other hand, it should be used very sparingly to make a point. Similarly, unnecessary use of quote marks can confuse the reader. If a shoe manufacturer puts the word 'shoes' within quotes in his promotion letter, the reader would be confused whether the businessman is really selling shoes, or something else he refers to as shoes.

One mistake often seen is closing the letter with the statement 'With regards'. When the letter is addressed to a company and opens with sir/Madam, a personalised ending like this is not in order. 'Warm regards' should be strictly reserved for those persons whom the writer holds in respect, in which case the letter opens with a personalised salutation or greeting. The closing should be appropriate considering the nature of the letter, whether it is a friendly one or a formal one.

The following is an indicative list of expressions that should be avoided:
- We beg to acknowledge the receipt of your letter. OR, We beg to differ. (Why beg?)
- In due course of time… (gradually)
  At your earliest convenience…. (as quickly as possible)
- Thanking you in anticipation (incomplete unless followed by 'We remain, yours sincerely')
- With your kind permission…. (why kind permission ?)
- Your favour (letter) duly to hand … (We have received your letter)
- Attached herewith please find… (We attach the following documents)
- Contents duly noted…. (We note the contents.)

Some more wrong usages:
- He *made* an interesting speech (delivered)
- The *male members* of my family are well employed (men)
- My leg *is paining* (I am feeling pain in my leg)
- *See* the word in the dictionary (look for)
- He never *hears* my advice (listens to)
- It is bad habit to *speak* lies (tell)
- I'll spend my *remaining* life in Pune (rest of my)
- This water is *good for drinking*. (good to drink)
- You should return *before* two hours (within)
- *It is exact five in my watch*. (by)
- I will dine with them *on next Sunday*. (Sunday next)
- *Due* to illness I cannot come *(owing)*
- His illness is *owing* to street food consumption. *(due)*

2.6.3 Physical Appearance of a Business Letter

The physical appearance of a letter should be attractive, impressive and pleasant, such that the reader should want to read and consider the message contained in it. A person who can produce attractive letters is considered as an asset to the organisation.

Care to be taken to make business letters attractive:

1. **Quality of Paper used:** A business letter exhibits the personality and the culture of the organisation. Naturally, paper of standard quality should be used. It should be appropriate to the type and nature of the business and the stature of the organisation. It should be suitable for typing or printing. Cheap paper creates a poor opinion of the writer and his/her organisation. A simple letter-head makes a good impression. It should be attractive and decent. Within an organisation, papers of different colours may be used to identify letters originating from different departments or to prepare copies that go into the files of relevant departments. For instance, copy of the production department notices can be in yellow for its own file, pink for the finance department file, blue for purchase department file etc. A similar colour code can be followed by all departments, so that it becomes easy to identify the file from which a document has been sourced.

2. **The sizes of the paper used for business correspondence differs from country to country.**

   In U.K.:
   1. 8" × 10" (Standard Size)
   2. 5" × 8" (For short communications)

   In the U.S.A.:
   1. 8 .5 × 11" (Standard A 4 size)
   2. 5 .5× 8.5

   In India, generally the standard A 4 size is used.

3. **Typing:** Writing letters by hand is outmoded and so is typing. Ordinary typewriters gave way to electronic typewriters and now computers are used extensively. However, the basic format of the key board has remained the same. Unlimited variations of font style and size are available. Similarly, variations can be made in the margin space, space between lines, indent, lay out etc. The use of carbon paper for making copies has become obsolete. Multiple copies of a letter can be obtained by running the printer so many times or by taking photocopies. The letters can be stored as files in relevant folders and can be retrieved whenever required.

4. **Paragraphs:** A long letter should be divided into short paragraphs. Every new idea should be written in a new paragraph. Spacing between paragraphs should be adequate to differentiate them.

5. **Address:** The name of the city and pin code number should be typed in block letters. In the case of mass circulation, printed stickers of addresses may be used.

6. **Folding:** Letters should be folded carefully such that they fit in the envelope comfortably. There should be minimum number of folds to a letter. If window envelopes are used, the inside address of the receiver should fit into the transparent window area.

7. **Envelope:** The envelope also creates an impression upon the receivers. The envelope should be thick, attractive and impressive. The size, quality and colour of the envelope should be commensurate with that of the paper of the letter.

2.6.4 Layout of a Business Letter

Business letters must be faultless in appearance, matter, style and tone. Otherwise they will fail to create a favourable impression. Generally, organisations allow each of its departments or individuals to adopt their own style. However, large companies adopt a particular type of layout and standardise its use throughout the organisation. This style becomes symbolic of the company's personality. A lot of deliberations go into finalising a standard letter format. Aspects like clarity, space utilisation, style etc. are considered in this exercise.

A letter generally consists of several parts depending on how formal or informal it is and the nature of business to be communicated. The structural parts of a letter may be divided into two parts, viz., essential and optional features.

(a) Essential	(b) Optimal
Heading	Reference line
Date	Attention line
Inside address	Subject line
Salutation	Enclosures
Body of the letter	Identification initials
Complimentary Close	Post script
Signature	Extra Copies

1. **Heading:** The letterhead carries the name, address and monogram of the company, its contact details and its web address. Some organisations may opt to give details of branches, but this may consume too much space. On the other hand, the web page would have links to all its branches and other information that the organisation would want to communicate to the readers.

2. **Date:** The business letter must contain the date on which it is written. The date of dispatch may be different from the date on the letter, depending on when the dispatch section completes the process. Date of writing is essential for reference to the reader. Letters without date do not carry any legal significance. Generally, the date is written on the top right side of the letter, though, as a matter of style, some may prefer to left-align it. There are various methods of writing dates, such as:
   - 30th March 2013 - dd/mm/yyyy (date/month/year)   (British style)
   - March 30, 2013 - mm/dd/yyyy (month/date/year)   (American style)

3. **Inside address of the Recipient:** The inside address consists of the name and address of the party to whom the letter is addressed. It is written on the left-hand side of the letter above the salutation line. It is generally completed in three lines. The inside address is useful for future reference.

   (i) Position on the page: The inside address is aligned to the left margin. It is typed using single space. In government correspondence, the name and address of the recipient is often placed in the lower left hand position of the first letter.

   There could be a lot of discussion whether it is necessary to give the entire postal address of the recipient at all, as it takes up too much space and typing work. The argument is the recipient knows his own address.

   (ii) Punctuation: Usually, a comma is placed at the end of each line except the last, which ends with a full stop. This is called "closed punctuation". In many organisation, pressing the comma button is considered wasteful.

4. **Reference:** In a large organisation, where innumerable letters are sent out every day, it is essential to give a reference number to each letter. Generally, the reference number contains the initials of the department, serial number and the year. It helps in tracing the letter.

5. **Attention line:** This is to draw the attention of a particular person in the recipient organisation and ensuring that the document reaches that person's desk. However, if the person is on a long leave of absence or has left the organisation, it may remain unattended.

6. **Salutation:** The salutation is the greeting from the writer. The degree of formality depends upon the personal relationship between the writer and the addressee.

   The following points should be noted while typing the salutation:
   - It should be typed two or three spaces below the inside address.
   - In very formal letters, Dear Sir/Dear Madam are used.

- If it is being addressed to a particular person, depending on the gender, Dear Mr.... /Ms... is used.
- Use a comma after the salutation.
- The salutation and the complimentary close should agree.
- In the case of departmental letters, office memoranda etc., salutations are not used.
- When a circular is issued, the salutation should be 'Dear Readers' or 'Dear customers' or 'Gentlemen'.
- 'Gentleman' is the proper form of salutation while addressing a post box or a newspaper number.

7. **Subject Line:** The subject in the letter should be written in brief, after the salutation. The purpose of the subject line is to indicate the main theme of the letter. It is generally placed between the salutation and the first paragraph of the letter.

8. **Body of the Letter:** The body is the most important part of the letter. It contains the message that is being communicated. The purpose of writing a letter is fulfilled through this part of the letter. Usually, the body of the letter is divided into three parts:

    (a) The Opening Paragraph: Here the writer is trying to draw the attention of the reader to the subject. It should be brief and give reference to the letter received from the addressee if any. The opening paragraph must arouse the reader's interest.

    (b) The Main Paragraph: In this part, the subject is discussed in details. The entire subject may be discussed in one paragraph or if different points are being addressed, it may be divided into 2-3 paragraphs accordingly. The paragraphs could be numbered or bullet points can be used. Avoid writing on too many issues in a single letter. "One subject, one letter" should be the guiding principle of business correspondence. Make the contents of the letter as clear as possible. The message should be communicated in an interesting and courteous manner. It should be kept brief, simple and to the point.

    (c) The Closing Paragraph: This is the concluding part of the letter. The writer should convey very clearly his/her expectations by way of response or action. The writer should close the letter by thanking the recipient for his/her attention, and if necessary, assuring him/her of continued support.

9. **Complimentary Close:** The complimentary close is a kind of courteous leave-taking, or farewell in a business letter. It is written after the letter is completed. There must be an agreement between the salutation and the complimentary close. A comma should follow the complimentary close.

Example:	**SALUTATION**	**COMPLIMENTARY CLOSE**
	Dear Sir / Madam	Yours faithfully
	Dear Gentleman	Yours truly,
	Dear Shri	Yours Sincerely,
	My Dear	Yours truly/Yours sincerely

Abbreviations such as "Yrs ffly" or "Yrs try' should never be used in the complimentary close.

10. **Signature:** The signature comes below the complimentary close. It should be written by hand and should be legible. Sufficient space should be left below the complimentary close for the signature. Below the signature, name should be typed within brackets, below which, the official position of the person signing the letter should be typed.

    The signature should not be stamped or typed. In the case of a circular letter, the signature can be printed. In computer generated letters sent out digitally, signatures may not be possible. In such cases, the scanned signature of the sender is used.

11. **Additional Points**

    (a) **Enclosures:** Very often, to complete the objective of a letter, certain documents like receipts, cheques, documents to indicate title to goods, sales literature, price lists, testimonials etc., are sent with the main letter. These enclosures must be numbered and specifically mentioned in the main letter at the left hand bottom corner. The enclosures must be arranged according to the number given to each of them, and they should be checked before the letter is sent. The abbreviation "Encl" is used for indicating enclosures.

    (b) **Initials of the person dictating the Letter and the Typist**: These should be in capital letters, typed on the left hand corner at the end of the letter.

    (c) **Post Script:** This is an addition of a small message to the letter. Generally, it is not advisable to write post script. It may indicate that the letter writer was not careful in drafting the original letter. Generally, as letters are typed on computers, editing is easy and so even the latest piece of information can be incorporated in the body of the letter. However, in exceptional cases, when an urgent telephonic message is received and it has to be acknowledged in the letter, and the letter has to be dispatched immediately, a post script may be added. The post script should be very brief, and written two spaces below the Identification Mark on the Margin. No complimentary close is required. After writing the postscript, the letter should be signed again.

(d) **Notations:** Notations indicate the nature of the correspondence, such as 'Personal', 'Private', 'Urgent' 'Confidential' etc. The notations should be typed and underlined.

12. **Page Layout:** There is no standard page layout or form for a business letter. It is a matter of individual choice or taste. In order to have uniformity, some organisations prescribe a standardised layout or form to be used by all the departments.

    Normally, the following forms are used in business letters:

    (a) **Indented Form:** The indented form is the oldest, traditional form. The date and the complimentary close are right aligned, while the inside address, body and the salutation are left aligned. The first line of each paragraph is indented five spaces from the left margin. Each line of the signature is indented three spaces from the beginning of the complimentary close.

    (b) **Full Block Form:** The main feature of the full block is that all the structural parts of the letter are left aligned. There are no indentations. The main advantage of the full-block style is speed. This form is simple and very useful when there are many letters to be typed. However, computers allow the letter writer to pre-set the indentation and style type without any loss of speed.

    (c) **Semi-Block Form:** All structural parts of the letter are left aligned, but the first line of each paragraph is indented five or ten spaces. All lines of the typed signature are aligned with the complimentary close. The date is typed in the conventional position.

    (d) **Hanging Paragraph Form:** This form is rarely used. When novelty and visual effect is required to be created, then this form of letter is used. This form is the opposite of the indented form. The first line of each paragraph is flushed with the left-hand margin, but all other lines are indented five spaces in the hanging paragraph. Block form is used for the inside address and the signature lines. It takes longer time to write a letter in this form.

    (e) **Official Form:** The inside address is placed below the signature at the close, instead of before the salutation. The identification lines and the enclosure notations, if any, are typed two spaced below the last line of the address.

    (f) **Simplified Form:** In the simplified form the salutation and complimentary close are left out. "Copy to" before the names of persons to whom copies of the letter are to be sent is also removed. All structural parts of the letter are left oriented. The subject line is placed between the address and the body of the letter. This form is very common.

Types of Letter: Routine letters, Bad news and persuasion letters, sales letters, collection letters:

(a) **Routine letters:** These are letters that a manager will be writing to convey some information. For instance, the manager informs the customer that "product # ....., with following as required by them has been dispatched on ...., and the dispatch notice # is .... You can track it on your computer."

Format for a routine business letter:

ABC Company
3519 Front Street
Anna Salai, Chennai
October 5, 2013

Mr.....
Accounts Officer
XYZ Company
312, Affinity Plaza
Pimpri

Dear Mr.......

We have noted that there is delay in your payment for our services for the last six months. As you are our regular customer for the last ten years, we are making the following offer to you, to help you clear all the outstanding amounts and streamline your further monthly payments.

- One-time discount of 5% for the outstanding amount,
- 2% discount for payment of our monthly charges within 10 days of receiving the invoice.

We appreciate your business and hence we are making this offer to you. If you have any questions, please feel free to contact me.

I hope that everything is going well for you and your company.

Sincerely,
Signature
PQR
Accounts Receivable Dept.

> **Format for a complaint letter**
>
>
> TRPSOQH
> 5, Market Street
> Andheri (W)
> Mumbai
> June 26, 2013
>
>
> Customer Service Dept.
> XYZ Company,
> Pune
>
> Dear Sir or Madam:
>
>   I have recently ordered a new pair of sports shoes (item #654321) from your website on June 21. I received the parcel on June 26. Unfortunately, when I opened it, I saw that the shoes were used. They were not clean and there was a small tear in the front part of the left shoe. My order number is OP38902. I had communicated this matter to your executive on your help line. As instructed by her, I am returning the shoes to you along with the document you had sent with the product, duly filled in and signed.
>
>   I would like you to resolve the issue by crediting my account for the amount charged for the shoes. I do not want a replacement as I have already bought a new pair of shoes at the local sporting goods store.
>
>   I am sure there was some error while packing the item. My previous experience with your company has always been very good.
>
>   I request you to send me an advice as soon as you credit my account with the refund amount.
>
> Sincerely,
> *Signature*

Format for Letter to Convey Unpleasant News

    Bad or unpleasant news letters require special attention as they are not welcome by the receiver and the writer also does not cherish writing one, as they contain negative messages. There are varying degrees of bad news, from informing that a product being sought is temporarily out of stock to informing an employee that his services have been terminated.

    Generally, when business managers have to deliver bad news, they want to retain goodwill with the reader. For instance, while informing a prospective client that the product he wants to buy is temporarily out of stock, the company would want the readers to think that it is a reliable supplier and that it treasures the order. The company can offer alternatives available with it. Thus, it uses a soft and neutral tone.

However, there are situations when a manager has to deliver a strong negative message and no longer cares to maintain goodwill, such as eviction notice, job termination letter etc. A typical bad news letter contains the following elements:

- A neutral non-offensive opening.
- Clear statement of the bad news.
- The reasoning behind the decision, which is clear and logical. It should not be cover-up type of a general statement.
- Suggestion of a positive alternative if available.
- A closing that is as encouraging as possible. The writer should apologise for any inconvenience if caused. A restatement of the bad news may also be in order.

A word of caution while writing a bad news latter: Never write it when you are very angry, as anger clouds one's thinking. Even if it is written in that mood, take your time to calm down, reread the letter and refine it if necessary before you dispatch it.

Sample Termination Letter

Mr. ....,   August 23, 2013
48, Bishop Street
Mumbai

Dear Mr. ....,

This letter confirms our discussion today that your employment with Stanley Brown Co. is terminated with immediate effect. Please sign and return the attached copy of this letter to indicate your receipt of it. Along with that, please deposit at the reception desk your security pass, your office key as well as the laptop and mobile phone given to you by the company.

As informed to you, since you have been with us for two years, you will receive severance pay equivalent to your current salary for two months. This amount will be given to you by cheque once you have signed and returned the enclosed document pertaining to your release. All other dues, benefits and accrued funds will be given to you by a separate cheque along with a detailed statement. You may pick up this check from the reception desk or we can mail it to your home.

You are requested to keep the company informed of your contact information so that we are able to contact you if needed.

Please let us know if we can assist you during your transition.

Signature

Name and position of the signatory.

Format for a Cover Letter

Dr. TSPWTKSQ
27 West Street.
Jayanagar
Bengaluru
October 28, 2013

Mr. Michael Black
Director, Human Resources Dept.
XYZ Pharmaceuticals
3456, Apex Street
New York

Dear Mr. Black:

It is with great interest that I am applying for the position of Chief Scientist in your organisation. I note from the job description posted in your advertisement in the New York Times of October 12th that it very well matches with my qualifications and career aspirations. I have always wanted to work for a reputed Fortune 500 company like yours.

My CV is attached with this letter. I believe that I am the ideal candidate for the position of Chief Scientist in your organisation. At my current position at DEMAG, I perform all of the tasks that are described in your advertisement. I have the reputation of being innovative and hard working. My team at DEMAG has always completed our projects on time. My presentations have been hailed at the various international conferences that I have participated in.

Please contact me at the earliest on phone # 9143286585 to setup an interview. You can also reach me by way of e-mail at tspwtksq@nadate.com. I look forward to meeting you to discuss my future with XYZ Pharmaceuticals.

Thanks for your time and consideration.

Sincerely,

Signature

Enclosure: résumé

> **Essentials of Email Letters for Job Search**
>
> **Subject Line:** Make sure to include a subject line. Otherwise, the reader may not open it.
>
> **Salutation:** If you know a contact person, address your email to Dear Mr./Ms. (Last Name). If not, address it to 'Dear Recruitment Manager'. Alternatively, do not include a salutation but simply start with the first paragraph of your message.
>
> **Email Message:** If it is a job application, copy and paste your cover letter or write your cover letter in the body of an email message. You can send your résumé as an attachment either as a PDF or a Word document.
> If you are enquiring about job openings in the organisation, write a clear message to say what you are looking for.
>
> **Format Your Email Message** like a typical business letter, with paragraphs, spaces between them etc. Include an electronic signature. Give your full name, your email address, and your phone number in your email signature, so the reader can see, at a glance, how to contact you.

2.7 Résumé / CV / Bio data

The first official communication related to a student's career is the job application. It is the picture of the applicant, expressed in words. As such it has to be prepared with great care. Until recently, the conventional method of drafting a job application was simple and straight forward. It was in the form of a letter addressed to the employer explaining or giving personal details such as name, address, qualifications, experience (if any) and references. This information used to be general and presented in a single page. However, the current trend is to make it into two parts, viz., the résumé or a more detailed CV and the covering letter.

In the United Kingdom, a CV is short (usually a maximum of 2 sides of an A4 paper), and therefore contains only a summary of the job seeker's employment history, qualifications and some personal information. It is often updated to change the emphasis of the information according to the particular position for which he is applying. Key words may be highlighted to attract the attention of the potential employers. A CV can also be extended to include an extra page for publications if these are important for the job.

In the United States and Canada, a CV is used in academic circles and medical careers and is far more comprehensive than a résumé, which is used for most other recruitments. A CV elaborates on education to a greater degree than a résumé and is expected to include a comprehensive listing of professional history covering every term of employment, academic credentials, publications, contribution or significant achievements. In certain professions, it may even include samples of the person's work and may run into many pages.

Some companies standardise the information they would like to receive by producing their own application form. They may or may not ask for a separate CV to be attached.

> ***It is reported that some employers spend as little as 45 seconds skimming a résumé before branding it "not of interest", "maybe" or "of interest".***

Tips for Job Search

- Write every word in your résumé yourself. Do not copy anybody else's résumé. It could land you in trouble later. Write only the truth.
- Do not make spelling and other silly errors in your résumé.
- Do not proclaim, "I am a hard working person" etc. You are expected to be so.
- Select the right fonts and style.
- Customise your résumé for particular jobs to show how well suited you are for that job.
- Have four to five different versions of your résumé highlighting your qualifications and work experiences. Even if you are just starting your career, you might be applying for different job roles in different industries.
- Create a *LinkedIn* profile. This professional website gives you scope to elaborate on your résumé if you want to. You can also restrict the privacy of your page or make it public to allow recruiters and employers to search and contact you.
- Write a good covering note for your application to indicate that you are really interested in the position and explain how you are the right person for it.
- Update your résumé every time you add a new skill.
- Make use of the Internet for job search and use all the tools the Net provides for this. Look at all the job boards, including those for freshers. Sign up for job alerts.
- Maintain the same profile in the social networking sites.
- Do not get into any controversial topic or make derogatory statements on the social networking sites. The recruiters may be just looking for such things.
- Pay close attention to each employer's or recruiter's instructions for submitting your résumé in response to a job posting, regarding the type of résumé required and also how it should be sent.
- Many job sites and employer's websites ask résumé in text format Maintain a text only copy as well, as copying and pasting your content from a word document leads to alignment problems and wastes precious time.
- If the job site provides ready formats, fill in the relevant information with care. Ensure that it tells the reader something meaningful about your personality.
- After uploading your résumé, visit the respective job sites regularly to search for relevant positions.
- Visit each employer's website individually and browse current job openings, review the employer's requirements, and apply to each employer directly.

- Apply only for jobs for which you meet the eligibility criteria. It wastes your time and the employers' tracking system.
- Do not be attracted to scam job postings with fat salaries in spurious companies. Understand the authenticity of the job post before applying. Consult more experienced persons, search for the company on the Net etc.
- Online platforms are just part of your strategy to get a job. There may be other avenues like press advertisements, job fairs, networking etc.
- If you are shortlisted, prepare carefully for the next step, viz., interview.

> *Your résumé must speak to the employer for you. Without being excessively boastful it must accurately mirror your true strengths, potential and interests and create a favourable first impression.*

The **forwarding letter** is in a simple form addressed to the prospective employer. It contains your name, date, address to whom it is to be sent, the job you are seeking, the source through which you got to know about the vacancy and a sentence indicating that a copy of the résumé is enclosed. The covering letter should not be a dull or lifeless note. On the contrary, a well-drafted covering letter reflects the personality of the writer, his/her attention to detail, communication skills and enthusiasm. Coupled with the résumé it helps the prospective employer to decide whether to invite the applicant for an interview or not.

Tips for writing a good covering letter:

(i) Use a good quality paper for the application.
(ii) It should be a formal letter, properly typed unless a handwritten application is specifically asked for.
(iii) The name and the address of the employer should be written carefully.
(iv) The applicant should express his desire to be considered for the position.
(v) It is essential to mention the source of information regarding the vacancy.
(vi) The applicant should use an active and positive tone.
(vii) The applicant must express enthusiasm and optimism towards receiving a favourable reply from the employer and an opportunity to discuss more details in an interview.
(viii) The applicant must mention that the résumé and other papers, if any, are enclosed.

The second part is the **Bio-data or résumé** presented in a tabular form covering different aspects of your personal details. This is the most important document in the process of job application as it provides an overview of your education, experience and other qualifications. Hence, this has to be prepared with utmost care. It should emphasise the details to show your suitability for the job you are applying for. Tabulation ensures

disciplined and orderly presentation and allows no omissions. In general, the information to be included in the Bio-data is classified into the following five broad categories:
1. Personal details.
2. Educational Qualifications.
3. Extra curricular activities.
4. Experiences of work.
5. References.

1. Personal details

This should generally cover the following:
(a) Name in full, typed in block letters, in the order of first name, middle name and last name. Some require the family name first, and then the first and the middle names.
(b) Contact details: Apart from postal address, email ID is essential these days. Hence, open an account even if you do not have Net connection at your residence. One can access the account from any communication centre.
(c) Date of birth (In many companies which follow the policy of Equal opportunities, this is not required.)
(d) Marital Status (married or unmarried)
(e) Mother tongue (Peculiar to India, where there are many languages)
(f) Other languages known
(g) If applying for a job outside the country, include the following details:
   (i) Nationality
   (ii) Passport number
   (iii) Period of validity of the passport
   (iv) Knowledge, skill level and academic achievement in foreign languages

2. Educational Qualifications

(i) A complete record of academic qualifications with ranking positions beginning with matriculation, giving details of institutions attended, universities from which diploma/degree obtained etc. The current trend is to begin with details of the highest level of education and projects undertaken. Whatever the order, each item should be numbered.
(ii) Additional courses, trainings.
(iii) Awards, scholarships etc.

However, application for very senior posts will carry educational qualifications at the end.

3. Extra Curricular Activities

They may be relating to sports, drama, study circles, workshops, seminars etc. and prizes, awards and distinctions achieved in those fields. These achievements add to your personality aspects such as teamwork skills, inter-personal skills, organisational skills etc.

4. **Work Experience**
   (i) Current employment status and job description.
   (ii) Previous employment stating the name of the companies and periods of employment and job description. This may be internship or voluntary work done for any social, cultural, charitable organisation, short period work during vacation etc. This is important especially for fresh entrants to job situation. Mention specific achievements, if any.

Useful tips for writing about work experience

(a) Use action words, such as developed, organised, executed, spearheaded etc.

(b) Do not mention routine work details. Aspects like working in a team, quality service, leadership role etc. catch the attention of the reader.

(c) Try to relate the skills to the job you are applying for. A finance job experience involves numeracy, analytical skills, problem solving skills etc. Focus on persuading and negotiating skills if applying for a job in the marketing department etc.

---

5. **Interests and Hobbies:** This segment should be short, and to the point. Show a range of interests. Bullets can be used to separate interests. Avoid writing about passive, solitary hobbies like reading, listening to music etc. Hobbies which are out of the ordinary make you stand out. Any interest related to the job could help. Being the captain of a sports team or the leader of a biking group helps in demonstrating leadership qualities. Any activity with opportunities for demonstrating employability skills, such as organising, team work etc. will add to your acceptability.

6. **References:** Generally, two references are expected. One should be from the academic field, like a teacher, a guide, or a respectable individual in the society who knows you. The second should be a former employer in the case of those with work experience. Name, title, address, telephone number should be given indicating your relationship with them. It is necessary to obtain permission from these people to include their names as references.

2.8 Memorandum

The term 'Memo' is derived from the Latin word '*memorate*' meaning 'to mention' or 'to tell'. It is a short form of the word memorandum and its plural form is or 'memoranda'. The literal meaning of the word memorandum is 'a note to assist the memory'. A memo is generally used for internal communication between officers of the same level (equal ranks). Whenever an office or a company executive wishes to issue certain directives or instructions to his staff, he writes a memo and sends it to the concerned persons. A memo has to be very brief and to the point. It is written directly in a less formal style. Since it moves from one department or employee to another, it must contain words like 'from' and 'To'. A memo has only a heading, body and signature. It does not contain a salutation such as 'Dear ... ' or a complimentary close such as 'Yours ...'. It is the most convenient and inexpensive device for communication within the organisation. A memo can be used for the following purposes:

1. To seek or give suggestions.
2. To communicate policy changes.
3. To issue instructions to the staff.
4. To request for help or information.
5. To confirm a decision arrived at on the telephone.

Sometimes, it becomes necessary to instruct subordinates to refrain from certain undesirable habits. The most common among them is being tardy, spitting in the office premises etc. Such an attitude disturbs office discipline. Under such circumstances, an office chooses to issue a memo, which is a sort of mild warning, which also sets an example for other subordinates.

There is also a category of memo, known specifically as 'warning memo'. It is generally served to subordinates whose work is unsatisfactory or against the rules and regulations, and in spite of several oral instructions, they have not shown improvement in their attitude or behaviour. A warning memo is not a threat of removal from service, but is included in his personal records. It categorically indicates that better behaviour is expected from him. Failure to show improvement may result in holding up of incentive, increment, promotion etc.

While issuing a warning memo, the manager has to make sure that there is enough documentary evidence to show the uncooperative behaviour of the recipient. The evidence could be by way of attendance register, leave register, work/performance record/reports etc. Issuing warning memos based on vague charges may lead to conflict, which the unions can escalate.

2.9 Minutes
Meaning of the term 'Minutes'

The term *'minutes'* means a concise and accurate record of the decisions taken at policy level meetings. These could be at the corporate level or meetings of board of directors. There is a statutory format for recording the proceedings. Even within an organisation, important policy matters could be discussed and their minutes prepared as a means or recording the decisions taken, action to be taken and persons responsible for those actions. Though in such cases, there is no need for a statutory format to be followed. In short, minutes indicate the business transacted at a meeting. The main purpose of the minutes is to preserve an accurate official record transacted at a meeting, which will serve future reference. For each type of meeting, minutes are to be kept in separate minutes book. Minutes enable a member to get a clear idea about the previous discussions and decisions with respect to various matters. It is, therefore, essential that the minutes should be free from ambiguity but at the same time they should be concise.

Tips for Drafting of Minutes

1. **Draft immediately:** The secretary should write the minutes immediately after the meeting is over. If it is done immediately, he will be able to recall every transaction and record it accurately.

2. **Consultation with the chairman:** The secretary should consult the Chairman while drafting the minutes. He should prepare a rough draft, and after it is approved by the chairman, he should prepare the final document.

3. **Concise:** Minutes should be concise. Unnecessary information should be dropped.

4. **Complete:** Minutes should not be incomplete. Absent members should be in a position to understand the business transacted at the meeting. Minutes can be accepted as authentic evidence, hence they should be written very carefully.

5. **Clear:** The minutes should be written very clearly. Information about ordinary resolution, special resolution, dates, numbers, quantities, shares, debentures and names of persons etc. should be clearly written.

6. **Compliance with provisions in the Companies Act:** The minutes of general body meetings should be prepared according to provisions of the Companies Act.

7. **Form of Minutes:** Minutes may be drafted in a tabular form or in the form of a series of paragraphs. The paragraphs should be numbered. They should have appropriate sub-headings.

Contents of Minutes

The details in the minutes depend on the level and nature of business transacted. An indicative list of points to be covered is as follows:

1. **Particulars of the meeting:** Name of the meeting, place, date and time of meeting, constitution of the meeting, names of the chairman, directors, auditors, secretary.
2. The names of the members present at the meeting.
3. Serial number of the meeting.
4. Brief subject heading.
5. All the resolutions passed at the meeting.
6. Specific business upon which decisions were taken.
7. In case of special resolution, number of votes for and against.
8. Objections and protests raised by members together with the chairman's rulings.
9. All details about appointments of officers, their salaries, remuneration etc.
10. The Chairman's signature and date of verification of minutes as correct.

Types of Minutes

1. **Minutes of Resolutions:** All the resolutions passed at a meeting are recorded without any reference to other matter. Minutes of Resolution may be accompanied by a statement indicating the names of proposer and the person who 'seconds' or supports the proposal. Minutes of resolution usually start with the words 'RESOLVED THAT' followed by the text of the resolution.
2. **Minutes of Narration:** Relevant facts and circumstances are mentioned in a narrative form along with the resolutions passed at the meeting. A summary of the discussions, the method of voting, number of votes cast for and against a motion etc. are recorded with or without a formal resolution.

2.10 Circulars and Notices

A circular is a communication meant to notify or convey to all the customers, business friends, shareholders and employees, certain fundamental changes or important information. It is a letter which contains common information about the business. Sufficient number of copies of the circulars is prepared and sent to all the concerned parties.

Generally, circulars are issued on the following occasions:

(a) Establishment of a new business.
(b) Starting a new department.
(c) Business expansion, acquisition of new business, new collaboration etc.
(d) Downsizing, break-up in partnerships/collaborations etc.
(e) Change in business location.
(f) Starting of new branches of business.
(g) Admission of a new partner into the business.
(h) Clearance sale.
(i) Sale of a business

A notice is a written communication of the date, time, place and the business to be transacted at the meeting to all persons who are entitled to get it. Sending a notice is the first stop in convening a meeting.

2.11 Executive Summary of Documents

Whether it is a report, a business plan or an investment proposal, a brief executive summary forms the preface to the main document. The purpose of an executive summary is to get the report read. It is like putting a foot in the door, a gateway for informing the executive about the details presented in the main business report. It is aimed at grasping the reader's immediate attention and indicating what the report contains. It involves taking out the essence of the report and presenting it in brief. An executive summary should include the major details of the main document, but not too many details. It should be prepared keeping in mind the fact that the top executive who reads it has very little time and has too many tasks to attend to and too many decisions to take. These busy executives may have enough time to read only this part of the report for taking decisions. Hence, it requires great skill on the part of the manager to decide what is important from the point of view of the top manager and how to present it.

An executive summary should not be a mere 'copy-paste' type of a document, with smaller font size to make it appear smaller. On the other hand, it should be unique and have a professional look. There is no set structure for an executive summary, but there are a few guidelines that can be followed.

- The size of the executive summary will depend on the size of the main report. However, the thumb rule is to limit an executive summary to maximum four pages.
- If it is a two-page summary and printed back to back, it may look like a brochure. This should be avoided.
- Understand the readers and their background and expectations. If the readers are not technically qualified, they may be more interested in knowing the broad implications and risks involved. Use language that the readers can connect to.
- If the report goes to people with different backgrounds, consider creating different versions for each party.
- Use clear, concise and relevant language and explanations. Avoid any superlatives, clichés, or over-used expressions that cannot be supported.
- Use bullet points to present your ideas.
- Do not clutter the executive summary with analysis, charts, numbers etc. Give appropriate reference to the details presented in the main report. Give all links and citations so that the executive can refer back if necessary.
- If it is a business plan or an investment proposal, describe the current activities and the strengths of the business by way of the expertise available in the management team, any new technology or patents, unique marketing plan etc.
- One effective structure is to summarise each section of the main report and present it in the same order as in the main report.
- Explain in brief, the problem, the solution suggested in the report, the action plan to be initiated. Highlight the urgency of implementing the suggested action plan.
- Give a brief summary of the financial implications, risks involved and the expected outcomes.
- Make sure there are no errors. Read, re-read and edit the executive summary to ensure that there are no factual and language errors.
- An executive summary should reflect the confidence of the author. A professional looking executive summary reflects well on the company,

Example

An executive summary for a marketing research report can include the following sections:

- Name of the company which has commissioned the study and its business activities.
- Mission Statement or statement of the problem, objectives and coverage and the period when the study was conducted.
- Overview of the competition and supply situation – current and emerging. It is necessary to mention the names of the companies already in the market and their status as well as newcomers if they can be identified.
- Expectations and concerns of the consumers.
- The market opportunity – demand estimates, current market size and market potential for the next five years. This is the most crucial part and the reader should be able to go to the core and understand the marketing viability of the product or service it has proposed.
- Technological developments and demographic changes taking place, which can influence both demand and supply, and scenario analysis. All details should be in the main report with cross-references in the executive summary.
- Risk analysis.
- Conclusions and recommendations. This includes the salient points in the 'Conclusions' segment of the main document which support the recommendations. However, the recommendations should be reproduced as in the main document, as it is vital for taking decisions.
- The proposed marketing plan along with the risks involved. If a business plan forms a part of the main report, the executive summary will include management and financial implications and expected revenue before and after tax calculations.
- Strategic relationships.
- Sources of information and contact details.

2.12 Preparing Press Release and Press Notes

Organisations issue printed news items periodically to the media to inform the public about major events, decisions and actions proposed or undertaken by it, visit of experts etc. They are termed as press notes. They are prepared by someone in the organisation with the authority – generally in the public relations department or section. Most of the newspapers provide some space for corporate news. The news may be regarding opening of a new business or a new branch, achievement of the target set for a period, a conference, lecture series, social responsibility projects etc. Non-government organisations also conduct a variety of events and inform the public about these activities through press releases.

The basic principle to be followed is that the matter should be news-worthy. The press release should contain the following:
- Name of the organisation.
- Purpose of the press release or news being covered.
- Date and place.
- Main speakers, including the person who gave the vote of thanks if he is an important member of the organisation.
- A brief summary of the main speech.

The order may be changed, to give the summary of the main presentation at the opening, so as to catch the attention of the readers and the rest can follow as given above. Students should read some important press releases in newspapers to see how the matter is presented.

The note should be self-explanatory, brief, complete and correct. The language should be simple, without any cliché. It should strengthen the image of the organisation. There should be no scope for editing by the media persons, as that will delay matters and hence the urgency is lost. It may not meet the deadline for the day's printing. Generally, there is a press club in each city. The required number of copies of the note along with the prescribed fees is sent there for circulation among the members.

2.13 Creative Writing

It is very difficult to define the term 'creative writing'. It can only be described as writing that expresses the writer's thoughts and feelings in an imaginative, often unique, and poetic way. Creative writing is guided more by the writer's need to express feelings and ideas than by restrictive demands of factual and logical progression of expository writing. (Expository writing is writing that is designed to convey information or explain what is difficult to understand.) It goes outside the bounds of normal professional, journalistic, academic or technical forms of literature.

Creative writing serves such needs of the writer as:
1. The need for keeping records of significant experience,
2. The need for sharing experience with an interested group, and
3. The need for free individual expression

Works like instruction manuals, legal documents etc., do require some amount of creativity, as the person who drafts them have to imagine the questions that may arise in the minds of the readers, but they certainly cannot be termed 'creative writing', as their sole purpose is to convey facts, rules etc.

Thus, the purpose of creative writing is to express thoughts, feelings and emotions rather than to simply convey information. It is generally associated with fiction and poetry, where imagination is dominant and the emphasis is on description associated with language skills and the craft of writing. Hence, creative writing is more difficult than technical writing, drafting legal documents etc.

Apart from fiction, many other types of writing which managers would handle in their work life can also be classified as creative, such as essays describing something as in creative product or service brochures, travelogues, food writing, biographies, feature stories, press releases, an attractive punch line or caption for an advertisement etc., which will make the reader visualise the situation or place and enjoy reading the piece. Even in preparing business cards and fliers, one can use a lot of creativity.

Creative Writing Skills for Managers

Business writing does not have to be boring, with standard formats, or extremely formal in style. On the contrary it can be creative in its unique way. With the new information and communication technologies, business writing has become even more interesting. In addition to acquiring the necessary communication and technology skills, a little linguistic imagination should make business writing more than a routine chore. It should be remembered that imagination cannot be taught. But using it in the right context however requires training and experience.

Elements of Creative Writing

- **Research:** Research forms the foundation of all creative writing. Without getting the facts together, the manager will not be able to decide what and how to present them. The reader will easily know if adequate research has not been done. It will sound shallow. Hence, the manager has to gather information from both secondary and primary sources, including experts in the field if necessary. The Internet has opened a huge pathway to acquiring knowledge from various sources online. Being good at writing not only helps you do your tasks faster, it brightens your career path.

- **Organising the facts:** The manager will have to put the entire information together, brainstorm with peers if necessary, and prepare a brain map or a broad scheme to ensure a smooth flow of information/analysis and thought.

- **Building a roadmap, so your readers do not get lost:** Managers have to know their readers, understand their level of understanding of the subject and accordingly develop the structure of the write-up copy. He has to decide how much of technical and other details should go into it. A news handout has to read like a story, but an advertisement copy has to be like a dialogue. An article in a technical journal should be more informative and interesting. An invitation for a corporate event has to be prepared keeping in view the prestige of the organisation. A business proposal should impress the other party and lead to a successful deal.

- **Write for your readers and not executives:** The manager will have to try and make the article interesting. This can be done by using appropriate quotes, diagrams with captions etc., to catch and sustain the attention of the reader. The manager has to identify the attention grabbers and use them judiciously.

- **Speed of writing:** The manager will have to develop the skill for writing and with experience, he will be able to produce interesting works with sufficient speed.

- **Take care of context, grammar and spelling:** The need to prepare a perfect copy can never be over emphasised. Whether it is a small note or a lengthy article, perfection should be the ultimate objective. The definition of perfect grammar varies with context – for instance, in a conversational type of advertisement copy, colloquial usage may be required to attract the audience.
- **Writing requires revising:** It is said that *'writing is rewriting', 'writing is polishing'* etc. This clearly highlights the importance of revising, looking at the word choice, editing, and proof reading to improve the quality of the work and make the writing clear and presentable. It means that the first draft will focus on the flow of ideas. Only when the entire article is written as the ideas flow will the manager be able to realise if the topic has been adequately addressed. All the refining work will happen thereafter. In fact, the polishing stage may take more time than the initial writing, but it is worth the time and trouble. Even the most knowledgeable and creative writer will spend some time to revise, proof read and correct.
- Revision and Rewriting is the process of making deep, contextual changes to a piece of written work. To make the work readable, the author may want to drop certain sections, change the order of presentation or introduce new elements. He may want to change the tone of the piece.
- Editing focuses on making the work readable. It is all about the organisation of the points in different sections and paragraphs and making sure that the sentences convey the meaning properly to make it more readable.
- At the Copy editing stage, the text is reviewed and adjusted before it is taken up for formatting.
- Proof reading has a limited focus of checking the grammar, spelling, punctuation and eliminating typing errors.

2.14 Poster Making

A poster is a very good way to get your point across to the audience quickly. Posters have become one of the most important vehicles for presenting work at conferences. Poster sessions provide a useful forum to discuss scientific work on a person-to-person basis.

The two characteristics of a successful poster are:
- It has conveyed a clear message to the audience, and
- It has generated valuable comments or feedback to the presenter.

While preparing posters, the presenter has to be crystal clear about the objectives, the approach, the main results and the major conclusions of the work. He will have to communicate his message, using minimum number of posters, within the proper perspective of existing knowledge on the particular subject.

Though there is no standard structure for a poster, the presenter has to take good care to make it interesting and relevant for all sections of the audience. The work and the content presented may be interesting work, but they become difficult to follow because the speaker unknowingly makes a number of presentation errors. By far the largest mistake is that the speaker does not know his audience, their attention curve and how they listen. The audience can get distracted very easily. Only a few may take keen interest in the poster. The rest who visit the poster gallery may be whiling away their time for various reasons. The presenter has to identify the factors that distract the audience and deal with them. It may be an inadequate sound system, poor overhead projector, or a noisy conference area or limited attention span of the visitors. Researchers have made the following observations about the attention span of the audience:

- Almost everyone listens in the beginning. The presenter has to take advantage of this and state his message loud and clear.
- Divide your presentation in several parts, each ended by an intermediate conclusion. So even if there is some distraction, the audience will get back to the poster with interest and catch up as they know the structure of the presentation.
- Repeat your message loud and clear at the end. They will remember the message better.

If you are well aware of what errors you should avoid, the chances are high that you will be able to greatly improve the effectiveness of your presentations. Errors can fall in two classes: speaker's errors and presentation errors.

1. The speaker assumes that the background information needed to clarify the meaning of his work is common knowledge and so need not be included.
2. The structure of the presentation is not clear, and hence the audience cannot clearly follow the contents.
3. Adequate care has not been taken while planning the visual aids. They may be inadequate, confusing, unreadable, too small, too crowded, etc. Some speakers are too enthusiastic and load a lot into the slides. They choose smaller font size and compromise on line spacing. It becomes impossible for the audience to read and understand them within such a short time. They lose the flow of thought.
4. The speaker uses long, complicated sentences, unnecessary jargon, abbreviations or difficult words. His rendering while explaining the posters may be unattractive. Monotonous sentences, spoken either too fast or too slowly, lack of emphasis, unclear pronunciation, all make it difficult for the listeners to stay attentive. Some speakers turn their back to the audience and watch the poster/screen while they are talking. They do not make visual contact with the audience.

Care the Presenter has to take while Preparing Posters

> *A good poster enables the reader to grasp the message within a minute. If he finds the subject of interest he will stay to learn about the details, and discuss the work with the presenter.*

- **Avoid too much text:** This will reduce the impact of the visuals and the audience will spend too much time reading the text.

- **Formulate your goal:** As far as possible, the essence of what you want to present should be stated in a single sentence. This should help determine the data to be included in the poster.
- **Plan the content meticulously:** Apart from the content, pay attention to making the poster attractive with appropriate pictures, visual presentation of the theme, captions that attract the attention of the audience etc. Plan the content carefully, review the contents, get peer opinions, revise where necessary and make sure the poster conveys the message you want and creates the right impact on the audience.
  - **Introduction:** containing a few short sentences which help identify the subject being addressed, knowledge you have obtained about it, the objectives of your work and your approach in investigating the problem. It is good idea to use bullet points while presenting them.
  - **Results of your study:** Should be relevant and pertinent to the subject, with facts and figures, presented in an attractive manner. Statements or tables should be avoided as it will take time for the readers. Figures with appropriate captions and a brief conclusion below every figure will make it easy.
  - **Conclusion:** It should be short, clear statements, preferably presented as a list with bullet points. It should indicate your achievements in relation to the objectives set and your future plans in this regard.
  - **Layout:** Plan all the parts of the poster around the main theme. Add headers for each section of the poster. If any reference is made to others' works, make sure to acknowledge appropriately. Give your name and position, and give details of the organisation you represent.
- **The structure has to be clear.** The key elements such as objectives, approach, conclusions, or perspectives should be well organised. Otherwise, it will be lost on lay persons, i.e., those who are not insiders to the subject matter.
- **The structure should be appropriate.** There is no standard structure for a poster. However, the presenter should remember that it is not a miniature article or report. Hence, he should not use the standard structure of a written report blindly, as that will automatically add to the text.
- **Figures should be designed properly to convey the message clearly and not confuse the audience.** They should be audience-friendly. Captions should be clear and appropriate. Legends should be used sparingly, and where used, the letters should be legible when projected. In a chart, labels should be shown on the figure itself, not in a label to enable the visitor to understand the theme without taking time to look at the legend each time. Abbreviations should have proper clarifications.
- **Language** should be simple, easy to understand and without any spelling or grammatical errors.
- **Information overload should be avoided.** The average visitor may not be willing to spend so much time at each poster.
- **The presenter has to be present** near the posters to answer any questions or obtain valuable feedback. He should be actively involved in explaining the concept and initiating discussions.

2.15 Framing Advertisements, Slogans and Captions:
(A) Advertisements

Advertising is a form of mass communication aimed at encouraging or persuading an audience (viewers, readers or listeners, either general or specific target groups) to (a) make a new decision, (b) take some new action or (c) continue with the action that has already been initiated. Advertising messages are usually paid for by the sponsors.

One definition of advertising is *"Advertising is the non-personal communication of information usually paid for and usually persuasive in nature about products, services or ideas by identified sponsors through the various media."* (Bovee, 1992, p. 7)

The **purpose** of advertising could be many, such as:
- For commercial purposes or for political or even ideological purposes. **Commercial advertisers** are aimed at generating increased consumption of their products or services through the process of branding. This involves the repetition of an image or product name and message to bring about instant recall by the consumers regarding the association of the name, the product and its specific qualities. **Non-commercial advertising** is when an organisation pays for advertising items other than a consumer product or service. This category includes political parties, interest groups, religious organisations and governmental agencies.
- Corporate advertisement to reassure employees, shareholders or the public about the intentions of the organisation, its reputation or its viability.

The **medium** of advertisement may be many, such as: (1) print, (2) traditional mass media such as newspapers, magazines, radio, television, outdoor advertisement like hoardings, and direct mail or (3) the new media such as web sites, drop-down advertisements on other sites, social interaction sites like Face book, Twitter, blogs, etc., as well as text messages. Whatever the medium, the overall objective is to drive consumer behaviour or influence decision.

In economic terms, advertisements add information value to products and services.

Curiously enough, the history of modern advertisement can be traced to the 1920s, which marked the growth of the American tobacco industry and the innovative techniques used in their advertisements, most significantly the campaigns of Edward Bernays. As the tobacco industry took to mass production, they developed strategies for mass marketing to create demand to match the tremendous increase in supply. Another development during that time was the establishment of radio stations for the first time. To promote these stations and to increase the sale of radio sets, more programmes were needed. In due course, many non-profit organisations also set up their own radio stations. This led to sponsoring of programmes in exchange for a brief mention of the company's name. This led to selling sponsorship rights, allocating time for many businesses.

With the entry of public service broadcasting, non-governmental agencies started using it as a powerful educational tool for promoting their own concepts and welfare programmes. This sector is also referred to as 'public service advertising', 'non-commercial advertising', 'public interest advertising', 'cause marketing' and 'social marketing'.

With the advent of television in the late 1940s and early 1950s, the same concepts of advertising, such as sponsorship and selling advertisement time to multiple sponsors were extended to this mode as well. The 1960s saw the emergence of multi-media advertisement campaigns for creating brand awareness, involving huge expenditure. Cable television was introduced in the late 1980s and early 1990s and the concept of music videos and interactive media took shape. TV programmes became diverse in nature. Special channels were also introduced for advertisements. Advertisements started becoming integral parts of news and entertainment programmes.

The advent of the Internet in the 1990s opened a new arena for advertisements. Companies specialising in advertising on the Net emerged. Search engines, on-line marketing portals, social networking on the Internet etc. have given a new edge to the advertising industry. The 21st Century has witnessed the appearance of a whole new range of interactive advertising. From modest newspaper advertising, this industry has seen many unusual approaches to product placement, brand building and carrying messages, scaling new heights in spending.

Advertising Media

Advertising can use any medium the sponsor pays to deliver their message.

TV commercial is generally considered the most effective mass-market advertising format, as is reflected by the high rates per second the TV networks charge for commercial airtime during popular TV events such as IPL. Some television commercials feature a song or jingle that listeners soon relate to the product. Computer graphics are used to enhance the impact of the advertisement message. Some companies sponsor 'infomercials, which are long-format (about five minutes or longer) with the objective of creating impulse purchase decisions by using the toll-free numbers or web site flashed on the screen. As they describe, display, and often demonstrate products and their features, and also have testimonials from consumers and industry professionals, the viewers get convinced easily.

Apart from TV, the other media used include the following:
- **Radio:** here the lack of visuals is the limiting factor.
- **Internet (online advertising), or digital signage.** It has advantage of huge coverage world-wide, with no extra cost, audio-visuals, attention grabbing drops on web sites, portals that can also be used for e-commerce, feedback etc. Consumers from any part of the world or any time zone can access them at their convenience. A lot of product information can be given at very little expenditure.
- Product placement in entertainment programmes (guerrilla advertising),
- **Press:** (advertisements and articles in newspapers, magazines and special journals), etc. The advertisers can choose the vehicle to suit the target audience and the cost per insertion.
- **Billboard advertising:** This involves using large structures located in public places, preferably on main roads with maximum visibility, to display advertisements to passing pedestrians and motorists.

- **Mobile billboard advertising:** The billboards are mounted on vehicles. Mobile displays are used in large cities throughout the world, for various purposes such as, target advertising, one-day and long-term campaigns, conventions, sporting events, store openings etc.
- **In-store advertising:** It includes placement of a product in visible locations in a store, such as at eye level, at the ends of aisles and near checkout counters etc. It is also known as point-of-purchase advertising.
- **Other media** like coffee mugs, carry-bags, on moving public vehicles such as taxicabs, buses etc.
- **Celebrity endorsements:** especially for TV and press advertising, generally seen in promotion of sports accessories, soft drinks, cosmetics, luxury items etc., where the readers/viewers could be impressed by the fact that a favourite star is endorsing the product or service.

Implications for Managerial Communication

For a manager, these developments open up innumerable opportunities for connecting with the consumers. He should be clear about the objectives of an individual advertisement or an advertising campaign. He should understand the steps a consumer or a business buyer moves through when making a purchase, such as:

1. Awareness
2. Knowledge
3. Liking
4. Preference
5. Conviction
6. Purchase

An effective advertisement is one where the message, along with the manner of communication and the media used, should lead the prospective customers to a desired state, by moving them from understanding the benefits of a product/service to liking it, getting convinced an finally purchasing it.

As a form of communication, advertisements use repeated verbal messages and/or visual images to develop and alter the pinion of the public and ultimately shape their beliefs and values. The success of an advertisement depends on a clear understanding of the target audience, their socio-economic and cultural background, their purchasing power, their saving and investment habits, current opinions or habits, the manner in which purchase decisions are made, their exposure to various media and the factors that influence their decision process. This requires in-depth marketing research and advertisement impact surveys which will help the manager outline the entire advertisement plan. This is more so in these days of globalisation, when advertisement messages are meant to cross cultural barriers.

In these days of the Internet, advertisements combined with entertainment, and information, most delivered digitally, offer tremendous opportunities for managers to consider various options of staying connected with the target audience. Niche marketing is another term used very often while designing such targeted advertisement messages.

The choice of the visuals and the language used should be based on this clear understanding of the target audience and should be such that they do not antagonise the society or hurt their sensitivities. Humour should be used with care and concern for the feelings of the audience. The words used should be simple and easily understood by the audience so that they can connect the unique selling proposition of the product and the message. Too much importance is not given to grammatical construction of the sentences, but the important consideration is to making the message catchy. Spellings of words are often intentionally distorted to give the message uniqueness. The increasing trend in India is to add local language words along with English to make the messages appeal to the 'happening' generation next.

By repeating the messages often, the advertiser creates a top-of-mind recall for the product/service being advertised. Considering the power of such repeated messages which are intended to make a deep impact on the minds of the target audience, the manager has to be extremely careful while creating the messages.

Managers have to be aware of the various regulations with respect to advertisements, the manner in which spam messages are dealt. Managers should take into consideration that the public has become more empowered and vocal and so understand their levels and should not do anything to arouse their mistrust or disapproval.

(B) Slogans and Tag Lines

Definitions:

- **Oxford Dictionary:** *"A catchphrase or slogan, especially as used in advertising, or the punchline of a joke."*
- **Dictionary.com:** *"A phrase or catchword that becomes identified or associated with a person, group, product, etc."*
- **Wikipedia:** *"A tagline is a variant of a branding slogan typically used in marketing materials and advertising. The idea behind the concept is to create a memorable phrase that will sum up the tone and premise of a brand or product (like a film), or to reinforce the audience's memory of a product."*

All campaigns, be they for commercial advertisement or for political or religious purposes, have a slogan, a motto or a catch phrase which impresses the audience and helps them connect with the respective product, service or a concept. These phrases are rhetorical and simple and are repeated such that the audience remembers them. As they are short and simple, there is no scope for detail. Slogans could be written and presented visually or they could be chanted. A chanted slogan may be more useful as an expression of a unified purpose, than as communication to an intended audience. Even the defence forces have their own slogans, which help the officers and men to rally round a campaign. 'Satyameva Jayate' is a slogan used by the government of India. Similarly, on the occasion of Independence Day, the Prime Minister of India calls the audience to join in and chant 'Bharat Mata ki Jai'. This is more a rallying phrase, than a form of communication to the audience.

A slogan can thus be described as a repetitive expression of an idea or purpose.

In marketing terminology, slogans are powerful brand messages delivered by companies with the objective of promoting their products and influencing purchase decisions. They are compact and consistent, so that the consumers associate the product with these messages. They are called taglines in the United States, straplines in the U.K. and baselines, signatures, claims or pay-offs in Europe.

Difference between Taglines and Slogans

Though both are used effectively as marketing tools and have a number of commonalities, there are some points of differentiation:

- Slogans can be any expression, saying, idiom, phrase, or trademark that can be associated with a product. They express a company or product's stand or goal. They form the foundation of a company's marketing strategy and have a single objective of informing the consumers, drawing their attention and developing an environment of trust in the company and its products. They are constantly changed to suit the current trends in the market. As such they may even be used to define a campaign and may last only for that duration. Thus slogans can be short-lived.

- Taglines are brief messages, repeated frequently to provide identity to a product or a company. They are used in marketing and advertising to promote a company's name and its products. The purpose of taglines is to use a memorable phrase as a tool to make a product known and reinforce it in the consumers' memories. Thus, they aim at making a lasting dramatic effect in the minds of the consumers. In these days of severe competition, these tag lines are important in providing prominence and distinction to a product or a company, thereby giving it a marketing edge over the competitors. Tag lines usually last for a long time, as they are meant to create distinct impressions, associations and memories.

(C) Captions

The reading habits of people vary significantly. Whereas some read the articles completely, scanning each and every word, while others look for captions to tell them what to look for. In presentations, if the person presents a series of pictures or paragraphs without captions, he would be wasting his time and effort, as the audience will not be able understand their relevance or the context in which they are being presented.

A caption, also known as a cutline, is the text that appears below an image or as the head-line for an article. It is relevant to the image or the text and generally draws attention to something in the image that is not obvious. Thus they add meaning to an image. They can be a few descriptive words, or contain several sentences.

Captions need not be grammatically complete sentences. They may be noun phrases, such as "Busy Street on the All Bus Day". They have succinct reference to the surrounding text or context. The caption can have a title and a sub-title, separated by a colon.

Writing good captions is difficult, as they have to be succinct, short and snappy, imaginative and also informative. If there is no caption to highlight an image or an article, then there is no justification for keeping it there.

Guidelines for Framing a Caption

1. **Determining the Need for a Caption:** The author has to decide where captions are necessary and where they are not. For instance, if in a statement, information boxes are provided, captions are not necessary. Group photographs should contain list of persons in the order in which they are located in the picture. In maps and diagrams, if different colours are used, a caption and legend explaining the usage of colours would help the reader understand the information better. Portraits should show the name of the person, artist, place and year and also the medium.
2. Understanding the salient features of the picture or article. Not all of it may be presented in the caption. They may be presented in a note accompanying a picture or as a foot-note to the article.

The Criteria for a Good Caption

1. It clearly identifies the subject of the picture, adds value to it, but does not describe the obvious. One of a caption's primary purposes is to identify the subject of the picture or provide a headline to a text. The readers should not wonder what the subject of the picture or the article might be. In this respect, the caption should be clear and unambiguous. It may have to provide some context to the picture or the article, such as the name of the author or artist, date, place etc.
2. It should be succinct. Succinctness stands for brevity. If the caption is too long, it is necessary to carefully remove all excess words, and add power to the caption. This process of editing is far more important while preparing captions than in other forms of writing, as it is necessary to convey a lot with minimum number of attractive and powerful words. As a general rule, a caption should not be more than three lines. Otherwise, it can distract the readers. The caption should be presented in a very attractive style to make it look distinctive.
3. It establishes the relevance of the picture to the article. As the headline for an article, it draws attention to the content immediately and rouses their curiosity. A good caption explains why an image is depicted in the article, why it belongs there or what the article is trying to say. For instance, a news release of a new automobile model introduced in the market would be meaningless without a picture of the vehicle. However, if the picture has no caption to tell the readers about the model and the company, the picture would make no sense.
4. It provides context for the picture or the article. A picture is frozen in some time frame, without any information about the happenings outside its frame. In the advertisement for a new automobile model, the caption would create more curiosity if it gives the model name and year, name of the company and some relevant information about fuel efficiency, interiors etc. Similarly, the caption of an article should lead the reader to the article by rousing his curiosity and attention. For instance, a caption like "Eleventh Century Structure Restored to its Pristine Beauty" would want the readers to know more about the ancient monument and its maintenance issues and also the manner in which the restoration work was undertaken.

2.16 Maintaining a Diary

> The development and running of a successful business often translates into being in control of all issues pertaining to the day to day operations. This requires sound organisational and time management practices and techniques.

A diary is a book that functions as an important tool in time management. It is useful for recording the daily events or thoughts, such as phone calls, client meetings, communication within the organisation and decisions taken, invitations received, meetings to attend, personal commitments etc., as well as the follow-up actions to be taken. Thus, it helps in keeping track of events and organising one's activities in a systematic way. Especially if a person is forgetful or has extremely crowded work weeks, it serves as a useful aid to memory. There is nothing like a diary as a reminder of appointments or something that the person is supposed to do within some specific time frame. It can be of great assistance to a busy person who has a number of engagements to keep every day. It gives a lot of confidence to the manager if he develops the habit of writing a diary of daily events and things to do. For instance, top level managers are very busy as they deal with a variety of issues. From his diary, his secretary will be able to find out the date and time when he would be able to attend a meeting or grant an interview.

From a time management point of view, it is advisable for a manager to write down the details of any event and the follow-up action needed, so he can set his targets, prioritise his activities and plan his day and week ahead. A little time spent in writing a diary can go a long way in making one's professional and personal life, to that extent, stress-free. He can colour code certain events, like correspondence with customers, staff meetings etc.

Secondly, if this system is followed by all, it brings in the necessary discipline within the organisation and the day-to-day working becomes smooth. The managers' desks will not become war zones with clashing time commitments, frustrations etc.

The manager can use an electronic diary by using a computer or a pocket note book in which he writes. The advantage of an electronic diary is that his secretary can access it and schedule further events for him. This is the general practice where there are a number of senior managers who may need to attend either internal or external meetings with others from their same office. Coordinating the timings of so many with the help of electronic diaries is known as "meshing". One limitation in this is, that unless all members elect to accept (or reject) the meeting attendance, it cannot be automated into the diaries of the other members invited for the meeting.

A diary can also give an intimate glimpse to the personality of the writer. If the writer has noted down events of national importance along with his activities, it may even become a sort of historical record.

Tips for Maintaining and Using a Diary
- Before you start work on each Monday, ensure your diary of 'to do' activities for the week ahead is complete, which may include addressing issues raised by clients, marketing calls to be made, administration issues to be sorted out, travel arrangements to be made, accounts of previous travel to be sent to the accounts section, meetings to attend etc. It may also include personal matters to attend to.

- Prioritise your activities, giving importance to client interactions or major commitments within the organisation. Set the target such that as early as possible in the week all these matters are set in motion and they have the entire week to act on it.
- Before you start any written/computer work on each day, make all your phone calls first, marketing calls, clients, administration and other matters etc., in that order of priority. It would be preferable to ask these people to respond on your direct phone and not through the receptionist or secretary. This saves a lot of time and leaves the other person satisfied.
- After the call or meeting, write the details in the diary. Next to each item in your diary, note down whether you are expecting a response back from the other party or whether you are expected to take some action. It avoids the confusion as to who is expected to follow-up
- While taking necessary actions according to the proritised list in the diary, keep at hand the necessary back-up information. This should be available without your having to get up from your chair, or mess around with a number of files to look for the details you need to refer to. This saves a lot of time and also embarrassment.
- As far as possible, schedule your external meetings for the early hours of the day or as late as possible in the evening, thus eliminating wastage of time during the day for reaching the venue and getting back to office. Many managers use the travel time to make easier business, social and family calls using a hands-fee mobile phone.
- You do not have to meet with a client, a peer or a superior every time something needs to be discussed, unless it is very necessary. For instance, if you already know the client fairly well and have met with them several times before, a conference call should be sufficient. This will save an enormous amount of otherwise wasted in travelling. A similar approach can be used for developing contact with prospective clients as well.
- Do not waste your time meeting with people with whom you do not expect to do business, unless it is for personal reasons.
- If you are doubtful about attending a meeting or a function for which you have received invitation, you can politely indicate that you are busy by saying that you would consult your diary and respond.
- The diary should contain information about all monies that are due to you and those that you owe. If the amount is due to you, follow up on them personally. For instance, if you are on an hourly contract, your diary will help you prepare the invoice according to the payment schedule and mode mutually agreed. Your diary will also help you send out polite reminders if the other party is tardy in making payments. Maintain a schedule of all payments you are expected to make, and stick to the schedule. Thus the diary helps you to save a lot of time and frustration in financial matters.

- Similarly, if a matter has not moved very far and no conclusion has been arrived at, your diary will tell you that you have spent enough time on it and there is no need to pursue the matter any further.
- In the entire process, always focus on the quality and effectiveness of your time. Use the diary effectively to complete all that needs to be done within normal business hours, so that family and social engagements are not disturbed.

Case Studies

1. A multinational corporation selling cola drinks in India, intending to enhance its market share, decided to adopt the celebrity endorsement strategy. Cricket being a cult sport in this country, a star cricketer was selected to be the brand ambassador. The visual in the TV spot showed a group of poor children playing cricket on a hot afternoon. The star enters the scene to urge the children to enjoy the xxx drink, irrespective of whether they had the essential things in life or not. This advertisement was withdrawn hastily soon after it was introduced. It would be useful to analyse the situation and answer the following questions:
    - Was it the right decision to use the sportsperson as the brand ambassador for a cola drink?
    - Were the visuals and the message offensive in a commercial for selling cola drinks?
    - Did the message show that the company had done adequate research into the socio-economic background of those who consume cola drinks in the country?
    - How relevant was the ad message for fulfilling the objective of the company while introducing the advertisement?
2. The poster presentation was being given by a brilliant young engineer who was appointed very recently by the company. She had just completed her round of tests for a new product and was going to present the findings at a company workshop. The audience included a number of senior managers from the marketing, production, purchase and quality assurance departments, as each of these departments had a stake in the product. As the presentation progressed, the audience seemed bored and distracted. Some managers came in as the speaker was well into the third and fourth poster. They had driven in from some other location of the company and had to get back after the presentation, to attend to other pressing matters. Some had squeezed in this meeting in their busy day at the workshop. The speaker's voice was hardly audible as some announcements were going on and people in the adjoining corridor were talking loudly. As the light from above was shining into the eyes of the audience, they could hardly keep their eyes open and focus on the screen. The speaker had not kept any hard copies for the audience. It was an important presentation, but there was no feedback forthcoming. Gradually, the presenter started feeling disheartened. She had prepared so many posters and tried to

incorporate so much information into her presentation. She very much wanted to create a good impression. What could the young engineer have done to make the presentation really effective?

3. The company HR department was flooded with applications from enthusiastic candidates for the post of a trainee manager in the department. The advertisement was in the 'Classified' section of a couple of leading English newspapers. As there were no details in the job advertisement regarding the job location, years of experience expected etc., even those with 8-10 years of work experience had applied. Each application had a covering letter, with the résumé attached to it. Some had a photograph attached to it; some were brief one-page résumés, while some others had sent their detailed autobiographies as résumé. Some had given their educational qualifications in the beginning while others had mentioned it at the end. In many, the address for correspondence was missing, while others were very meticulous in giving all details including telephone numbers, email ID etc. The HR manager had a tough job ahead to review each application and make a short list and a comparative evaluation for the final selection. Time was of essence, and he had many other pressing issues to attend to. What do you think are the steps the HR manager could have taken to expedite the process? Give at least five suggestions.

Points to Remember

- **Objectives of Written Communication:**
    - Inform
    - Respond
    - Request
    - Report
    - Develop goodwill
- **Types of Written Communication:**
    - Letter
    - Office Memorandum
    - Circular
    - Inter-departmental note
    - Office order
    - Notification
    - Report
    - Resolution
    - Press communiqué/note
    - Endorsement or expression of support
    - Advertisement

- **Media for Despatch of Written Communication**
  - Telegram
  - Fax facility
  - Registered Post, Speed Post
  - E-mail
- **Process of Effective Written Communication**
  - Planning
  - Organising
  - Drafting
  - Revising or editing
  - Proof reading to eliminate errors.
- **Writing Skills**
  - Avoid being verbose
  - Subject lines
  - Decide your audience
  - Prepare an outline of the document
  - Purpose statement
  - Format
  - Organise the contents in paragraphs
  - Pay attention to the Structure of the document
  - Be effective and persuasive
  - Address one reader rather than many
  - Engage the reader's attention
  - Take care of spelling and grammar
  - Check before sending (Proofing):
  - Communicate with confidence
- **Importance of a Business Letter**
  - Permanent Record
  - Promotion or Business
  - Creates Goodwill
  - Useful in finding out the Creditworthiness of a Customer or vendor
  - Collection of Overdue Payments
- **Essential Qualities of a Good Business Letter**
  - Completeness
  - Clarity
  - Accuracy
  - Brevity or Conciseness
  - Courtesy
  - Sincerity
  - Simplicity
  - Style

- **Physical Appearance of a Business Letter**
    - Quality of Paper used
    - The sizes of the paper used for business correspondence differs from country to country.
    - Typing
    - Paragraphs
    - Address
    - Folding
    - Envelope
- **In general, the information to be included in the Bio-data is classified into the following five broad categories:**
    - Personal details.
    - Educational Qualifications.
    - Extra curricular activities.
    - Experiences of work.
    - References.
- **A memo can be used for the following purposes:**
    - To seek or give suggestions.
    - To communicate policy changes.
    - To issue instructions to the staff.
    - To request for help or information.
    - To confirm a decision arrived at on the telephone.
- **Tips for Drafting of Minutes**
    - Draft immediately
    - Consultation with the chairman
    - Concise
    - Complete
    - Clear
    - Compliance with provisions in the Companies Act
    - Form of Minutes
- **The press release should contain the following:**
    - Name of the organisation.
    - Purpose of the press release or news being covered.
    - Date and place.
    - Main speakers, including the person who gave the vote of thanks if he is an important member of the organisation.
    - A brief summary of the main speech.

- **Elements of Creative Writing**
    - Research
    - Organising the facts
    - Building a roadmap, so your readers do not get lost
    - Write for your readers and not executives
    - Speed of writing
    - Take care of context, grammar and spelling
    - Writing requires revising
    - Revision and Rewriting
    - Editing focuses on making the work readable
    - The Copy editing stage
    - Proof reading
- **The two characteristics of a successful poster are:**
    - It has conveyed a clear message to the audience, and
    - It has generated valuable comments or feedback to the presenter.
- **Slogans and Tag Lines: Definitions**
    - **Oxford Dictionary:** *"A catchphrase or slogan, especially as used in advertising, or the punchline of a joke."*
    - **Dictionary.com:** *"A phrase or catchword that becomes identified or associated with a person, group, product, etc."*

Questions for Discussion

1. Explain the significance of managerial writing.
2. What are the characteristics of an Executive Summary? Explain its significance in a report.
3. You are the marketing manager of Company ABC. Write a reply to letter # XYZ54/Nov 2012 from client XYZ, assuring him that the QA department will attend to his complaints with respect to specific quality issues in consignment ABC# 87/2012, dispatched on November 08, 2012.
4. You are the accounts manager in RST Company. You have noticed that the credit period extended to printing and publishing house PAC for purchase of paper, is expiring shortly. Write a letter to the Accounts Dept of PAC Company drawing attention to the expiring credit period and request him to make the payments within the due date to avoid penalties.

Chapter 3...

Effective Presentations

Contents ...
3.1 Introduction
3.2 Principles of Effective Presentations
3.3 Principles Governing the Use of Audiovisual Media
- Points to Remember
- Questions for Discussion

Learning Objectives ...
➢ To be aware of the principles of effective presentation when making and giving presentations
➢ To develop an understanding of the principles governing the use of Audiovisual Media

3.1 Introduction

Very often, managers are called upon to make presentations. These presentations may be to communicate the facts to superiors, or to peers from various related departments with respect to a project to be undertaken as a team effort. They may be for training programmes. They may be to address customers about a new product or improvements in a product. Whatever the occasion, the two key issues in the preparations are:
- **The message:** What the audience need to know.
- **The audience:** Making an effective talk such that the audience will understand and remember the message.

While preparing a presentation, managers should understand the difference between written communication and oral presentation. In a written report, the reader can choose the portions he wants to read and the order in which he goes through the document. He can go back and forth as and when he wants. Hence, written reports follow a well demarcated structure where the information flows from the introduction to method of study, results, interpretation or discussion and conclusions, followed by references.

On the other hand, in presentations the listener, by necessity, has to follow the order in which the speaker presents his material. **Here the format followed in a written report is totally unsuitable for an oral presentation**, as the audience will have to remember the earlier sections and relate them to what is being presented in the discussion or conclusion sections. This makes it very difficult for the audience.

Grouping of relevant aspects of the study along with necessary facts and figures to support the conclusions arrived at can help the audience to understand each issue properly and completely. If details regarding the 'why', 'how', 'what' and their meaning with respect to each aspect of the research are brought together, it will help the presenter also to fit the individual issues properly in to the larger picture. A conclusion at the end of each segment will convey the complete message with regard to that segment, and a general conclusion at the end of the entire presentation will put the entire message in the right perspective. For instance, if the presentation is about entering a new market, the various aspects such as linguistic issues, cultural issues, infrastructure available and that to be created, marketing strategy etc., should be treated as separate units with a brief introduction, to be followed by the main presentation and a brief conclusion.

3.2 Principles of Effective Presentations

Effective presentation is all about staying connected to the audience, engaging them continuously throughout the delivery and achieving the objectives set forth for the presentation. The presenter does so by projecting his personality as a professional who possesses certain unique characteristics. In fact, his personality is the medium as well as the window through which the message is sent to the audience. The audience receives this message, understands and interprets it in the context of its own reference points and frame of mind, and takes action on it.

The key to making a good presentation is staying relaxed, and being alert and observant. An individual communicates better when he is most relaxed. Hence, the presenter has to make sure that he can have a stress-free conversation during presentations, irrespective of whether he is addressing a small group or a large gathering. Through his oratory skills and body language, the presenter has to make the audience comfortable in order that they receive the message in the right perspective, react and take the decision expected of them. The presenter should demonstrate his commitment to the ideas and thoughts that he is presenting and this commitment should be felt by the audience all the way. Towards this, the presenter has to take care of the following principles:

- The presenter must be **sure of the objective of the presentation, prepare accordingly** and stay focused. Remember that the audience does not have the facility to go back and forth to understand the subject. Make an orderly presentation, with a smooth flow of ideas.
- Work towards a **relaxed conversation**. This can happen if the presenter has made all necessary preparations and so is not under any sort of stress or anxiety regarding the content and the format of presentation. The presenter should remember that he is not 'downloading' information, but is communicating a message with an objective. Communication is a two-way process. The audience sends its response immediately by way of body language and the presenter has to identify it and respond immediately. For instance, if the presenter perceives a puzzled look among the

audience, he should address it immediately, just as he would do in a one-on-one conversation. He should find out if some additional explanations are required and offer it forthwith or assure them that the matter will be answered in the subsequent part of the presentation. These questions can pave the way for better mutual understanding. It may be a good practice to allow the audience to raise questions during the presentation instead of a Q/A session at the end.

- The presenter should remember that in a relaxed environment, it is possible to achieve a **meaningful two-way interaction**. By definition, all conversation is a two-way exchange of messages. In a relaxed conversation, the presenter should be looking for clues from the audience, such as nods, blank expressions, puzzled look etc. The presenter can change his tactics, pause a little or find out if they have any questions. He can also use examples, anecdotes etc., to lighten the mood. He should adopt a style of delivery which will make the audience comfortable. In short, he has to treat the audience with respect and adjust his approach, answer their questions clearly and concisely. He will then stand a better chance of ensuring that the audience has understood his message and will act on it.

- In a relaxed conversation, **the receiver gets all the importance**, as the outcome depends on how he receives the message. The speed and manner in which information goes from sender to receiver is driven by the receiver's needs, and not that of the sender. There is a lot of difference between hearing and listening. During a one-on-one conversation, the receiver signals by a nod or an appropriate sound that he has understood the message. If such a response is not forthcoming, it means that the sender has failed in creating a good level of mutual understanding before moving on to the next point. The receiver will stop listening and the conversation breaks down. Similarly, in presentations, if the presenter continues to talk without stopping to gauge the reactions of the audience, it becomes one-sided, and the presentation will lose its purpose.

- The presenter should adopt a **conversational style of delivery**, which appears to be more spontaneous and interesting and not memorised. For instance, in a relaxed informal conversation, the sender thinks about what he is going to say, forms his idea, frames it in appropriate sentences and delivers it. He then stops and allows the listener to absorb the idea, relate it to his own perceptions and biases and form his responses. Through this process, the sender waits and observes the reaction of the receiver and continues after he gets it, and so on. Similarly, if the presentation is in a conversational style, both the presenter and the audience will take their own time to formulate their messages/reactions and communicate them meaningfully.

- The presenter should be very **natural in his behaviour**. Any attempt at being extra polite or over-confident, arrogant and offensive will show and the audience will react accordingly. Obviously, he should know that he has to be on his best behaviour and there are some norms and standards of addressing the members of the audience. However, he should know his own strengths and use them to his best advantage. His dress and style should be appropriate for the occasion. He must follow the protocol in introducing distinguished members. He must be attentive when a participant is asking a question and answer it properly, without showing any signs of disapproval or despise. His body language should be very natural. However, considering that there are differences in how people interpret hand movements, many trainers suggest that the presenter should limit hand and finger movements to a great extent.

- The presentation should be as **simple and brief** as possible. If it is too lengthy, the audience will not remember what the presenter has communicated. One of the basic rules of presentation is that the presenter should not overshoot the attention span of the audience. If the delivery is short, the audience will remember what has been said. If the presenter, in his anxiety to use the occasion to the best, may try to load it with too much information. But such a presentation will defeat its purpose. This contradicts the principle that the speed at which information travels from the sender to the receiver is determined by the need of the latter, and not the need of the presenter to communicate as much as possible. The receiver will absorb only what he needs to. A lengthy presentation will distract the receiver so much that he may not even receive what he needs. To be effective, the presenter should limit his delivery and allow time for interaction and networking.

- At a point of time, the audience can listen or think, but not do both simultaneously. Hence, the presenter should intersperse his presentation by reasonably frequent (but not too frequent) **pauses** to give time for the audience to absorb what they have heard and think about it. If the presentation is non-stop, the audience will not catch everything. At some point, they may lose track, and try to catch up with the presentation. This may happen once or twice, but if there is no time in between, they will give up this effort and lose interest. The presenter will have lost the opportunity of achieving the main objective of the presentation.

- Brief periods of **silence or pauses are essential** to make the presentation effective. A presentation is not an occasion to prove that the presenter can make lengthy presentations, non-stop. The main purpose of the presentation should be to pass on information in an effective manner. These pauses give the presenter the time to gather his thoughts and get back to the basic theme. The audience also need time to digest what has been presented thus far and react to it. The message is important for the presenter and he cannot afford to lose his audience due to lack of attentiveness or boredom.

- The audience will not remember the exact words said in the presentation, and what they remember will be coloured by their perceptions or their frame of reference. For this, they **need some break in the presentation**. If the presenter does not give the break, they will take it, and stop listening to the delivery.
- The presenter should **think before he speaks**, so that the delivery is correct and focused and not confusing or distracting. The presenter can keep with him a brief note or a checklist of points to cover, and in the same order in which he wants to convey. Addressing one idea at a time makes the presentation organised and purposeful. To get over an anxiety or stress situation, he can encourage the audience to ask questions. This will make the presentation clear, concise and focused.

3.3 Principles Governing the use of Audiovisual Media

Communication, especially with presentation materials, is an art. There are no rules. Armed with the right graphics, an ordinary speaker with extraordinary ideas can teach, persuade, sell or inform the audience without too much stress. However, it should be remembered that the objective of preparing presentation material is not the creation of a beautiful art piece, but a useful aid for conveying a message effectively. For a presenter, his ideas are important to him and through the presentation, he wants to communicate that same importance to his audience.

The tools to be used for the presentation depend on the nature of presentation. If it is a formal, large gathering, audio-visual aids like slides with or without animation would be the most practical and helpful tool. But if it is a small workshop or in Q & A sessions, where it is necessary to maintain eye contact most of the time, overhead projectors and flip charts may be more appropriate. However, the current trend is to make spreadsheets or PowerPoint presentations even for small group presentations or even on-line sharing of screens.

The four areas where managers have to develop audio-visual presentation skills are:

1. Understanding the needs of the audience.
2. Developing good content, that is informative, relevant, complete and credible and editing it to make it simple and effective.
3. Preparing a presentable design, which is pleasing, attractive and readable considering the ambience where it is presented.
4. Conducting the entire presentation, keeping in mind all aspects of oral presentation.

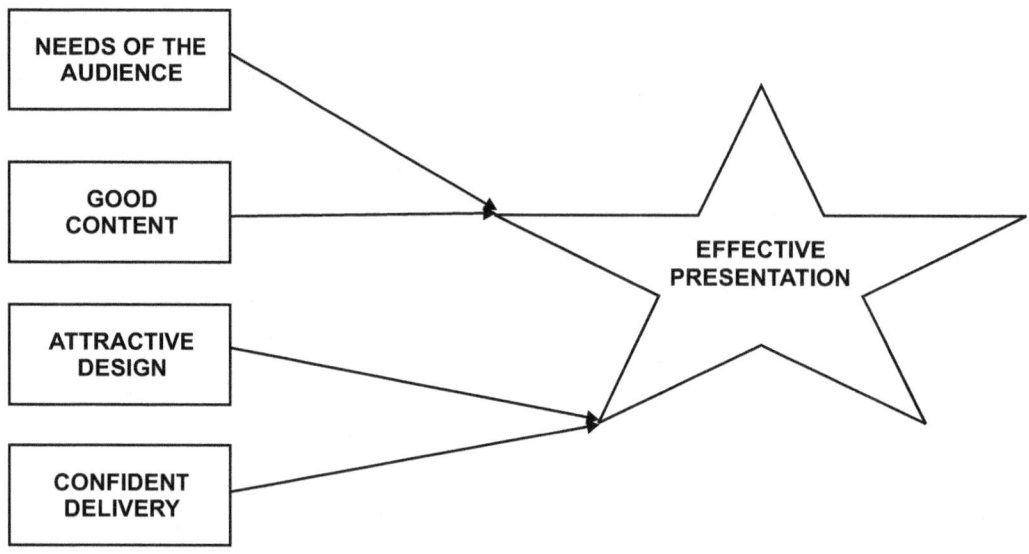

Fig. 3.1: Elements of an Effective Presentation

Developing Strong Content

1. **Be clear of the objectives of the presentation**: It could be to inform, to make a request for project grant or for training.

2. **Know your audience**: The manager has to know the audience and their background before preparing the presentation so as to keep them engaged throughout and get the necessary outcome. The presenter should know the following about the audience:

    - Names with proper spellings.
    - Their needs by way of information in the presentation, and decision making.
    - Gender, as the approach and choice of words will have to be appropriate and gender sensitive.
    - Language and culture they belong to.
    - Educational level.
    - Their other interests and hobbies, as this will make it easier for the presenter to introduce them to the audience and also take some examples from those fields to make them comfortable and connected.
    - Years of experience in this field and in other areas.
    - Organisation and department they are in.
    - Their position in the organisation.

- Whether they are the influencers or decision makers. This is crucial when the presentation is meant to garner financial support for a project.
- Papers they have published, and the patents they have.
- Their attitude towards the subject being discussed.
- The action expected from them.

All this will help the presenter make appropriate seating arrangements and introduce the participants according to an accepted protocol, and in a professional manner. The presenter will also be able to know the extent of technical information that should be included, the depth of information to be given, duration of the entire presentation, number of slides, balance between text and visuals to be included, any abbreviations used and the need for explaining them, supporting documents and references to be cited or presented, any take away hard copies to be prepared etc.

3. **Collection of relevant data:** The presenter will then work on collecting all relevant data keeping in view the information regarding the audience and their background. Depending on the amount of information already available with the presenter, he/she should work backwards to determine the time required to collect the information and putting it in the required sequence and format, and start working accordingly.

4. **Preparing a presentation outline:** The presenter will organise the data in the order in which they should be presented. This outline will have a logical sequence of presentation which will help the audience move from slide to slide without any confusion. The presenter will have to review this order of presentation and finalise it with care.

5. **Structure of the presentation:** The structure of a presentation should be designed keeping in view the need to keep the audience connected on a continuous basis, so that the arguments and conclusions are understood by the audience and the presenter gets useful feedback.

> *In an oral presentation you should group together what belongs together.*

6. **Designing the content:** While designing the content, the presenter has to remember the basic principles of presentation, viz.,
    - **Appearance**: This includes use of various elements of design such as:
        - **Size of letters or images:** The audience should not have to struggle to read the contents. Various size fonts are available and should be used judiciously for the headings, text, legend boxes, foot notes, references etc.
        - **Contrast:** This can be achieved in many ways, such as use of background colour, space, line, colour choice, selection of font size, colour, texture and style, positioning of the text either in the top or bottom, isolated or grouped etc. It can also be used to highlight the dominant item, theme or focal point so that the viewer gets the point immediately and remembers it. Contrast is a very powerful and effective way to effectively highlight the focal point.

It should be remembered that anything that looks beautiful on the computer screen may not show up the same way when it is projected. For instance, light backgrounds look wonderful on a colour monitor, but when projected in a dark room, anything placed on it will appear dull or washed out. Hence, the greater the contrast, the greater is the impact. It is a good idea to have a black background. The most important thing to remember is to keep the background dark and the foreground light. That gives the designer plenty of range in the colours he can use for the text.

While preparing the text, use bright, light colours. Reds and blues always look great on a computer screen, but not for projection unless it is boldly outlined in white. Pastel shades like yellows, pinks, light blues and light greens look best on black or any dark colour. For instance, on a bright blue background, bright yellow letters would make it pleasant and readable. Use lighter colours to accentuate the major points. The hierarchy of colours is white, yellow, beige, orange etc. Vary the colours to break the monotony and for highlighting certain points. The audience will be interested and know what to expect.

In the text, if everything is given the same look, nothing will be clearly dominant and it becomes difficult for the audience to give appropriate weightage to the main theme or objective of the presentation. However, too many font sizes, styles and colours in a slide may be confusing and the audience will be distracted from the main focus of the presentation.

> ***Designs with strong contrast attract interest, and help the viewer make sense of the visual. Weak contrast is not only boring, but it can be confusing.***

- o **Title Page:** Put special thought into the design of the main title slides. A good title slide attracts an audience's attention, and tells them about not only the content of the presentation, but also how the speaker is going to approach it. A title slide also signifies the quality of a presentation. For instance, a sloppy one communicates the fact that the presenter has just put together some material and has not given it much thought or planning. The audience would perceive it as an insult. But a classy title slide, with a different coloured background, a frame or a piece of clip art placed just right, can tell the audience that the speaker regards them with respect. In general, good speakers display a good title slide for about 5 minutes prior to the scheduled beginning of the presentation. If in a conference, the audience has a choice of presentations to participate in, this title slide would be a good guide for choosing the session that interests them most, even if they have not decided which one they want to attend.

- **Alignment:** A lot of thought has to go into arranging the elements in a slide systematically. Nothing in the slide design should look as if it has been placed there randomly. The slide should be prepared by dividing it into grids, and the texts and visuals should be placed such that the elements are linked even if they are placed far apart. Every design element should be connected by an invisible line so that the presentation is a visual treat. Such slides look cleaner, extremely professional and sophisticated. The audience may not be conscious of it, but the overall effect of such careful presentation can be very pleasing.
- **Repetition** of same header/footer and other basic design elements throughout the presentation to bring a clear sense of unity, consistency, and cohesiveness. As against contrast, which is used for differentiation, repetition is used to indicate that the slides belong to a larger whole. The presenter can use anyone of the standard templates available in the software application for this purpose, or create one to make the presentation unique. It must be remembered that the standard templates would have been used very often and so the audience may find them tasteless and so lose interest.

- **Proximity:** The readers should be drawn to the content and made to think about the information presented, rather than on the flow in the presentation. Audiences will naturally tend to look at similar items that are near to each other as a single unit. The principle of proximity is about keeping related items grouped together so that they will be viewed as a group, rather than as several unrelated elements. This involves organising the flow of information such that the audiences do not have to struggle trying to connect the caption with graphic or trying to find out if a line of text is a subtitle or it is a line of text unrelated to the title. It would be a good exercise to sit back and see what path human eyes take while looking at a slide and design accordingly.
- **Clarity:** Use of all capitals can make it difficult for the readers. Mixed case is better. Similarly, italics would be difficult to read on the screen. This style should be used very sparingly. Avoid any fancy styles. Some of them may look absolutely beautiful on the monitor, but not while projecting. It is a wise policy to stick to simple typefaces used in newspapers or magazines, as they will have been chosen as a result of a lot of expensive research aimed at finding out what the readers are comfortable with.

Use large fonts for texts. The thumb rule is, if you have any difficulty at all reading something on your monitor, your audience will not be able to read it. Do not use compressed text, as it is almost impossible to read.

For highlighting some points, different colours may be used. But underlining may indicate hyperlinking and so should be avoided for emphasis. Numbers should be used to show the sequence if there is a list with priorities attached to the points. But if there is no priority, hierarchy or sequence in the list, bullet points should be used. However, if too many such bulleted lists are used, it may become very clumsy.

- **Consistency:** There should be consistency in using the style, size, colour etc. Differences should be used only to attract attention and not distract the readers. For instance, if each point in a slide has a different style and colour of bullet, it can be distracting and considered poor in taste.
- **Progression:** The slides should lead the audience to the conclusion in a systematic way without any need to go back and forth.
- **Simplicity**: Follow the 6 x 7 rule: No more than 6 lines per slide and No more than 7 words per line. It is better to use a larger number of simpler slides which move faster than a few slides crammed with text. Please remember that a slide is not a page in a book or magazine, and so do not have more than a few elements or groups of elements in a slide.

  It is good practice to give the gist of a point in a few sentences and lines. Too many details should not be crammed into a slide. For instance, in a table, the unit of measurement can be given in the title line and the details in the columns should be presented as briefly as possible using decimal points to shorten them. Similarly, the charts should be clear with colour codes used and explained appropriately.

  Sound effects should be used sparingly, as they distract the audience. It is too amateurish and will fail to impress the audience.
- **References and Citations:** In the presentations, if the information content is built on the works of others, the sources of information should be acknowledged and credit given appropriately.

  Citations to appropriate sources show that the manager has done his homework and is aware of the background and context into which his work fits. They help lend validity to his arguments. The presentation looks more professional. Additionally, citations help interested readers by providing avenues to enhance their understanding of the subject. Thus, the knowledge circle grows wider.
- **Good summary** either at the end of each segment to indicate a shift to a new segment or at the end of the entire presentation will help the presenter to wrap up and open the floor for discussion if it is part of the strategy of the presenter.

- **Review and Editing:** Even an experienced manager should take time to review the slides and edit them in order to make a perfect presentation. At this stage, the presenter will view all the elements from the point of view of the audience and refine it. If possible, he should use the projector, microphone etc. at the presentation venue at this stage to check and make sure that apart from the content and the flow of thought, size, colour, alignment, lighting, seating arrangements, verbal delivery etc. together make the presentation a pleasant experience. Glitches of all types should be removed, and the audience should be able to follow and understand the content without any distractions or confusion. If necessary, a back-up copy of the presentation can be kept ready to take care of any problem with the computer the presenter is using.

7. **Content Delivery:** The presenter should remember that he is not acting or delivering a prepared speech. Nor is it intended to manipulate the audience. It should minimise conflicts by promoting a better understanding of the subject. It is aimed at informing the audience and giving them proper choices so that the decisions are based on genuine information and judgment. Hence it is necessary that the presenter is well informed and is comfortable with the content that he is presenting. There is cohesion in his thought and conviction in his words. The audience should be taken through the presentation and led to take the expected decision or action.

Body language is important, and if the comfort level is high, the self-confidence becomes very much evident in the body language. However, attention should be given to all aspects of communication like eye contact, tone and pitch of voice, facial expressions, posture, movement etc.

Proper lighting is important. It could be extremely frustrating for a speaker if after careful preparation of the slides, he has to present it in a room without proper lighting. The audience should be able to see the presenter as well as the slides clearly without eye fatigue. The presenter has to make eye contact and get immediate non-verbal feedback from the audience. The rule here is to have the screen area darkened, but the rest of the room bright enough for the presenter and the audience stay connected.

The presenter should take care not to read from the slides. The audience can very well do that. He should explain or provide context to the text and graphics being presented. Audiences appreciate attractive slides with good graphics, but that does not make up if the presenter does not have command over the subject being presented. Know your material backwards and forwards, and try to remember which slide comes after which. The presenter should know where a few key slides will come during the presentation. It can really enhance the impact of a point if he knows how to highlight that special slide.

Constantly evaluate your effect. Watch your audiences for their non-verbal feedback. Ideally, nobody should fall asleep and nobody should leave during your presentations. If you notice that some in the audience are losing interest and are distracted, it means that you are going slow, the room is very cool or extremely hot, there is noise outside, or the participants are preoccupied with their own issues and concerns etc. It may also mean that there are some shortcomings in the slides that distract them or make it difficult for them to read. The presenter should be alert to such feedback, so that maximum corrective measures possible, given the circumstances, can be taken. Such experiences can be useful as lessons for future presentations.

Maintain a pleasant demeanor and a comfortable stance. It is appropriate to quote from personal experience, as the presenter then develops emotional connection with the audience.

Technology like projectors, microphones and so on, should be used to enhance the presentation quality. The presenter should be well versed with the functioning of these systems and not fumble and say 'oops!' and try to cover up.

These are not rules for effective presentation, but some guidelines to help managers to communicate those valuable ideas of theirs. What makes the presenter special is his own style, voice, mannerisms, inflections etc.

To sum up, the characteristics of an effective presentation are:

Communication is the key. The presenter should know the content very well and be confident and relaxed. Preparations should be complete. The passion of the presenter can create favourable audience reaction.

- Text should support the presentation.
- Pictures should be used to simplify complex concepts.
- Animations can be used for explaining complex relationships.
- Visuals should support, and not distract. Use all elements of slide design effectively.
- Sound effects in the slide show should be used only if necessary.
- Comfortable ambience and proper seating and lighting arrangements are necessary.
- Presenter should be comfortable with the technology for presentation.
- Confident oral presentation using the slides, applying all principles of verbal and non-verbal communication to maximum advantage.

Tips for Successful Presentation

The two basic principles of a successful presentation are: (1) The message (2) The audience and how they understand this message best. Awareness of how the audience would listen and remember is the key behind a presentation that will be appreciated by many.

1. **Submission of abstract:** Submit the abstract to the conference organisers well in time, as they have to allot time slots for each presenter and manage the time.

2. **Start your presentation in time:** As soon as your abstract has been accepted, start thinking about how you will organise the material. Read about the subject and related work, review the facts and think about the most relevant conclusions. Try to imagine the type of audience you would be facing and consider the details to be included as background information and in the text.

3. **The Message:** As an introduction, try to portray your message in a single sentence. This is not easy unless you are confident of the subject you are talking about.

4. **Select the facts to be presented and order them:** How much you need to explain and how much detail should be included depends on the purpose of the presentation and the audience. There are no hard and fast rules regarding this. Even if the facts are known to the audience, they will sit through if it is presented in an interesting way. If it is a presentation of the results of a scientific experiment, determine the order in which you should present it. Be very critical of the content. Any experiment or result that does not contribute to your main message should be left out. Decide where you want to discuss the highlights. It could be at the beginning, near the end or they may be dispersed through the entire talk. If it is a training programme, consider the need to consistently retain the excitement among the participants by adopting various ways like games, puzzles etc.

5. **Opening and Introduction:** Address the Chair and the audience appropriately, followed by a few seconds of silence just to look around and see if the audience is attentive. It also raises the curiosity of the audience. Use this time to see if the sound system is carrying your words adequately. Catch the attention of the audience by an appropriate question or a catchy or may be even provocative statement. Perhaps you could already give the conclusion of your work too. Prepare and rehearse the opening carefully.

6. **Structure of the Presentation:** Sketch the background of your subject matter in a concise manner and space your talk with a short pause at the end of each point to allow the facts to sink in.

7. **Visuals:** They should be readable, relevant, attractive and self-explanatory. Using tables with a lot of numbers take a lot of time to read and remember. Use colours and contrasts effectively.

8. **Style of Presentation:** Try to speak slowly, confidently and in a relaxed manner, with appropriate emphasis, and look at the audience all the time. Do not read from the slide or from your notes. Do not use fancy words or a flashy style.

9. **Conclusions and Ending:** Announce the conclusion properly to regain complete attention. The conclusion should answer the question posed at the introduction stage. End by acknowledging those who have helped you, such as your co-authors if any and your sponsor. Conclude with a 'take home' message, which reiterates your conclusion.

10. **Timing:** Close your presentation well within the time allotted. Rehearse, edit and then finalise the presentation keeping adequate time for the introduction and conclusion. It is not a good practice to wait for the moderator or the chairperson to keep track of the time for you. It is an offence to the audience. You will be more organised and look more professional if you stay within the time slot.

Steve Jobs, the Late CEO Apple, was a leader in the technology industry, who led the company into great heights year after year. His tenure saw the release of many innovative and exciting products, which gave the company record profits. He was known for his vision and great passion to pursue that vision. Under his dynamic leadership, Apple grew to be a very strong brand. No doubt he had very clear business sense, but more than that, he was known for his charisma, showmanship and flair for great presentations. With his impressive speaking skills and ability to persuade people, convince any audience, be it the corporate world, media or the public, about the prospects for his company and its products and also about his own ideas. His strength to captivate the audience even when he spoke for a couple of hours, came not only from his style, but also his mastery over the subject and his humility. For managers, it is a good exercise to analyse the fundamental characteristics which distinguished him from others:

1. **Passion:** Jobs had an undying passion for Apple and its products. He displayed this enthusiasm and communicated it while describing his new innovations by using terms as 'Thrilled', 'excited' etc. His excitement was reported to be contagious. He used variations in tone and pace of speaking to convey his excitement. So much so that the audience waited for his presentations in hushed anticipation and broke into wild cheers when he closed.

2. **Clarity:** Steve Jobs had the superior ability to communicate his message with great clarity, such that the audience could understand and relate to it. He could explain in simple, non-technical terms, terms even the most complicated company or product related statistics. For instance, he explained market size and share by using simple pie charts, which the audience could understand easily. This established the credibility of the company and its prospects and Jobs gained the admiration of the consumers. This simplicity and clarity of speech made him accessible to the audience at large.

3. **Humour:** Though there are reports of his huge ego, it never showed up in his presentations, which were interspersed with light humour, which endeared him to the audience. His style was that of an ordinary person with extraordinary experiences, which he shared in colloquial style and casual tone. This helped him to connect beautifully with the audience. His child-like simplicity, excitement and laughter eased any tension in the environment and ensured that the mood remained light. He clearly demonstrated that he was in command. Amidst all this, he stood out for his dignity, composure and adaptability, qualities essential in a great presenter.

4. **Engagement:** His keynote addresses were known for the manner in which he stayed connected with the audience and kept them engaged. This he did not only through his excellent oratory skills but also through impressive product demonstrations and assurance that the consumers would be thrilled with the products. The manner in which he communicated his excitement is legendary.

5. **Hyperbole:** He raised the pitch and praised his products by using a number of adjectives such as 'incredible', 'magical', 'cool', 'hot' 'amazing, 'awesome' etc. These are expressions commonly used in colloquial American style, and this helped him stay connected with the consumers.

6. **Congruence:** It is significant to note that in all his presentations, Steve Jobs stood for the company's vision, mission and message, which is about cutting edge innovation, purity of user experience, and aesthetics.

"That passion, vision, and commitment to ideals is the foundation of legendary presentations."

Excerpted from: Say it like Steve: Principles for Powerful Presentations – September 8, 2010
Posted in: General, Story Archive.
By Joseph Quan, WJYC Writer

Points to Remember

- Very often, managers are called upon to make presentations. These presentations may be to communicate the facts to superiors, or to peers from various related departments with respect to a project to be undertaken as a team effort. They may be for training programmes. They may be to address customers about a new product or improvements in a product.
- Effective presentation is all about staying connected to the audience, engaging them continuously throughout the delivery and achieving the objectives set forth for the presentation.
- It should be remembered that the objective of preparing presentation material is not the creation of a beautiful art piece, but a useful aid for conveying a message effectively. For a presenter, his ideas are important to him and through the presentation, he wants to communicate that same importance to his audience.

- The tools to be used for the presentation depend on the nature of presentation. If it is a formal, large gathering, audio-visual aids like slides with or without animation would be the most practical and helpful tool.

Questions for Discussion

1. What are the basic principles of successful presentation?
2. What are the elements of an effective presentation?
3. Explain the basic considerations while making an audio-visual presentation.

■■■

Chapter 4...

Interview Skills

Contents ...

4.1 Introduction
4.2 Meaning and Objectives of Interview
4.3 Types of Interview
    4.3.1 Job Interview / Placement Interview
    4.3.2 Discipline Interview
    4.3.3 Appraisal Interviews
    4.3.4 Exit Interviews
    4.3.5 Promotion Interviews
    4.3.6 Qualitative Research Interview
4.4 Videoconferencing and Tele-meeting
- Points to Remember
- Questions for Discussion

Learning Objectives ...

➢ To be aware of the objectives of Interviews
➢ To know the different types of Interviews
➢ To be familiar with Video-conferencing and Tele-meeting

4.1 Introduction

An Interview is a meeting between persons for a discussion. It is a conversation between two people, viz., the interviewer and the interviewee (the interviewer may be one person or a panel) where questions are asked by the interviewer to obtain information from the interviewee. Thus, it is a form of two-way communication.

The word interview is derived from the French word *'entrevoir'* meaning 'to glimpse', which indicates seeing each other. It endeavours to discover as much information as possible in the least amount of time about some relevant matter. While the interviewer is seeking information, the interviewee will also be assessing the other party. For instance, in a job interview, the candidate will also be seeking clues about the overall environment and culture of the organisation, and whether he would like to commit a major part of his professional life to it.

An interview is usually conducted in four phases which can be easily remembered by the acronym 'WASP'
- Welcome,
- Acquiring Information,
- Supplying Information,
- Parting.

At the end of each interview, the interviewer or the interviewing committee will prepare a detailed report on the interview for maintaining transparency and also for future reference.

4.2 Meaning and Objectives of 'Interview'

"An interview is a formal meeting in which a person or persons question, consult or evaluate another person or persons." **– Murphy and Peak**

An interview reveals the views, ideas and attitudes of the person being interviewed as well as the skills of the interviewer. It is a medium of two-way communication between people. There are various purposes of interviews.

According to **E. C. Eyre**, *"an interview is a face-to-face verbal exchange which endeavours to discover as much information as possible in the least amount of time about some relevant matter"*.

According to **Vivien Palmar**, *"an interview constitutes a social situation between the two persons, the psychological process involved requiring both the individuals mutually respond through social research. The purpose of the interview calls for a varied response from the two parties concerned"*.

Depending on the company background, purpose, level etc., the depth, style and location for the interview can be decided. For instance, for a graduating class, campus interview would be the best method, while for senior levels, the interview will be held at the senior-most level and it can be held over a lunch or dinner.

4.3 Types of Interviews

4.3.1 Job Interview/Placement Interview

In the context of a **job interview**, the candidate and the interviewer each have a need: the candidate wants the job and the interviewer wants to find the right person to fill a position. Companies need to recruit people at various levels. This need may arise due to internal promotions, normal retirement process, when the older employees make way for the younger generation or due to attrition, when the serving employees leave the organisation looking for greener pastures.

Job/Placement interviews are conducted to recruit new employees in the organisation. It is a formal discussion between a hirer and an applicant or candidate, in which information is exchanged, with the intention of establishing the applicant's suitability for a position.

They are aimed at assessing the strengths and weaknesses of prospective candidate. Though these are typically held in person, the current trend in many companies is to have a telephonic interview prior to a face-to-face interview, especially if the candidates are from far off places. Employing a new candidate for a company is a very challenging task for a manager. The job market is becoming extremely competitive and so, newer interview methods are being introduced to sift the candidates.

There are many types of job interviews such as:

(a) **The Screening Interview:** Companies use screening tools to ensure that candidates meet minimum qualification required. Some organisations use computer programmes to weed out unqualified candidates. This is the reason why they require a digital resume that is screening-friendly. However, in most companies, professionals are assigned the role of gatekeepers who are skilled enough to determine whether there is anything that might disqualify a candidate for the position. They do not need to know whether the person is the best fit for the position, but only determine if the candidate fits in. For this reason, screeners tend to be very critical in looking for gaps in the employment history of the candidate and look for pieces of information that look inconsistent. They also will try to find out if the candidate is over-qualified and hence be too expensive for the company.

(b) **Face to Face Interview:** This is the traditional interview method in which job seekers meet the employers in person whether it is a fresh recruitment or the candidate is being considered for a higher post requiring some experience. The advantage of this is that the employer and the job seeker can get to know each other. The candidate also gets to assess the work environment. The questions generally pertain to the candidate's academic qualifications and experience, and are aimed at evaluating the strengths and weakness of the candidates. There may also be questions about the expected salary and other benefits. Before interview the candidates should gain as much knowledge about the company as possible, including their product or service range and financial positions.

(c) **Group interview or Group Discussions (GD):** These are part of the recruitment process for fresh candidates. These are conducted by most large companies for graduates who are all evaluated at one time. As they all come from similar educational background, it is easy to compare them and pick the best for further interviews. They may be given a topic for discussion or some exercises to solve in a group and the moderators observe how the candidates react with each other. Group interviews are helpful in assessing the candidates on the following parameters:
- Knowledge level,
- Communication skill,
- Listening Capacity,
- Leadership qualities,
- Team work,
- Reaction under stress.

Normally a group consists of 8 to 10 students. The normal time duration for any GD is about 10 to 15 minutes. For a GD relating to any particular topic, 2-3 minutes thinking time may be given. For GDs relating to case studies, 15 minutes time should be given for studying the case. The valuation of the participants is normally done by experts (usually professors from business schools). All these experts possess vast experience and expertise in their respective fields.

Tips for Effective Participation in GDs:
1. Give proper respect to the views expressed by the other speakers.
2. Be courteous while speaking.
3. Do not use very insulting, harsh or aggressive language.
4. Speak clearly and pleasantly to all the members of the group.
5. Stick to the main point of the GD. Do not speak irrelevant matter in the discussion.
7. Do not use loud and angry tone while speaking.
8. Do not interrupt other members of the group while they are speaking.
9. Learn to disagree politely.
10. Use positive body language while speaking.

Note for Participants in GD

There are no fixed rules for a GD held for candidate selection. The participants are generally eager to be the first to speak. The first speaker should mention the topic and state the issues. He should not give any opinion at this point. Later, the person may offer clarifications. This should be in the form of a statement, and not a question. Care should be taken to address the entire group. The candidates should maintain calm even if there are opposing arguments. The candidate should acknowledge this viewpoint using a meta language.

Situations may arise, when one's point of view has already been expressed by someone else. The best approach would be acknowledge the contribution of the other person and then add to it and thus become the centre of attention.

If there is interruption from someone else, the approach should be to request the person to allow you to complete your statement and offer the field to that person.

The group should move towards a consensus but due to the all round anxiety to make one's point, this may not happen at all. The idea is to exhibit some leadership qualities in steering the group while making one's contribution. A person with leadership qualities will look at the clock and when it is almost nearing closing time, will start summing up. If the group is too noisy, the facilitator may allot one minute to each candidate to sum up the discussion. This is an opportunity to put on one's best effort. Without criticising the group, one can sum up and give one's own views. The candidates should not stray from the topic.

> The candidates are evaluated on how they speak. Fluency, meaningful contribution, depth of knowledge on various topical issues, and leadership qualities are what the selectors would be looking for. Whatever personal views one may have, it is important to know both sides of the argument. One must be able to defend one's viewpoints convincingly and therefore the need for acquiring knowledge about a wide range of subjects.
>
> As preparation for a GD, candidates should select some topics, prepare and talk in front of the mirror, family members and friends to understand where they need to strengthen their arguments or presentation skills. They can also record their speech to know where they falter, and this will indicate the areas for further improvement. The voice quality, body language etc., can also be assessed during this process. The practice sessions can be used for ensuring that the thought process is well organised. One way to practice this is to write down the points and keep it in front of you. By periodically looking at it, you can arrange your thoughts mentally.

- **(d) Behavioural interview**: These are intended to gain insight into the personality traits and attitude of the candidates. The interviewer will attempt to predict their future behaviour based on their past experiences. The candidates are asked to explain their skills, experience, activities, hobbies, school projects, family life etc., as examples of their past behaviour. This interview shows the candidate's self-confidence, creativity, motivation, self-discipline, willingness to learn, train, work effectively in groups, and undertake travel etc.

- **(e) Stress interview**: A stress interview is aimed at creating discomfort for the candidate with the objective of testing his ability to function under such situations. It may take the form of making the candidate wait for an hour or more, asking questions continuously without giving the candidate time to think and answer, openly challenging his beliefs or judgement etc. The interviewer is not negatively inclined, but is performing a task.

- **(f) Panel interview**: In Panel interviews or Committee interviews candidates will meet several persons holding higher authority. This method is used when top positions are being filled. Questions may be asked by all the panel members. The candidate can expect any type of critical questions from them. He must establish eye contact with each member of the panel while answering the question.

  The Panel members may be:
  - The supervisor,
  - The manager,
  - The human resource officer,
  - The union representative,
  - Employees who are in the recruiting team.

(g) Telephonic interview: The main purpose of conducting a telephonic interview is to save the time and expenses for those who live very far from the location. A telephone interview is conducted in a professional manner like other interviews. The most important aspects for the candidate are his mastery over the subject, tone of voice and confidence in speech. The interviewer may ask all sorts of questions about the candidate's academic achievements, hobbies, interests, references etc. This method is adopted in the globalised scenario, where the company can hire suitable candidates from across the globe. Especially in the IT sector, many companies including Microsoft adopt this method to their advantage.

As a preparation, the candidate should do adequate research about the company. He should take the phone call in a quiet place. He should be comfortable and relaxed. He should have his resume in front of him to answer the questions arising from it. He should inform the referees ahead of the interview and keep their names and addresses ready, though the information is already given in the application. Right in the beginning, he should ask the interviewer's exact name with spelling and title as also postal address or email ID, so that a 'thank you' note could be sent. The advantage for the interviewer is the opportunity to judge the capability of the candidate to respond to an interview set up at a very short notice. Most companies use this method to eliminate those who fall short of the expectations and call only those who do well for the next level of interview. Even universities use this method for selecting students for professional courses.

(h) Campus Interviews: As a source for entry level recruitment, and depending on the nature of their requirement, the personnel department of various companies visit campuses towards the end of the academic year as an opportunity for screening the outgoing students. This screening process help the interviewer to form an impression regarding the candidates and their suitability for the organisation in terms of qualifications, personality, poise, attitude, ability to communicate etc. The candidate may be confident of his specific job-related skills and knowledge, whereas the interviewer may be more interested in the candidates' capability to understand the job requirements, whether his knowledge is based on realistic understanding of the job content and also his level of motivation. The interviewer may also want to know the other accomplishments of the candidates apart from the academics and how they value these accomplishments, and how they relate these experiences to their career interests. This campus selection gives the interviewer an opportunity to make a short list of candidates for a second round of more in-depth interview, prior to final selection of the candidate. However, if the interviewer is convinced of the suitability of a candidate at this stage, the job offer is made immediately.

Significance of Interviews as a Process of Selection:

As can be seen, interviews involve high cost and time, and require that the interviewer is highly skilled in this technique. There is a lot of preparation involved. Secondly, sometimes, even with the best interview techniques, the result may not be error-free. For instance, the candidate at the job interview may impress the interviewer by a super display of flashy communication skills, supreme self-confidence, random knowledge about the subject and excellent references. Hidden behind this façade may be a loser, an inefficient and ineffective employee, who is not capable of taking even routine decisions. Though such outcomes cannot be ruled out, by and large, interviews provide the best possible opportunity to understand and evaluate the prospective employees. The advantages far outweigh the occasional setbacks.

Advantages of the interview method

1. As has been discussed, for hiring and other HR related issues, interviews provide an excellent opportunity for both the parties to evaluate the situation. In research, it can prove to be a very good technique for getting necessary information about complex, emotionally laden subjects. Apart from the core subject of the interview, the interviewer is able to observe the body language of the interviewee and thus, is in a better position to judge the overall situation better.
2. It can be easily adapted to the ability of the person being interviewed.
3. It yields a good percentage of returns.
4. In marketing or social research, it yields perfect representation of the general population if the sample is selected judiciously, and the tools are properly prepared and vetted. The data collected by this method is likely to be more correct compared to the other methods that are used for this purpose.

Role of the Interviewer while setting up the Interview

Hiring a new employee is like asking an unknown individual to come to the hirer's home to spend some thirty years or more there. The new employee will be expected to join the team and show results. Hence, choosing an employee based on a person's or a panel's very brief interaction in a single interview has its risks. Thus, with the authority for hiring comes a lot of responsibility.

The interviewer starts the entire exercise with a purpose and in order to make it a success, he will have to approach it with adequate planning, preparation and execution. The interviewer has to take care of the following:

1. The interviewer must be very clear in his mind about the purpose of the interview. He should come fully prepared for the interview and does not waste either his own time or that of the candidate.
2. The interviewer must ensure that the conditions are suitable for a fair assessment of the candidates called in, so that the purpose of the interview is fulfilled.
3. The interviewer should welcome the candidate with courtesy and make him feel at ease.
4. The interviewer should not abuse his position by asking personal and irrelevant questions.

5. The interviewer should go through the bio-data of the candidate carefully before framing the questions.
6. The interviewer must conduct the interview in a carefully planned manner.
7. The interviewer should adopt a positive attitude towards the candidate while interviewing him and not intimidate him/her.

General Tips for the Interviewer
1. Use a quiet and comfortable place chosen by the interviewer. (In contrast, in the case of marketing research, the meeting place can be decided mutually.)
2. Put the interviewee at ease. (In marketing research, give a brief background of the company, and explain the objectives of the interview. Sometimes, the respondents are offered some monetary incentive for answering all the questions. This has to be stated clearly. If the conversation is being recorded, it should be told to the respondent.)
3. Be interested in the person as well as the purpose of the meeting.
4. Outline clearly the requirements of the job or purpose of the interview.
5. Explain fully the conditions of employment.
6. Tell about the benefits, development and promotion opportunities and so on. Do not make false or flashy promises just to attract a particular candidate.
7. Avoid questions which are sensitive to the feelings of the respondent, issues like gender, religion etc. For instance, it is generally reported that women are asked how they would balance both personal and career related activities. This would put the candidate on the defensive, unless she has been called for the interview only as a formality, without any serious intentions.
8. Encourage the applicant to ask questions. This will tell the interviewer how casual or professional the interviewee is. It will also tell the interviewer about the candidate's communication skills, and level of self-confidence.
9. Guide the interviewee through the interview.
10. Listen and let him/her talk freely.
11. Be natural, and use a conventional, neutral tone. Body language should indicate a pleasant demeanour.
12. Know when and how to close the interview.
13. Announce your decision, or explain your next step. The interviewee should be sure of what to expect and when.
14. Part with goodwill.

The Interviewer should avoid the following:
1. Keeping the applicant waiting.
2. Building false hopes.
3. Overselling the job.

4. Interrupting the candidate while he is talking.
5. Rush through the interview.
6. Repeat questions already answered on the application form. However, some interviewers may deliberately repeat a question just to make sure that the written communication is not random.
7. Use a phony excuse for rejecting him/her.
8. Use bad words and send him away with a bad taste in his mouth.

Role of Interviewee in the Interview Process

The interviewee at the job interview has a lot at stake. Hence it is necessary for him/her to prepare for the interview and go with a positive approach. The questions asked and the order in which they are asked may not match the method worked out by him/her. This should not disturb the candidate. He should realise that the interviewer is a representative of the organisation where he is seeking a placement and comes with a lot of experience and also the authority either to accept or reject the candidate. Along with that, the person (or interview panel) has a tremendous responsibility on his shoulders and so will be very observant throughout. The interviewer will constantly be on the lookout for warning signs or red flags, such as lies, lack of preparation, poor attitude, insincerity and so on.

The candidate should realise that an interview is a major part of a well-thought-out, consistent, employee selection process. This realisation should make the candidate take utmost care while preparing for the occasion. Some indicative list of things on which care should be exercised are:

1. **Exhibit appropriate Communication Behaviour:** Though the employers realise that the candidate would be anxious, they would not appreciate poor communication skills. Effective communication is critical for success in most jobs. In fact, it is one of the skills most frequently listed by employers in their job postings. If the candidates talk too little, the interviewers would not be able to learn enough about them to make a favourable hiring decision. Others may talk way too much, which would appear to be aggression. Eye contact should be maintained with the interviewer or the panel, whether the interviewer is a woman or a man. The candidates should remember that the person who conducts the interview could be a man, but the candidate may have to report to a lady. Hence, the candidates should develop good communication skills appropriate both for women and men.

2. **Respond Effectively to Follow-up Questions After The Initial Answers:** Most candidates prepare answers to questions pertaining to the resume very meticulously. They are very articulate about it. However, it is the follow-up questions that provide an opportunity for the interviewer to assess the candidate adequately. The proof of experience, appropriateness, and knowledge is demonstrated in these answers. They provide the specific details the organisation would be looking for in order to assess his or her competence in the area for which he is being evaluated. If the candidate

shows signs of panic or the answers are not up to expectations, it would give the impression that the candidate had got his resume prepared by someone else, even a professional agency and there is nothing beyond that.

3. **Plan to Stay Very long at the Job:** It is obvious that the organisation would be looking for a stable work force, as hiring and training involve costs. Clues about how long the candidate may work for the organisation can be obtained in answer to questions about their family, the location of close family members and the reasons for the candidate choosing the particular location. In case a candidate is over-qualified for the job offer, it is likely that he would consider this as only a stop-gap arrangement. Candidates provide all sorts of clues about their plans in their answers.

4. **Talk Appropriately About Former Employer:** It is likely that the candidate has had a bad experience at the previous job. It could be a stifling experience in a hierarchy driven organisation or the boss was irrational or biased. There could be many such reasons for job switching. The interviewer may ask leading questions, like - Why are you leaving your current job or employer? Why were you fired from your last job? Describe your relationship with your former boss. How did you handle your relationship with a difficult co-worker? The candidate should be diplomatic and not waste precious interview time dwelling on bad experiences.

Unfortunately, if the candidate falls into this trap and gives a negative picture, he is sending a powerful message. The interviewer may think that he would do the same with this organisation as well, perhaps even during his employment tenure. A reputed organisation would stay clear of such candidates.

Dress with Care and Dignity for The Interview: Neat appearance, appropriate accessories, cleanliness and good taste matter a lot. Dirty, unkempt, wrinkled, and inappropriate clothes are loud signals to skip this prospective employee.

General Tips for the interviewee

(A) Preparation Stage for the Interview:

1. At the preparation stage, the interviewee should collect all relevant information about the organisation in which he seeks a job.
2. The interviewee should try to visualise the sort of questions that may be asked keeping in mind the nature of the post and the qualifications required. This will help the candidate prepare for the interview.
3. The candidate should make sure that the dress and style are appropriate for the occasion. He should carry his resume, certificates and testimonials in a neat binder or file.
4. The interviewee must arrive ahead of the scheduled time of interview, so that he can be calm and composed. There are many factors to be considered, such as traffic situation, weather conditions etc., while determining when to start and what mode of transport to take, so that he reaches the venue ahead of time. The interview venue

may be many stories above and the lift could be out of order, requiring the candidate to use the staircase. This situation should also be factored in while setting the estimated time for departure for the interview. In short, all eventualities should be considered and nothing should be left to chance.

(B) At the Interview:
1. The candidate should not be nervous while entering the interview room. He should greet the interviewers with a polite smile and occupy the seat in a natural, composed manner. The body language, such as the way person sits (either on the edge of the seat or too relaxed), can convey a lot about the personality and attitude of the candidate. He should not do anything to indicate nervousness, such as playing with the papers in the hand, shaking the legs continuously, fiddling with the fingers, wiping the face unnecessarily etc.
2. The interviewee should pay minute attention to the surroundings during the conversation without interrupting the interviewer. This should be done so casually that the interviewer will not think that he is distracted.
3. The interviewee should answer all the questions in a clear and natural voice. The answers should be to the point. Unwanted or unsolicited information should not be given. It is not a friendly conversation but a professional meeting.
4. The interviewee should answer the questions with confidence. He should speak slowly and clearly, maintaining eye contact with the interviewer during the entire course of the interview. If the candidate is facing a panel, he should address all the members while answering, with special attention to the person who has asked the question. If the candidate does not have the answer for a question, it is better to acknowledge it instead of giving an irrelevant answer.
5. During the entire interview, the candidate should project a confident and positive image about himself.
6. At the end of the interview, when the interviewer thanks him, the candidate should get up, shake hands (if it is appropriate), thank the interviewer with a smile and leave.

4.3.2 Discipline Interview

These types of interviews are conducted to maintain discipline in the organisation. These interviews can be either to explain the standards of discipline followed in the organisation and answer the questions that arise out of them, or to chastise in case of repeated breach of discipline by an employee. The former type of interview is on a more positive note and there is no unpleasantness in the interaction. On the other hand, an interview to point out breach of disciplinary norms of the organisation can be stressful for both the parties. The disciplinary interview can be conducted by an individual or by a committee. Such an interview should be conducted behind closed doors, away from prying eyes of other employees.

The Interviewer will have prepared a dossier of all events of indiscipline by the employee, and the notices issued to him from time to time. He will have also studied similar cases in the organisation in the past. With this evidence, the interviewer confronts the erring employee and tries to find out the reasons for such indiscipline and why action should not be taken against him. The interviewer should limit his statement to the specific cases in front of him and not depend on any hearsay. He can read out from the file, but not repeat what others have said orally, as that can lead to perception of bias, favouritism etc. The objective here is to give a chance to the employee to explain his position and not to hurt him or antagonise him. Hence, even while asking for an explanation, the interviewer should be respectful. He can start by praising the employee for his overall contribution for the growth of the department or the company and then say that notwithstanding all that, it his duty to enquire into the complaints.

The interviewee or the erring employee called to face the interview should have his objective clear – whether he is going to continue with the organisation, or is preparing to quit. Either way, he should aim ay maintaining goodwill in the company. If he wants to continue, he will stay calm, listen to the charges and answer them clearly. He may also have his own justifications. He might be facing some personal problems, or some shortcomings or obstacles within the organisation which is forcing him to adopt devious methods. His problems may be totally unrelated, such as attitude of some colleagues, parking space for his vehicle etc., but may be disturbing him emotionally. He will have to put forth his arguments convincingly, apologise if called for and seek help if necessary. He should limit his arguments to the situation on hand and not rake up unconnected issues. Any indication of aggression, raising of voice or temper can ruin his chances of continuing in the organisation.

4.3.3 Appraisal Interviews

This type of interview is also called as assessment interview. It is conducted to evaluate the achievements of subordinates during a set period, to provide the basis for promotion, salary increase, production bonus etc. Such an interview is more in discussion form rather than question-answer form. It provides the organisation an opportunity to have an in-depth dialogue with the subordinates to not only assess their performance but also obtain a feedback about the overall work environment, working conditions, hiring policy etc. This information could be used to bring in policy changes aimed at improving the efficiency of the work place.

The following matters are usually discussed at these interviews:
(a) Objectives and targets set for the review period and achievement,
(b) Review of the organisation policy, work environment and conditions etc., which have contributed positively or negatively to the performance levels observed,
(c) Any lacuna by way of training, staff strength etc.,
(d) Any innovative intervention by the employee and the way it was received by the organisation,

(e) Targets for the ensuing period and the support expected by the employee,
(f) Suggestions for improving the performance of the individual, the department and the company,
(g) If the employee is expecting better rewards, the basis for such expectations etc.

These appraisal interviews can be successful only if there is an environment of mutual trust and both the interviewer and the interviewee adopt a positive and constructive attitude. The manager should not misuse the information, personal or about the work environment, provided by the subordinate, during the course of these discussions.

4.3.4 Exit Interviews

An exit interview is a kind of grievance interview. It is held when the organisation is severing relation with an employee. The exit of an employee can be voluntary on the part of the employer and employee, or involuntary, i.e., when an employee retires after attaining a certain age, when he cannot contribute to the organisation any more.

When the exit is involuntary, and the employee has been dismissed, the interview should be held in a pleasant atmosphere or not at all. If it is voluntary, i.e., the employee has decided to seek greener pastures, the organisation should aim at knowing the circumstances leading to the resignation. This interview can help the organisation obtain valuable feedback about its policies, based on which it can design improvements to gain employee loyalty. Hence, the manager in such interviews plays the role of a listener. Such interviews should be held after the farewell party is given by his colleagues. The chief advantage of this type of interview is that it enables the management to make a proper assessment of the real working of the organisation.

4.3.5 Promotion Interviews

Promotion Interview is conducted when the organisation is trying to fill vacancies internally. If there are a number of candidates for promotion, the organisation can use this to gauge the suitability of each contestant and the time and energy required to train him for the higher post. Even if there is only one candidate, a promotion interview can be held, in which case the interview is likely to be more informal. During the interview, the organisation obtains vital clues about the candidate, such as the nature of work he does, targets achieved, any innovative ideas he has implemented for improving the work environment or efficiency, the group or team activities he has participated in, customer responses about his work and working style, personal issues he is facing, his expectations from the organisation etc.

4.3.6 Qualitative Research Interview

In detailed marketing research or social research, apart from quantitative data collected through questionnaires, there is need for qualitative research to describe the situation and provide meanings of the central themes. The main objective here is to understand the meaning of what the interviewees say with reference to the prevailing context or circumstances.

One essential element of all interviews is the verbal interaction between the interviewer/s and the interviewee/s. Hitchcock (1989:79) stresses that *'central to the interview is the issue of asking questions and this is often achieved in qualitative research through conversational encounters.'* Consequently, it is important for the researchers to familiarise themselves with the questioning techniques before conducting interviews.

Aspects of Qualitative Research Interviews

- The interviewer can use any of the following tools:
    - (a) Structured questionnaires which the interviewee answers in a very short time,
    - (b) Some structured questions and some open ended questions, so that the interviewee gets some scope to give elaborate answers,
    - (c) Checklists, for in-depth interviews, with the help of which, the investigator frames his questions and has the freedom to change the order in which the points are addressed and also add new ones in response to answers obtained during the interview. This requires a very highly knowledgeable and experienced interviewer to be able to go back and forth and yet cover all the points.
- In-depth interviews are a far more personal form of research than structured questionnaires administered by investigators or sent by post or email.
- In the personal interview, unlike in mail surveys, the interviewer has the opportunity to probe or ask follow up questions.
- Interviews are time consuming and are resource intensive.
- The interviewer has to be well trained in how to ask questions and respond to any contingency.
- Sometimes, an organisation may call a group of respondents together for the purpose of understanding their views. This may be prior to launching a new product or entering a new market or if the organisation is going through a critical period, to arrive at solutions. Questions may relate to their perceptions, opinions, beliefs, and attitudes towards a product, service, concept, ad message and format, or packaging. The role of the manager is more as a listener, though from time-to-time, he may interrupt to ask questions or obtain clarifications. As the views are expressed and responded to by the others, the manager gets a quick view of the situation, which can help him/her take decisions. Such interviews can be extremely stimulating and productive.
- As there is a time limit set, the moderator or the host will first explain the concept/product/service features and answer questions about it. He will then throw the meeting open for discussion. He will have a list of questions to be asked. To be effective, focus group questions should be open-ended and move from the general to the specific. The members are allowed to discuss both the positive as well as negative aspects of the issue. Care will have to be taken to ensure that all the members participate and all the questions listed by him/her taken up for discussion.

It is essential to ensure that sub-groups are not formed. Generally, a questionnaire is filled up by the participants, right in the beginning, giving information about their background. Analysis of this would yield a profile of the participants. The entire session is recorded for later analysis. For instance, today washing machines are an essential item in most urban middle and affluent class households in India. However, about a couple of decades ago, it was a rare acquisition for these households. Hence, prior to the launch of this product, a marketing consulting company was hired by a manufacturer of white goods to conduct a series of focus group meetings to find out the attitude of the consumers towards this product. Most of the participants, except for the very affluent, or those who had seen such machines on their travels abroad, had many doubts: Where is the assured water and power supply? It will add to our chores. It is too expensive, etc.

- After the meetings, each meeting is summarised and analysed as soon as possible, so as not to miss out on important observations made by the participants. These summaries are then brought together for further analysis and preparation of a report.

4.4 Videoconference and Tele-meeting

Teleconferencing or Tele-meeting: The word 'tele' means distance. The word 'conference' means consultations and discussions. Teleconferencing works by connecting by telephone, two or more locations situated at a distance so that the participants can hear each other. They can exchange views on real time basis, without having to go through the time-consuming exchange of notes. In some cases, the topic details or questions can be sent by fax or email, so that the participants at the tele-meeting know what the meeting is intended for and the basic parameters for discussions.

Audio conferencing or teleconferencing is a two-way voice communication among multiple locations that takes place in real time. This works through the public telephone network. Each location will have microphones and speakers. The number of participants can vary from three to thirty.

Tele-meetings or conferences are very common in the modern day business world as they help executives geographically dispersed, to be in continuous contact, get the latest information and analysis, and take decisions without loss of time. It saves travelling time and cost to a great extent. Companies can effectively take advantage of the strengths of different countries, such as low real estate costs, labour costs etc., and improve their profitability. In a sense, this has revolutionized the way businesses organise their activities and improve their margins.

For instance, a client company based in California can discuss the information or recommendations given by a consulting company located in Mumbai and get the clarifications needed based on which he can take appropriate decisions.

Customers can convey the specifications for the products they need, call for quotations and follow-up on their orders from multiple locations.

Managers can get progress reports from their subordinates through teleconferences. This provides flexibility for employees to reside in places of their choice and work by tele-commuting.

Managers can plan and coordinate their visits to multiple locations across the globe by having all the local coordinators in the loop through tele-meetings.

Call centers in various cities in Asia provide service support to businesses located in various developed countries to overcome huge personnel and establishment costs in their own countries. This is a win-win situation for both the companies. Thus, a whole new paradigm of providing service through telephone has emerged. The customers get the same quality of service as if they are in the same location.

Many large corporations in the developed world have thus off-loaded software development, back-office service etc. The various ways in which companies take advantage of this facility is innumerable. They have been able to overcome the differences in time zones effectively to do their business conveniently and inexpensively.

Videoconferences: It is also called 'visual collaboration' and is a type of groupware. In its most basic form, it is the transmission of speech and images back and forth between two or more persons located in different places. The components required at each end are, cameras to capture and send video from one location to another, microphones and speakers, computer systems, digital telephone systems and network connections. The sound and images are compressed, digitized and transmitted by using codec (compressor/decompressor) facility. Apart from sound and image, allied videoconferencing technologies can be used to share documents and display information on whiteboards.

Videoconferencing differs from videophone calls in that it is designed to serve a conference or participants at multiple locations rather than individuals. The history of the developments in videoconferencing is interesting. In the 1980s digital telephony transmission networks became possible, such as with ISDN networks. During this time, there was also research into other forms of digital video and audio communication. The first dedicated systems started to appear in the market as ISDN networks were expanding throughout the world. One of the first commercial videoconferencing systems sold to companies came from PictureTel Corp.

Computers became more powerful and CODEC application was developed during this period. Finally, in the 1990s, IP (Internet Protocol) based videoconferencing became possible and more efficient video compression technologies were developed, permitting desktop, or personal computer (PC)-based videoconferencing.

This technology was used commercially for the first time by AT&T Corporation in the early 1970s. As reported earlier, the development of this technology got impetus from improvements in computer processors and broadband telecommunication services in the late 1990s. Since then, this technology has found application in a number of ways in businesses, education, medicine and media.

High definition resolution has now become a standard feature, offered by major suppliers of videoconferencing equipment. Recent technological developments have extended the capabilities of video conferencing systems beyond the boardroom. Video conferencing system manufacturers have begun providing mobile applications as well. As a result, videoconferencing can now be used, independent of location, with **hand-held mobile devices** that combine the use of video, audio and on-screen drawing capabilities broadcast in real-time over secure networks. Thus, video collaboration has moved into the zone of mobile coordination. This facility allows people in previously unreachable locations, such as on an off-shore oil rig, to view and discuss issues with colleagues thousands of miles away.

Videoconference can be between two or more points. The participants can hear one another all the time, and the speaker takes control through a voice-activated switch.

Features of videoconferencing
1. Large group videoconferencing facilities are non-portable, large, more expensive devices used for large rooms and auditoriums. They have advanced features such as voice-activated camera controls, echo cancellation etc.
2. Small group videoconferencing facilities are non-portable or portable, smaller, less expensive devices used for small meeting rooms.
3. Individual videoconferencing systems are usually portable devices, meant for single users, have fixed cameras, microphones and loudspeakers integrated into the console.

Benefits of videoconferencing
- Improved work quality.
- Increase in productivity.
- Reduction in travel time and costs.
- It reduces frequency of travel by executives and managers, and thus contributes to reduction in carbon emissions and has environmental advantages.
- Critical meetings can be convened in very less time.
- More number of managers from various locations can be involved in information sharing and decision process.
- Improves communication among individual employees and teams.
- In the field of education, students can sit in a class room like set-up and learn from experts from various locations.
- For training purposes, this can be used to cover more number of staff without increasing training expenditure. Guest speakers can be brought in at minimum cost and integrated into the course. By making it interactive, the trainers can put forth their questions and get clarifications. The trainers get instant feedback.
- Medical practice has benefited greatly from telemedicine, which is a software based programme to promote interaction between patients and experts. The patients can also get real time information about availability of required patient treatment and care facilities closest to their locations.

Limitations of Videoconferencing

Mass adoption and use of videoconferencing is still relatively low, and is used mostly by corporate. The limitations of videoconferencing are:

- Complexity of systems. Most users are not technical and want a simple interface. Even simple problems with the hardware systems in a remote centre can be perceived as failure, or unreliability. Successful systems require dedicated support teams who can pro-actively support and provide fast assistance when required.
- Not all systems can readily be interconnected. Popular software solutions cannot easily connect to hardware systems. Some systems use different standards, features and qualities which can require additional configuration when connecting to dissimilar systems.
- Sometimes the cameras do not catch the correct angle to show eye contact of the current speaker, which may be misinterpreted by the audience. Technological developments have been able to address this to a great extent.
- Another psychological angle is that the participants may be uncomfortable facing a camera. However, people get used to this situation gradually.
- Some amount of time lag may be observed, with the result that there is no coordination between voice and images. Images may appear to be following the voice.
- The technology is fairly well established, but it should be available at all the locations.
- High quality telepresence is more expensive than teleconferencing, as the locations require sound-proof studios and expensive video cameras with all the controls. This is overcome by renting videoconferencing studios. Many event managing companies arrange for videoconference equipped meeting rooms with all technical support if needed.
- The success of videoconferences depends on the availability of uninterrupted power supply and bandwidth service at all the points. If the network infrastructure is not consistent, the participants will not be able to tune in. This is the major bottleneck in most developing countries. However, as Internet speeds increase higher quality and high definition video conferencing will become more readily available. With mobile telephones equipped with this facility, in limited applications, these limitations can be overcome to a great extent.

Impact of Videoconferencing

- **General public**: With computers and Internet connectivity becoming affordable and freeware applications like chat etc. available, people have started using this in their day-to-day interactions as well.
- **Governance**: Many state governments in India have videoconferencing facilities at the district levels, so that their activities can be coordinated by the state secretariat.

Similarly, media centre have this facility and so can organise panel interviews from multiple locations. This opens up opportunities for the government and other parties to connect to the public on a continuous basis.

- **Education:** Videoconferencing provides students with the opportunity to learn by participating in two-way communication forums. Teachers and lecturers worldwide can be brought to remote or otherwise isolated educational facilities. It also brings together students from diverse communities and backgrounds. They can interact and learn about one another, although language barriers will still pose limitations. They can have interviews with potential employers conveniently. Schools with multiple campuses can collaborate and share expert teachers. Researchers collaborating with colleagues at other institutions can interact on a regular basis. They can answer questions about grant proposals from funding agencies or review committees.

- **Health:** Terms like telemedicine and telenursing are no more strange to people any more. Transmission of diagnostic examination reports and images, consulting with experts at remote locations etc., can bring quality healthcare to even the remotest parts of the country. Recent developments in videoconferencing on mobile handsets has made healthcare accessible to even the most remote areas.

- **Business:** Videoconferencing enables individuals in distant locations to participate in meetings on short notice, with significant savings in time and money. Technology such as voice over internet protocol (VoIP) can be used along with desktop videoconferencing to enable low-cost face-to-face business meetings without leaving the desk, especially for businesses with widespread offices. The technology is also used to support employees who opt to work from home.

    Online networking websites help businesses form profitable relationships quickly and efficiently without leaving their place of work. This has been used effectively by banks to connect busy banking professionals with customers in various locations using video banking technology.

    Videoconferencing on hand-held mobile devices – mobile collaboration, is being used in industries such as manufacturing, energy, healthcare, insurance, government, public safety etc. Companies can connect to locations previously unreachable, such as a manufacturing plant floor a continent away.

- **Media relations:** The concept of press videoconferencing was developed in October 2007 by the PanAfrican Press Association (APPA), a Paris France based NGO, to allow African journalists to participate in international press conferences on important issues like developmental and good governance. Such meetings help journalists participate in press conferences in far off locations with the help of a computer connected to the Internet in order to ask their questions to the speaker. Since then, all TV channels use this to have live news and panel interactions, sporting commentaries with comments from experts in remote places, entertainment etc.

- **Web Teleconferences**: This works on Internet as its communication backbone and web browser as the participant interface. Interception and processing of their requirements is done by the web servers. In technology savvy companies, members use this method to conduct their live meetings and training programmes. Many universities conduct *webinars* or seminars on the internet, which can be downloaded and the students can absorb the content at their leisure. Each participant sits at his location with his computer connected to the others' through a web-based application, which can be downloaded from the Internet or through a link or invitation distributed by the convener by email. The participants enter the meeting and share their screens, so that the other members can look at the work being done, make suggestions, and even edit passages live on line. This is a very convenient way to share technical drawings, software codes, presentations etc. to pass on information and get feedback and suggestions.

Points to Remember

- *"An interview is a formal meeting in which a person or persons question, consult or evaluate another person or persons."* **– Murphy and Peak**
- An interview reveals the views, ideas and attitudes of the person being interviewed as well as the skills of the interviewer. It is a medium of two-way communication between people. There are various purposes of interviews.
- According to **E. C. Eyre**, *"an interview is a face-to-face verbal exchange which endeavours to discover as much information as possible in the least amount of time about some relevant matter".*
- **Job Interview/Placement Interview:**
    1. The Screening Interview
    2. Face to Face Interview
    3. Group interview or Group Discussions (GD)
    4. Behavioural interview
    5. Stress interview
    6. Panel interview
    7. Telephonic interview
    8. Campus Interviews
- **Role of Interviewee in the Interview Process:**
    1. Exhibit appropriate Communication Behaviour:
    2. Respond Effectively to Follow-up Questions After The Initial Answers:
    3. Plan to Stay Very long at the Job:
    4. Talk Appropriately About Former Employer:

- **Appraisal Interviews:**
    1. Objectives and targets set for the review period and achievement,
    2. Review of the organisation policy, work environment and conditions etc., which have contributed positively or negatively to the performance levels observed,
    3. Any lacuna by way of training, staff strength etc.,
    4. Any innovative intervention by the employee and the way it was received by the organisation,
    5. Targets for the ensuing period and the support expected by the employee,
    6. Suggestions for improving the performance of the individual, the department and the company,
    7. If the employee is expecting better rewards, the basis for such expectations etc.
- **Videoconference and Tele-meeting:**

  Teleconferencing or Tele-meeting:
    - The word 'tele' means distance. The word 'conference' means consultations and discussions. Teleconferencing works by connecting by telephone, two or more locations situated at a distance so that the participants can hear each other. They can exchange views on real time basis, without having to go through the time-consuming exchange of notes. In some cases, the topic details or questions can be sent by fax or email, so that the participants at the tele-meeting know what the meeting is intended for and the basic parameters for discussions.
    - Audio conferencing or teleconferencing is a two-way voice communication among multiple locations that takes place in real time. This works through the public telephone network. Each location will have microphones and speakers. The number of participants can vary from three to thirty.

  Features of videoconferencing
    - Large group videoconferencing facilities are non-portable, large, more expensive devices used for large rooms and auditoriums. They have advanced features such as voice-activated camera controls, echo cancellation etc.
    - Small group videoconferencing facilities are non-portable or portable, smaller, less expensive devices used for small meeting rooms.
- **Benefits of videoconferencing**
    - Improved work quality.
    - Increase in productivity.
    - Reduction in travel time and costs.
    - It reduces frequency of travel by executives and managers, and thus contributes to reduction in carbon emissions and has environmental advantages.
    - Critical meetings can be convened in very less time.
    - More number of managers from various locations can be involved in information sharing and decision process.
    - Improves communication among individual employees and teams.

Questions for Discussion

1. What is an interview? State its objectives.
2. Explain the various aspects of group discussions.
3. State the process of conducting (a) an exit interview and (b) discipline interview.
4. Write short notes on:
   (a) Role of the interviewer and interviewee in the interview process
   (b) Campus interviews and their significance in employee recruitment process.
   (c) Appraisal interviews
   (d) Exit interview.

Chapter 5...

Report Writing

Contents ...

5.1 Introduction
5.2 Objectives of a Report
5.3 Types of Business Reports
5.4 Report Planning
5.5 Developing an Outline, Nature of Headings, Ordering Points, Logical Sequencing, Graphs, Charts, Executive Summary, List of Illustrations
- Points to Remember
- Questions for Discussion

Learning Objectives ...

➤ To get acquainted with Report Writing and its objectives
➤ To be aware of the types of report and planning a report

5.1 Introduction

Reports are a routine way of communicating in a variety of professions and academic disciplines. Many scientists write reports about their observations in the laboratories and research findings. Social scientists are called upon to give field reports and research reports as status reports with or without analysis and suggestions. In their day-to-day activities, business managers are required to write a range of formal and informal reports. Each type of report has its own conventions regarding data analysis and presentation, and its own customary ways of communicating.

A business report is a standard form of business communication that combines qualitative and quantitative information presented in a logical manner to assist the organisation to take appropriate business decisions. Some may have actual solutions to a problem, others may just record past business information that can be used for trend analysis and future business planning. The more traditional business reports, such as business plans serve to communicate the business concept, business management model, commercial objectives, operational procedures and the perceived viability of certain operations. It is an essential part of the critical corporate documentation exercise in its pursuit of success.

Business reports present opinions based on information collected in a systematic manner, and presented to appropriate audiences. They can be industry related or customised by individual companies to serve their own decision making process. They can be prepared as an in-house exercise or the organisation may commission an expert or a third party consulting firm to undertake the research.

5.2 Objectives of a Report

Business reports are required for getting information and arriving at decisions by business organisations, business associations, chambers of commerce and industry, non-government organisations and the government. Depending on the objectives and scope, business reports could be as short as a couple of pages or may run into hundreds of pages. (The author of this book, during her tenure with a consulting firm, has prepared a number of lengthy reports, mostly pertaining to development plans for districts or groups of districts, covering all aspects of area development. All such studies were commissioned by concerned government departments or financial institutions. However, her marketing research reports were relatively much shorter.)

Business reports allow you to present pertinent facts, figures and information for analysis. This allows companies to create business plans and budgets, and make decisions pertaining to marketing and advertising, purchasing and human resources. It is important to format information in a business report so it can be read quickly and assimilated easily.

The specific objectives of research studies to support business decisions vary from organisation to organisation and the circumstances that warranted the research. These research projects involve extensive study of secondary data from various sources as well as primary data or information collected from the field. Some objectives are:
- To assess business performance, provide a status check, and monitor progress towards the strategic goals of the business.
- To use statistics, such as key performance indicators and financial ratios in order to prepare key business matrix.
- To summarise key business indicators and present them in the form of charts and graphs, easy-to-read grids and spreadsheets, documents, and in interactive sessions.
- To recommend future course of action for the organisation.
- They are needed by industry associations for providing information to businesses, for lobbying etc.

5.3 Types of Business Reports

Business reports can be **formal or informal** depending on the extent of formality, or the manner in which they are expected or received by the superiors or peers in the organisation. Formal reports are generally communicated in writing through notes, memos, letters etc. Informal communication can be oral or written. They can also be sent in hard copy form by hand, or as a soft copy via emails.

According to **function** they serve, reports may be classified as:
- Informational reports.
- Analytical reports
- Research reports.

They can further be classified as (i) routine reports and (ii) special reports.

According to **extent of formality** reports may be classified as:
- Statutory reports.
- Non statutory or voluntary reports.

There is no definitive number of business reports that can be produced in an organisation. Each business has its own specific requirements and practices, requiring different types of reports. Certain types of reports are common to most businesses, such as cash-flow reports, marketing reports, development reports and progress reports. However, reports required by the law of the land take overall precedence. The different types of reports are discussed below.

- **Informational reports:** They convey only the information (facts, data, results etc.) with no commentary. Whatever is gathered is reported without giving any thing by way of either explanation or any suggestion. For instance, minutes of meetings convey only the events and conversations of a meeting without any comments from the author.

  Generally informative reports are of routine nature specified according to time frames, such as weekly, monthly, quarterly or annually, or they may be for a particular situation. Sometimes they may fall under statutory routine category. The Registrar of Companies may ask for share allotment details within a stipulated period, say at the end of each financial year. This is nothing but an informational report, routine and statutory in nature. The methodology to be followed includes:

  (a) Understanding the subject, terms of reference and the end-time,
  (b) Brainstorming about the extent of the information to be provided in the report, sources of information, and personnel hours required,
  (c) Prepare a plan of action for collecting and collating the data and allocate persons and time for each activity,
  (d) Prepare the draft report,
  (e) Check for gaps and errors,
  (f) Refine, finalise and submit.

  Good reports are documents that are accurate, objective and complete.

- **Analytical reports:** These reports convey information gathered by the author along with his explanations, analysis or interpretations. For example, when a company is trying to solve a problem or make a decision, an analytical report might be necessary.

For example, a quarterly sales analysis might give a detailed account of corporate initiatives like advertisements, sales promotion etc., sales achieved, expenditures and profit and loss. It could include analysis of successful initiatives as well as the not-so-successful endeavours. The marketing department would base their further decisions on the conclusions derived from these reports.

A company chairman may ask for a report on competitors' activities or falling trends in sale in a particular area. He will in this case be naturally interested in knowing all the details including the opinion of the investigator or the author. Similarly, progress reports called for by department heads or project team leaders are usually analytical, covering not only what has taken place but also the writer's analysis of the factors contributing to the situation.

Typically they contain the narration of facts, collected data and information which is appropriately classified and tabulated, along with explanatory notes followed by the interpretations and conclusions arrived at. The author can add his own suggestions or recommendations.

- **Research reports:** These reports are based on some research work conducted by either an individual or a group of individuals on a given problem. The reports can be on scientific experiments or surveys to understand broad societal issues, including customer surveys, study of certain population segments and so on.

  When executives make decisions about new products and services, new markets, increasing staff strength or planning layoffs, they might require research reports. In-house research specialists or outside teams are given the issue and asked to create a report that provides all details about the topic, including relevant facts and statistics. The report typically offers the organisation the complete set of facts and figures analysed systematically, along with the conclusions and suggestions by the research team. The suggestions are all backed up by appropriate facts and figures.

  For instance, an oil company might sponsor an experiment to be conducted by its research division to find some substitute for petrol. The report then will be submitted by the research division detailing its findings and offering their own suggestions to the chairman of the company. Such a report will include the conclusions at which the research division has arrived along with application areas for the new product, economic and marketing feasibility etc. All details asked for in the terms of reference would be provided in the report.

  Similarly, a survey of a community to assess the affordability of piped water connection will cover the socio-economic background of the community, the price at which such a service can be provided and the capacity and willingness of the community to pay.

- **Statutory reports:** These in the nature of **compliance reports** are to be presented according to the requirements of a particular law or a rule or a custom which has over a period, become a rule. As such, correctness or accuracy of information contained in the report is of paramount importance. For instance, according to Company Law, every year, an audited report has to be submitted to the Registrar of Companies. This is a legal requirement. Similarly, a company has to submit reports to competent authorities, specified periodic reports regarding accidents in the company and compensation paid to the workers. These reports are generally prepared in the prescribed form as prescribed by the rules. In a dynamic society, many customs evolve into law over a period of time. For instance, by and large, all over the world, observance of festivals and memorial days has got official sanction and workers get paid holidays and the list of paid holidays is a statutory requirement.

- **Non statutory reports:** These reports are not in the nature of legal requirements or rules, but the organisation may want them for the following purposes: (i) for the administrative and other conveniences, (ii) for taking decision regarding a particular issue, (iii) formulating organisation's policies, (iv) for projecting the future or (v) for ensuring efficient and smooth functioning so that the objectives of the organisation are achieved with assured success.

- **Routine reports:** These reports are required to be prepared and submitted periodically on matters required by the organisation for its day-to-day functioning. For instance, the production department may call for progress reports at the end of each shift, number of pieces completed, work in progress, any disruptions etc. from the different shops where its activities are undertaken, so as to identify bottlenecks and ensure continuous supply of the product into the market. Similarly, the quality assurance department can be asked to prepare a daily report of the number of pieces checked from each shift, and percentage and nature of defects, so that deficiencies can be identified and the source of deviation pinpointed. The main objectives of routine reports are to let the management know the status in each department and measures that can be taken to remove bottlenecks if any. Routine reports are generally brief and help in taking corrective measures without much loss of time. Generally, formats are prepared for such reporting so that the information is standardised and easy for the supervisor to analyse and call for explanations.

- **Special reports:** These reports are more **investigative in nature**, targeted at non-recurring events, and required to deal with special situations. These special situations may be accidental or planned.

    For instance, the company plans to enter the market with a new product. For planning the launch and creating the brand identity, the organisation may commission a detailed market survey and also specify the terms of reference. This is a case of a planned special report.

    Examples of planned special reports are many, such as report after a special conference, training programme or event, tour report by employees etc. Such events do not have a specific pattern of occurrence. These reports are brief and limited in coverage. Such reports may have a predesigned format or may be open-ended. They are generally informative in nature, but depending on the situation, they can contain suggestions as well.

On the other hand, if there is an accidental leak of toxic gas from a pipe, the organisation may call for a detailed report about the time and nature of the accident, persons responsible for maintenance of the pipe lines and storage equipment, number of persons who suffered consequences, medical aid obtained at the spot, extent of damage to the property, down time estimated etc. These reports contain not only facts and details but they may contain comments, explanations and suggestion as well.

5.4 Report Planning

Since reports are a key to the success of any business, they should be carefully planned, organised, written and presented. A lot of planning should go into the actual writing of a report.

Reports are written after the problem is analysed and a solution to the problem has been found. The problem may be of a day-to-day nature, or, it may be a special one. In any case, the problem is the single fundamental issue to be addressed in the report. This and the time frame for the study should be clearly determined right at the beginning. Even if it is an in-house report, the manager should write down the various aspects of the study discussed and get the approval of the sanctioning authority. This becomes the starting point, runs through data collection and analysis and provides the necessary support to the author in case there is a dispute later about the coverage or time factor.

The report may be read by several people in the receiving organisation apart from the person sanctioning it. In order for the readers to understand why the report has been prepared, the writer has to have a purpose theme that runs through the report.

It should be remembered that the client party, whether in-house or outside, will all the time be trying to understand the problem in all its aspects. Hence the researcher has to anticipate the points that are likely to be raised at the time of data collection, analysis and report preparation.

A business report should be logically organised, clear, concise and easy to follow. The most important aspect is to check if all the issues covered in the terms of reference are adequately addressed. The type of the report determines the extent of information to be included as well as the analysis and conclusions. If it is an informative report, no analysis or conclusions are called for, nor do they require an executive summary. On the other hand, an analytical or research report will be elaborate and the manager will have to plan the contents accordingly.

The following considerations are important in this respect:
- **Purpose**: While planning the report, use the terms of reference as the thread that guides the entire report. Any deviation from that will have to be justified. In such cases, it is better to review the terms of reference with the client party before commencing the study, so that you are firm grounds.
- **Type of report and audience:** The first question to be asked before gathering information and writing the report, is regarding the type of report that is required and the audience it is intended for. Some reports may require a standard format to allow period-by-period comparisons. Others may require an elaborate presentation of data with analysis and interpretation.
- The **method for collecting relevant data** from various sources should be well thought out and followed impeccably.
- **Plan and collect all necessary information**, and organise them, so as to identify any gaps, which need to be covered.
- **Evaluation of data**: The raw data should be evaluated for its usefulness and organised in a form that is meaningful to understand.
- **Data analysis**: Tables, charts, graphs and summaries should be used to do this. Plan the methodology for data analysis, such as statistical formulae to be used, correlations to be observed, whether to present the analysis as statements, graphs etc.
- Once the information has been checked for its validity and reliability, it must be analysed, **interpreted and conclusions** drawn. Correct interpretation of the data is needed for the success of the report. Analyse the information, cover the gaps and complete the analysis.
- Study the findings, arrive at the conclusions and determine the solution to the problem being investigated.
- Sound conclusions cannot be made if the interpretation of the data is faulty. A common mistake made in the interpretation of data is the tendency of the researcher to use subjective judgements, instead of objective reasoning based on facts.
- The **conclusions** should stem from the analysed data, not from hearsay, analysis given in some other book or magazine or from the fertile imagination of the author.
- List out the **recommendations** based on the findings. Remember, they should be well considered, doable things, based on the facts, and not fancy items thrown in. The client party should not be under-estimated. Any report which requires a lot of back and forth discussions and rework diminishes the credibility of the manager who has prepared it.
- *Remember that a well written report that contains a bad solution to the problem is worse than a badly written report that contains a good answer.*

- Determine the **report format**. Again, the terms of reference should guide you in determining this. At this stage, decide the information and analysis to be presented in the report and that which can be presented as supporting data.
- The **flow of thought** should be logical and easy to follow.
- Be **flexible** to take account of random factors that affect business performance, even if it is not part of the terms of reference, but observed significantly during data collection.

Keeping all the above points in view, the manager writing the report should plan the report meticulously.

5.5 Developing an outline, Nature of Headings, Ordering of Points, Logical Sequencing, Graphs, Charts, Executive Summary, List of Illustrations

In their day-to-day work, managers are required to present reports on a regular basis. They may be status reports submitted on a regular basis, with a fixed, standard format or detailed reports, taking months to compile and prepare. There is no one universal format for writing a detailed business report. **Each report is unique and hence, the approach, the details included and presentation method are also unique**. Though a business report is based on systematic research and analysis, writing a report is a skill, which a manager can acquire from experience.

It should be remembered that the credibility of the author and the department or organisation he represents is at stake. If the customer rejects a report, it could be because: (1) The author has not planned data collection properly or is lacking in it, and (b) He does not have the skill to plan the report by organising its content and has poor writing skills. Once a report is rejected by the client, it becomes very difficult to rebuild credibility and trust.

The author should begin by preparing an outline of the report he is going to write. This should reflect the logic of the author and the flow of his thought and ideas. The time taken for this is well worth it, as it will help him put the data and analysis in a proper sequence. For instance, in a marketing research report, he will have to decide whether he would like to discuss the supply situation and competitors' activities before the demand analysis or after. With the help of the report outline, he will be able to sift the data as (1) crucial for conveying the main theme and hence forms part of the main report or (2) relevant but supporting the main theme. And hence can be presented as annexure.

A broad description of how a business report could be organised is presented below:

(A) Title Section: In a short report this may simply be the front cover, title of the report and the name of the author or consulting company presenting it. In a long one it could also include Terms of Reference, Table of Contents and so on. This section helps the reader establish an instant connection with the information in subsequent sections.

1. The **covering page** should be the starting point, where the author gives the name of the organisation undertaking the research and the organisation that has commissioned it. It should also indicate the topic covered and the period during which the study was conducted.
2. This is followed by a **table of contents**, which will inform the reader what to look for and in which page. It should also provide a list of annexures, numbered accordingly.

(B) An Executive Summary: This is the section that most of the senior personnel, who do not have enough time to go through the whole report, will read through. This gives an overview of the report along with the conclusions and recommendations. Give a clear, precise and very concise account of the main points, main conclusions and main recommendations. Use bullets and numbered lists to highlight important points.

As this is targeted at the extremely busy corporate heads, it should be very short, a few percent of the total length of the report. Extra care has to be taken to make it totally error-free. As these busy executives may not have the time to read anything else, the executive summary should almost be a stand-alone document. All the detailed information and analysis should be presented in the main report, which would be studied and analysed by other managers.

The executive summary should be free from jargon so that anyone can understand it and get the main points. It is obvious that it is written after all the other sections have been completed. However, the author should desist from the temptation of taking short cuts by copying and pasting certain sections of the main report. The pitfall in this is that the points may be disjointed and the report will lack the flow.

(C) Introduction: This is the first part of the main report. It contains the following information:
1. Description of the problem or issue being addressed, background to the organisation's perspective and why the report is important to the readers.
2. Detailed terms of reference,
3. Table of Contents which shows how the detailed content is arranged.
4. Research methodology adopted, experts in the field contacted and the coverage for primary data collection, geographically and also the number of competitors and other organisations contacted, with justifications. This would include the distribution network, suppliers of raw materials, parts and sub-assemblies, suppliers of utilities such as power, fuel, water supply etc., government departments which give licences, permissions and so on. (The detailed list of organisations contacted may be presented as an additional note at the end of the report.)
5. The organisation of the report and the issues addressed in each chapter. This is optional and since there is a Table of Contents, this may be redundant.

(D) Main Body: This is the heart of your report, and contains the information and facts collected during the study. Depending on the various aspects of the problem, it will have many chapters or sub-sections each with its own title/subtitle. This is unique to each report and will describe what the researcher has discovered about 'the problem' from various sources of information.

These sections are most likely to be read by experts so you can use some appropriate jargon but explain each special term as you introduce it.

The first chapter should contain an introduction to the study or the problem addressed, the hypothesis, the terms of reference, the industry/geographical coverage for data collection, and the method used for data collection and analysis. Broadly, information may be gathered using secondary research methods, such as books, magazines, newspapers, internet and other available sources, or through primary research methods, such as surveys that provide first hand information.

The subsequent chapters or sections put together the facts gathered and the analysis, followed by the conclusions arrived at. It should close with a set of recommendations if warranted.

Arrange the information logically, normally putting things in order of priority, the most important appearing first. For instance, in a marketing research report, the first chapter would give details regarding existing supply analysis and the total market size, with sub-sections on each of the competitors and their strategies, and their share in the market pie. This includes the client party sponsoring the research as well if the organisation is already in the market. The next chapter would be on demand assessment and the extent of unmet or latent demand. The expectations from the customers on aspects such as quality, price, availability etc., could be presented in a separate chapter. This could be followed by an analysis and explanation of the significance of your findings.

It is a good idea to insert **separators** at the beginning of each section or chapter. These could be of different colours with or without a flag. This helps the reader to identify the chapters and the report looks professional.

(E) Nature of Headings: The headings to various sections and chapters should give an insight into what it contains. Hence, an appropriate way of giving headings and sub-headings should be determined. This includes the numbering scheme, font size and style. Before finalising, the author should go through the report to check that there is continuity in the numbering scheme adopted.

(F) Logical Sequencing: The entire effort in preparing the report is ensuring that the report is clear and easy to follow. That is the reason why the report format has to be drawn out carefully, such that the subject matter flows from chapter to chapter and from paragraph to paragraph. The reader should not have to go back and forth in the report to make sense out of it. He will then lose continuity and get confused. For instance, while presenting the data analysis, the author should not mix up conclusions or suggestions. What is observed or studied is fact and should be presented as such in a distinguishable form, and what is interpreted should be presented separately. Everything has to have a place in the report that makes it readable. Nothing should be missing either. While planning the report, the author should make sure that there are no loose ends, or scope for the recipient to ask further questions. The report contents should be self-explanatory.

(G) Ordering of Points: Within a chapter or section, if the data is presented as covering well-defined points, they should be presented with bullet points or be numbered. The thumb rule is: if the points are sequential with a hierarchy of importance, a numbering system that is different from that used for headings and sub-headings, should be adopted. If not, bullets can be used. Avoid using fancy bullets which distract the readers.

(H) Illustrations, Graphs, Charts: It goes without saying that visuals convey a lot of meaning within the shortest possible time. The readers get to understand the figures if presented in the form of graph.

Thus, one important factor to be considered while writing the main body of a business report is data tabulation. Plan the tabulation formats and types of graphs (pie charts, graphs etc.) Presenting your data in lists or tables can help in readily understanding the report. Data tabulation makes the report look professional and neat. So, include necessary lists or tables and graphs in your report wherever possible.

The author should determine the number of such graphic presentations. The tables, charts and graphs should have an appropriate title which tells the reader what to expect. Each column/row in a table should have a heading. Similarly, the graphs and charts should indicate what they refer to. The unit of measurement should be mentioned clearly (₹ million or sq.km or ha (hectare) etc. If there is a legend, it should be clear. Each chart or graph should be numbered and the number should be mentioned at appropriate sections of the text, so that the reader can relate the figures and the text easily.

Make sure you use neutral colours for making the tables. Do not forget to give numbers for the tables, diagrams and charts, with appropriate reference in the text. No table, chart or diagram should be hanging free.

Determine if all the charts and graphs should form an integral part of the text or should be clubbed together and presented separately at the end of the report, with an appropriate separator. If there are too many charts and graphs, it would be a good idea to present them all at the end of the report. This way, the reader does not lose the flow of ideas in the text. This happens when a lot of demographic details are to be presented along with the core parameters of analysis as cross tabulation.

(I) Conclusions: The logical conclusions of your investigation regarding the problem or issue would be presented in this section. This section is very important as it will highlight the scope for the organisation and offer options for the way forward. Many people will read this section first. If important sections of the discussion from the main body are to be used here as the basis for the conclusions, they should be referred to in brief.

(J) Recommendations: The recommendations should be clear and not vague. They should stem from the facts and analysis in the report and not be picked up from some other report or analysis. They should be implementable and firmly anchored in the analysis of data collected, stated in an order of priority. If it is a new project and your findings indicate that it is not feasible, it should be stated so. The researcher should show his commitment to the project as the decisions of the client party would be based on this.

(K) Annexure: All supporting data or heavy details should be presented with appropriate references. These include information that only specialists are likely to read. As a general rule, details that are essential in the main report are retained there, but details which merely support the argument should not clutter the main report. They should be included as appendices. This includes references to secondary sources of data, tools used for data collection, list of organisations and individuals contacted with addresses and contact details etc. All these should have appropriate headings, should be numbered and referred to in the main body.

(L) Review and Proof-reading: While planning the report, allow some time for checking the report from all angles, such as flow of ideas, headings, references to graphs and charts, use of precise words, grammar and spelling. The objective is to make your report error-free and acceptable.

Tips for writing a business report:

1. In in-house reporting, following a standard business report format is what senior level managers and busy businessmen would look for, as they can be sure what to look for and where.

2. Follow the generally accepted format for a report: Executive Summary, Introduction, Main Body presented in well demarcated points or sections, Conclusions, Recommendations and Appendices.

3. Make sure you have all the information required, and no aspect of the problem is unattended. Ultimately, you will have to defend the report and so, make sure all the information collected is authentic.

4. Organise your information in each section in a logical fashion with the reader in mind, usually putting things in the order of priority. Remember, for top executives, who are the consumers of your report, time is money.

5. Use simple English and a straightforward style, without any hidden agenda in any statement. The report should be easy to understand, which means that the writing style should be comfortable for the reader. The objective is not to impress anyone with a high-flown language.

6. Support your statements by preparing graphs and charts as also where possible physical material that can be included in the report. This is not possible always.

7. Before finalising the report, check, proof and revise as many times as required to make you confident. Some consulting companies make it compulsory for the researcher to present to a select group of his colleagues, the arguments and the conclusions and recommendations. This brainstorming will help the researcher anticipate the client part's questions and prepare all his supporting arguments and the documents needed. Some organisations have in-house editors, whose job is to read and refine each and every report sent out. A well- compiled and well-written report enhances the prestige of the researcher and the organisation presenting it.

8. Although writing a business report is not all about creative writing, good writing skills are important in business reports, as it calls for giving comprehensive information using precise words.

Points to Remember

- **Objectives of a Report:**
    - To assess business performance, provide a status check, and monitor progress towards the strategic goals of the business.
    - To use statistics, such as key performance indicators and financial ratios in order to prepare key business matrix.
    - To summarise key business indicators and present them in the form of charts and graphs, easy-to-read grids and spreadsheets, documents, and in interactive sessions.
    - To recommend future course of action for the organisation.
    - They are needed by industry associations for providing information to businesses, for lobbying etc.
- **Types of Business Reports:**
    - Informational reports.
    - Analytical reports
    - Research reports.
- **Report Planning:**
    - Purpose
    - Type of report and audience
    - Method for collecting relevant data
    - Plan and collect all necessary information
    - Evaluation of data
    - Data analysis
    - Interpreted and conclusions
    - Remember that a well written report that contains a bad solution to the problem is worse than a badly written report that contains a good answer.
    - Report format
    - Flow of thought

- **Developing an outline, Nature of Headings, Ordering of Points, Logical Sequencing, Graphs, Charts, Executive Summary, List of Illustrations**
    - Title Section
    - An Executive Summary
    - Introduction
    - Main Body
    - Nature of Headings
    - Logical Sequencing
    - Ordering of Points
    - Illustrations, Graphs, Charts
    - Conclusions
    - Recommendations
    - Annexure
    - Review and Proof-reading

Questions for Discussion

1. Explain the different types of business reports.
2. Explain the significance of planning a report.
3. What are the different sections in an analytical report?
4. What are the criteria that a manager should consider while planning a business report?

Appendix

Business Correspondence (Only For M.P.M.)

I. Types of Business Letters

Some important types of business letters are:

(a) Letters of enquiry

(b) Placing order

(c) Complaint letters and Follow-up

(d) Sales letter

(e) Circulars,

(f) Application for employment with Resume,

(g) Notices,

(h) Agenda,

(i) Memo,

(j) Email

Whatever the type, the manager has to take care of the needs of the recipient, content, presentation style, and statement of purpose. The writer should be courteous, engage the attention of the reader and motivate him/her to comply with the request for response/action if any.

II. Letter of Enquiry

Letters of enquiry describe what the writer wants and why. The enquiry may be about some specific service, products, components etc.

After the usual format of a business letter opening, the first paragraph should tell the reader what the sender requires.

In the second paragraph give the reason why you are contacting that organisation. It could be in the vendor list of the organisation, an advertisement or on recommendation. Follow this by giving further details of your enquiry. This would include product specifications, quality expectations, last date for response, person whom the recipient should contact etc. If the request is unusual, the writer will have to convince the recipient with strong reasons.

The last paragraph will be used for a polite thanks. Here you can suggest that the reader can contact you for further details etc.

Example of a Letter of Enquiry

Deccan Engineering Company
64, Main Street
Kolkata

20 May 2013

Technology, Systems & Services Ltd.
48, Anna Salai
Chennai

Attn: **Mr. Selvam, Manager, Marketing**

Dear Sirs,

    Sub: Enquiry for Enhanced Supply and Just in Time Delivery of Components.

As you are aware, we have been using the components supplied by your company for the last ten years. We are very much satisfied with the quality of your products and the after-sale service offered by you.

We are in the process of scaling up our operations because of which our requirement is expected to increase by over 100%. Our requirement with respect to delivery period is also being revamped. As a cost reduction strategy, we have introduced a *'zero inventory'* system, which would mean that your deliveries will have to reach us within one week of placing of the order, which would take care of the loading, transportation and delivery time.

We would like to know whether your company will be able to (a) increase your production to meet our requirements, and (b) supply the components of the required quantity at a week's notice. In this respect, you may want to consult your logistics company before giving us the commitment.

We request you to give us your response within three weeks of receiving this letter.

We look forward to hearing from you in this respect.

Thanking you,
Yours faithfully
....
(....................)
Section Officer, Purchase Dept.

III. Placing Order

An order letter is a contract for purchasing a product or a service. Orders are considered one of the simplest types of direct request. The objective of an order is not to excite the reader's interest. It is a simple statement of the writer's needs clearly and directly.

Many companies use special forms for ordering merchandise or service. They have standard 'order forms', either prepared by them or provided by the vendor. These forms have blank spaces to cover all the necessary details regarding the order number, product or service specifications, packaging, quantity, rate, date of delivery etc. The advantage of pre-designed order forms is that they enable a company to maintain a record of the orders according to order numbers and so carefully file and analyse all costs of purchase made during a financial year.

However, a manager should know how to write an order letter for situations where such forms are not available and so an order must be put into letter format.

The cardinal rule for an order letter is that you must be sure to include complete and accurate information because incomplete orders result in a lot of enquiries from the receiving party and hence delayed deliveries. Inaccurate facts result in the receipt of wrong merchandise.

Tips for writing a good order letter

1. **Give the Information in a Clear Format:** To make your letter easy to read, do either of the following:
   - Write a separate, single-spaced paragraph for each item. Between paragraphs, allow double spacing.
   - Arrange your order in a tabular form similar to an order sheet. This is useful when several sets of numbers, items, and prices are given.

2. **Write Orders, not Just Hints: Be specific. Do not show just interest:** An order letter is a legal document indicating the "offer to buy" portion of a contract. The "acceptance" portion of the contract is completed when the seller sends the acceptance letter and/or dispatches the material as agreed. Do not be vague, by saying that you are interested in buying... or, you would like to buy...... Be specific and direct.

3. **Give a Complete Details for Each Item:** Be clear about the following aspects of the order:
   - Name of the product
   - Quantity ordered
   - Catalogue, model or stock number

- Description of the product as appropriate, such as (1) colour (2) size (3) material, (4) grade or quality, (5) pattern, (6) finish, and (7) packing, (8) any other details
- Unit price and discount if applicable
- Sales Tax, Service Tax, Credit Card charges, and other charges and duties, insurance and shipping charges if any
- Total price for the quantity ordered
- Date of delivery and possible penalty if this is not followed
- Documents required for meeting financial and regulatory authorities and where they should be dispatched
- Any other information, including the source of information about the company or the product.

4. **Payment Terms and Procedure:** This includes payment terms such as credit period, initial payments and installments if any, and mode of payment, such as credit card, online payment or physical movement of cheques. If it is credit card, give the name of the person in whose name it is issues, credit card number and its expiry date.

5. **Time and Place of Delivery of the Merchandise:** Give the shipping address. If you need the order by a certain date, and the time period during the day, be sure to include the specifics in your order letter. If you want the shipment urgently and are willing to pay for it, mention the details. Mention the method of shipment you prefer. If all these details are missing in the letter, the seller will choose the shipping method and will send the merchandise when it is convenient for him.

6. **Good practice:** Always be specific and use language appropriate to communicate direct statement of the request in a polite manner, such as "please send the items mentioned below", not "I need…" or, "I want…" This is rude and legally not correct. Give all details of the consignment you are ordering. Use a format which will help in easy calculation of total amounts. Double check the details given to make sure that it is complete in all respects.

7. **Justification, Explanation, and Details:** For complex orders, provide a general explanation of how the material ordered will be used, and provide all specifications regarding order quantity, price, and all information according to the above list.

8. **Courteous Close with Request for Specific Action:** While closing, give a brief summary of the desired action. Explain why it is important. If applicable, mention the benefit of complying with the order by way of repeat orders and a long period of mutually beneficial association. Close on a cordial note.

Business Communication Appendix

Example of Order Letter

Center for Socio-economic Research and Development
Pune 411001

May 21, 2013

Realtech Suppliers Pvt. Ltd.
Whitefield Commercial Center
Bengaluru 560007

Ref: 00345/5/13

Dear Sirs,

We thank you for your letter of March 23, 2013, along with your catalogue of computer hardware. Please send us the following items by TCPS Land Cargo Services:

  i. Hard Disk (60 GB): 6 Nos.
  ii. Ram (256 MB): 6 Nos.

We accept the price quoted by you. Please make sure that the consignment is packed in strong cases to withstand the shipping process. Please send the book receipt with other documents through our bank, as you will receive the payment directly from them.

As you are aware, we expect that all the voluminous research data will start flowing in from mid-June 2013 and thereafter, the data entry and analysis will begin. We are committed to complete this prestigious project by this year end. We request you to appreciate this urgency and send us the above items on or before June 10, 2013.

Thanking you,
Yours faithfully,
....
(..................)
Project Director

IV. Complaint Letters and Follow-up

Letters of complaint are written by both private consumers as well as business-to-business customers who are not satisfied with a product or service and seek positive outcomes from writing these letters. Complaints may also be registered by phone or email, although letters remain generally the most reliable and effective way to complain, especially for serious complaints. Many suppliers and organisations actually welcome complaints as opportunities to improve. They operate customer help desks to hear from them about their problems. The quality of answer provided by the help desk operators is also monitored by recording the conversations.

Effective complaints letters (and any other way of complaining) should be:
- **Concise**, as such letters can be understood quickly.
- **Authoritative**, as such letters will command better credibility and respect and hence will be taken seriously.
- **Factual:** The letter should contain all the relevant facts pertaining to the complaint. It could be pertaining to quality of the product or service delivered, as against what was ordered, order quantity, delivery date, etc. This statement should justify demand for corrective action by the supplier.
- **Constructive:** The letter should suggest and also encourage positive action, such as rework, replacement of the product, apology for delay and commitment to future prompt delivery etc.
- **Friendly:** The entire letter should be written to show that the writer is considerate. The writer could even offer to help the vendor. He should close the letter in a courteous manner. This will motivate the vendor to take up the matter on a priority basis and settle the issue to the satisfaction of the writer.

In short, the writer should be brief, to the point and considerate and his approach should highlight on cooperation, relationships and constructive problem-solving.

Example of a Complaint Letter

Global Imprint
D.N. Road, Mumbai

13 May, 2013

ABCD Polyesters Ltd.

Graphic Art Films Dept.

Andheri West

Mumbai

Dear Sirs,

As you know, to meet the rush for advertisements this IPL season, we had placed order vide our order form No. ...., date ...., 20 tonnes of graphic art film to be delivered at our company on or before 15 April 2013. We had specified our quality expectations in our order form.

---

cont'd. ...

However, our production team finds that the quality of the film supplied by you is not up to the specifications given by us and accepted by you in your letter dated 30 March 2013. We pointed this matter to your representative when he visited us on 2 April 2013. He accepted the fact that the quality issue was genuine, but expressed that your organisation would not be in a position to supply the required quantity at such short notice. It became imperative for us to import the required quantity from Seoul on an urgent basis. This created a lot of disturbance in our production schedules.

We enclose a still picture for a soft drink exposed with your product. A similar picture worked with the imported film is also enclosed for comparison. You can identify your product from the markings on the bottom edge.

You have been our trusted supplier for over two decades. Hence, we would not ask for a refund of the money paid by us. Instead, we will accept product replacement. However, since the IPL season is coming to a close, we will accept replacement in two installments to coincide with the advertisement season of Diwali/ Pooja, and Christmas and New Year respectively.

Please indicate the procedure for return of the product.

We look forward to a long and meaningful association with your organisation.

Yours faithfully,

....
(.....................)
Director
Global Imprint

Tips for Writing an Effective Complaint Letter
1. **Concise letters catch attention**: The purpose of a complaint letter is that it is read, the reader understands the facts clearly and knows what action is expected of him. In general, the only letters that are read fully and understood are those which are concise, clear and compact. Lengthy letters that ramble or are vague will not be read properly. So, to be read, make your letter concise. Make sure that you state the main point in less than five seconds. Your complaint letter may subsequently take a few more seconds to explain the situation, but first the main point must be understood in a few seconds.

2. **Structure of the letter:** The purpose of a complaint letter is to persuade the reader to take action. Remember the acronym AIDA - Attention, Interest, Desire, Action. This is the fundamental process of persuasion and applies to letters of complaints too. Structure your letter to include the following:
   - **A heading:** Which identifies the name of product, service, person, location, with code or reference number if applicable and the issue being raised.
   - Statement of facts in simple terms with relevant details indicating what was promised and what was delivered. If there is insufficient justification, the recipient organisation will not commit the investment needed to solve the problem. Hence, make sure you state all relevant facts in an orderly manner. Do not make it sound frivolous.
   - **Action expected:** State the action you expect - a positive request for the reader to react to.
   - **Soften and be Constructive:** As a closing point, mention the reputation of the organisation and previous record of satisfactory association. Even if you are very angry, make a positive, complimentary closing, as the objective is to make the respondent take positive action and resolution of the issue and not get into a long, bitter battle with him. Constructive letters and suggestions make complaints easier to resolve. Threatening people generally does not produce good results.
   - A friendly complimentary approach encourages the other person to reciprocate. He will want to return your faith, build the relationship, and keep you as a loyal customer. People like those who are helpful, nice and friendly. They would not find it easy to help who are nasty and attacking. This is perhaps the most important rule of all when complaining. Be kind to people and they will be kind to you. Ask for their help and they will help you.
   - **Try to see things from the recipient's point of view.** The person reading your letter is just like you, who wants to do a good job, be happy, to get through the day without being upset. The error must have occurred inadvertently or due to oversight by someone else, but definitely unintentionally. Hence, showing your anger at him will serve no good. Respect the worth and motives of your reader and make him your friend. You will see the result.
   - The customer service staff will be dealing with a whole lot of negative and critical statements all the time. This can be very depressing. Be different, positive and constructive. If the situation is complex and involves a lot of expenditure, be as flexible as you can to find a way forward, rather than terminate the relationship. Suppliers in general work harder for people who are understanding, stay loyal and are prepared to work through difficult situations.

- **An authoritative stance:** This does not mean that your tone should be intimidating or warning. But an authoritative tone which makes the recipient respect you is especially important for serious complaints or one with significant financial implications. A well-thought out professional presentation, good grammar and spelling, clarity and firmness in tone while putting forth your expectations are the characteristics of an authoritative letter of complaint. These help to establish your credibility. The reader will believe that you have a valid point. Blame game does not result in results.
- The use of **humour** often works wonders if your letter is addressed to a senior person. Senior persons dealing with complaints tend to react on a personal level, rather than at procedural levels. Hence, a good natured humour draws their attention immediately and helps in dissipating the conflict. It creates a friendly, intelligent and cooperative impression.
- **The look of the letter should indicate professionalism:** If you have one, use a letterhead. Otherwise, as in any business letter, type your address, communication details, date, address of the recipient etc., correctly, tidily, with proper line spacing, indents etc.
- If the letter has been **copied** to someone else, mention the details.
- If you have attached other pages giving further details, photocopies of documents, product being returned etc., state so at the foot of the letter by using the abbreviation 'enc.'
- **While returning a faulty product**, check all the facts properly and understand the terms and conditions of sale as well as the return policy of the supplier. Make sure you are within the specified policy limits. For certain consumer complaints it is helpful to return the packaging, as it contains all the production records. If in doubt, talk to the customer services department to find out what they actually need you to return.

3. **Follow-up:** Generally, the recipient of a complaint letter will acknowledge the complaint and thank the writer for bringing up the matter. While assuring the writer that he is a valued customer, he would take appropriate action, which will be (a) understand the quality issues raised and the circumstances that led to the supply of inferior quality product or service and take corrective action, (b) ignore the complaint if it is trivial and the customer is not of great consequence, (c) Contend or dispute the position taken by the customer in the complaint letter.

All this may take some time. The writer will wait for a reasonable period of time before sending a follow-up letter referring to the complaint letter. He will reiterate the issue raised in the complaint letter and then set a time limit for corrective action. This step will be taken only if the writer/customer is certain that he can take the dispute to a higher level.

V. Claim and Adjustment Letters

A claim letter is a letter that is written by a complainant to bring a mistake to the notice of that person who must take responsibility for them, whereas an adjustment letter is a letter that is written to answer a claim letter. This adjustment letter is also referred to as a compensation letter compensating for the wrong done to the complainant.

A claim letter is a persuasive letter sent by a customer to a business or agency to identify a problem with a product or service. It is also known as a letter of complaint. Typically, a claim letter opens (and sometimes closes) with a request for adjustment, such as a refund, replacement, or payment for damages. A reply to a claim letter is called an adjustment letter.

Main Elements of a Claim Letter

"A claim letter should generally contain the following four elements:

(i) A clear explanation of what has gone wrong. Give full information for quick identification of the defective product or faulty service. In the case of a product, details such as the exact date of purchase and arrival, the amount paid, order number, colour, size, model number, make, etc. are helpful in making a re-check by the supplier easier.

(ii) A statement of the inconvenience caused or the loss suffered as a result of the mistake or defect.

(iii) An appeal to the reader's sense of fair play, honesty, reputation or professional pride with a view to motivating him to take necessary action promptly to rectify the situation.

(iv) A statement of what adjustment you would consider fair.

To secure a prompt and satisfactory response a claim letter is usually written to the head of the unit or the department responsible for the mistake."

(R.C. Sharma and Krishna Mohan, Business Correspondence and Report Writing, 3rd ed. Tata McGraw-Hill, 2002)

"Make your claim accurately and tactfully. Assume in your letter that your claim will be granted and that the other firm will attempt to make a satisfactory adjustment. Avoid threats, accusations, or veiled hints about what you will do if the matter isn't solved promptly

"If possible, address your claim to a specific person in the company . . .."

(L. Sue Baugh, Maridell Fryar, and David A. Thomas,How to Write First-Class Business Correspondence. McGraw-Hill, 1995)

Adjustment Letters

Replies to complaint letters, often called letters of "adjustment," need to be handled carefully when the requested compensation cannot be granted. Refusal of compensation tests the diplomacy and tact of the writer. Here are some suggestions that may help in writing an adjustment letter:

1. Begin with a reference to the date of the original letter of complaint and to the purpose of your letter. If you deny the request, don't state the refusal right away unless you can do so tactfully.

2. Express your concern over the writer's troubles and your appreciation that he has written you.

3. If you deny the request, explain the reasons why the request cannot be granted in as cordial and non-combative manner as possible. If you grant the request, don't sound as if you are doing so in a begrudging way.

4. If you deny the request, try to offer some partial or substitute compensation or offer some friendly advice (to take the sting out of the denial).

5. Conclude the letter cordially, perhaps expressing confidence that you and the writer will continue doing business.

ADJUSTMENT LETTER: GOOD NEWS
• Begin by expressing regret over the problem or stating that you are pleased to hear from the customer, or both.
• Adopt the you-attitude; maintain a positive, cheerful tone.
• Explain the circumstances that caused the problem.
• State specifically what the adjustment will be.
• Handle any special problems that may have accompanied the letter; then close.
ADJUSTMENT LETTER: BAD NEWS
• Begin with a friendly opener—establish common ground; express regret over the situation.
• Avoid being discourteous, even if the customer has been downright abusive.
• Explain the reason for the refusal (and at some length, which indicates that you've considered the problem seriously).
• After the explanation, state the actual refusal (and inoffensively as possible).
• If possible, offer a partial or substitute adjustment.
• Close the letter in a friendly way.

[name]
[street address]
[city, postal code]

[date]

Mr. ABC
P.O. Box 3132
Pune

Subj.: March 24 letter about damaged freight

Dear Mrs. Hughes,

I have just received your March 24 letter about the damaged shipment you received through Green Tree Freight and regret the inconvenience that it has caused you.

From your account of the problem, I am quite sure that your request for the ₹ 2400 adjustment on the damage to the 2 crates of Bone china cups will be granted. A certain amount of breakage of this sort does unavoidably occur in cross-state shipping; I am sorry that it was your company that had to be the one to suffer the delay.

I must remind you to keep the damaged crates in the same condition in which you received them until one of our representatives can inspect them. That inspection should take place within 2 weeks.

If all is in order, as it sounds to be in your letter, you can expect the full reimbursement within 2 weeks after our representative's inspection. I hope this unfortunate accident will not keep you from having merchandise shipped by Green Tree Freight in the future.

Sincerely,

Customer Relations
Green Tree Freight Co., Inc.
Delhi 45453

VI. Sales Letters

A **sales letter** is a **direct mail** sent to a number of potential customers aimed at persuading them to purchase a particular product or service being offered. There is no sales person involved in the convincing process. Sales letters are ubiquitous. The corporate world, the medium and small production and service organisations as well as non-government organisations write sales letters to inform and attract prospective customers, donors etc.

These letters are sent to more than one person, and hence they are formal and impersonal in nature. An effective sales letter will have a very brief opening segment. As the readers can identify a sales letter as a form of advertisement, the writer should move quickly to the sales pitch. As a persuasive strategy, the writer can include an offer to encourage buying decision, such as an introductory price discount lasting two weeks and so on. Or he may raise a "pain point" or a problem situation that the prospects are facing and introduce a product or service that will take away the problem by providing a solution to their satisfaction.

Sales letters are distinct from other direct mail techniques, such as leaflets and catalogues, as these letters typically sells a single product, service or product line. They tend to be mainly textual as opposed to graphics-based catalogues. A sales letter is often, but not exclusively, the last stage of the sales process before the customer places an order. As such, it is designed to ensure that the **prospect** has decided to become a **customer**.

It is an integral part of **internet marketing** today. Sent on this format, it is much shorter than a normal sales letter. Typically these letters are unsolicited, i.e., they are sent as email even without a request for it from the readers. They are also delivered on the organisation's webpage. Unsolicited sales emails are known as **spam** or junk mail and deleted by the reader unless there is some very attractive offer.

Characteristics of an Effective Sales Letter: The components of an efficient/effective sales letter are designed to achieve the following:

1. Getting the reader's attention.
2. Creating interest and building a strong desire for the product or service.
3. Offering convincing proof regarding the product or service covered in the letter.
4. Persuading the reader to take buying decision.

As these letters aim at getting the direct response of the readers, their recall and outcome can be tested on an ongoing basis. For this purpose, a few versions of the letter can be prepared for comparison to determine which version performs best in terms of converting readers to customers. They can also be split-tested, i.e., each segment can be tested so that the entire letter emerges out of this. The copywriter can determine which headline, body text or graphic design gives the best results, and thus, he can build the letter incrementally. Sales letters on the Internet can be subjected to additional tests such as the open rate of emails, click through from opening to check out, bounce rate etc.

The AIDA formula that applies to any letter aimed at persuading the reader to take action applies to sales letters as well:

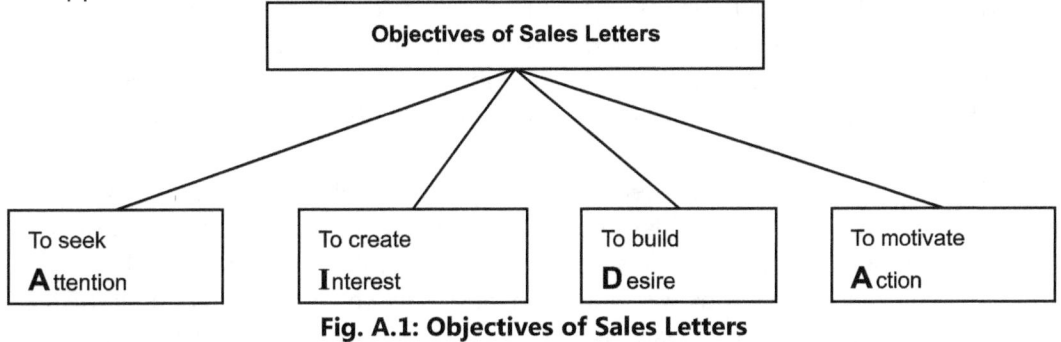

Fig. A.1: Objectives of Sales Letters

- **Attention: Headline:** Seeking attention comes first. Users want quick and easy things at lower prices. By highlighting this in an attractive and impressive manner, the writer hopes to grab the attention of the prospects instantaneously. This segment should be so impressive that the reader would want to read on and know more about the offer. It goes without saying that a lot of thought should go into preparing this. As it is the first thing the reader would notice, it should scream to the reader that the rest of the copy is interesting. So, make sure to make the headline strong.
- **Interest:** Attracting the reader with a strong headline is just the beginning. The rest of the copy should be such that the readers' interest is sustained. The effort of the writer is to hold the interest of the readers. He can do this by providing interesting and relevant facts, and offering a solution to the problem. For instance, as a statement of the problem, the sales letter of a water purifier manufacturer could include facts about water borne diseases and the disease load in various regions, or mention about the fuel cost of boiling water. It can then announce how the company's product can solve this issue and either contribute to better health and/at reduced cost. It can also announce how many units the company has sold so far, to build credibility.
- **Desire:** Once the curiosity and interest of the reader is aroused, the writer should move towards developing the desire of the readers to buy the product or service. This can be done by talking about the benefits of the product or service by giving actual examples. Talk about great after-sale service. People get influenced by the benefits of products and not their features. Of what use are great features if the products the consumers buy do not make their life easy?
- **Action:** This is of utmost importance to the marketing team. The entire efficacy of the sales letter rests on this. It should convert the interested readers into actual consumers, who would part with money to purchase the product or service being covered in the letter. The organisation can create that urgency to buy by giving specific benefits, such as a discount coupon for a limited period.

Components of a Sales Letter

The sales letter is split into several key sections and sub-sections within these.

1. **Headline:** The headline is the most prominent text on the sales letter, designed to attract the attention of the readers. It is the first item the reader sees and focuses on.
2. **Body copy:** This section is typically quite long, as it has the twin function of informing the readers and creating and sustaining their interest. Typically, it can run into 4, 8 or even 16 pages depending on the amount of information it carries. However, it is better to keep it as short as possible. This section will contain information about the problem the product or service aims to solve, features of the product or service, its various uses if any, as well as testimonials from existing customers who are happy with the product or service. It can also contain pictures of the product in use from various angles. For instance, a sales letter for a vacuum

cleaner can have pictures of the product in its various uses such as carpet cleaning, cleaning of the curtains and furniture, blowing dust off window panes etc. Sales letters on the internet can include audio or video presentation on the product, its features and uses, as well as testimonials.

3. **Call to action:** The final section of a sales letter is a call to action on the part of the readers. Converting the readers or the potential customers into actual customers is the end and aim of all this exercise of preparing and distributing sales letters. Typically, this action should be an outcome of the sales letter without any prompting or intervention by the sales persons. To gauge the efficacy of advertisements and sales literature, many companies ask the new customers about the source of information regarding the product or service.

Tips for Writing an Effective Sales Letter

1. **Know your customer:** This is the most important aspect of a good sales letter, but it is often ignored. The customer is the most important element. Know your customer by proper research. If you can imagine yourself as the reader of your letter, you can design it the way the customer would want to know, and not what you want to say. Use the opportunity and remember that customer's main concern is fulfilling his or her needs and desires, not increasing your sales.

2. **Organise your letter:** Sales letters need a strong introduction, a convincing body and a persuasive conclusion. Tell them why you are sending the letter. Include your "sales pitch," in the body and say why your offer is irresistible. Conclude by creating a strong urgency to act. Check the information you are going to include. For instance, in B-to-B communication, if you are sending the letters to top management, avoid leaflets and brochures. It is the job of the middle management to look at the details.

3. **Appearance of a sales letter:** The graphic design of a sales letter is an important aspect of building the brand image of the product or service. The font, layout, line spacing, paragraph formatting, images, etc. all have an effect on the efficacy of the letter.

4. **Make it easy to read:** You do not want your readers to throw away your letter without reading it.
    - For better effect, cover a single specific proposition, which is credible and believable.
    - Though these are formal letters, write in a conversational style, just as you would normally speak.
    - Avoid being clever or funny. They may feel insulted. Avoid posing puzzles. People cannot be bothered to waste their time.
    - Use short sentences. They are easier to read and understand. The chances of your making mistakes are reduced.
    - Write in second person: *'you, yours'* etc. For instance *'The product will save your time and effort.'* Avoid first person statements.

- Compose short paragraphs. The norm is to cover one point in each paragraph. It is easier for the readers. Check the flow of ideas. It should be smooth.
- Take your time. Edit and then re-edit your letter. Make sure there are no repeats. Check the spellings and grammar. A bad copy destroys the credibility of the organisation.
- Use a font size that easy to read.

5. **Aim to capture your reader's attention:** Your headlines should tell the readers something they want to know in a bold way that grabs their attention. The headlines can be up to three or four sentences depending on the important information you want to present. Always make the headline compelling for the readers. They should want to read the rest of the story.

6. **Get your readers interested:** The readers should feel engaged. The copy should be interesting and lively. Write in an active voice. Pay attention to how you compose the various sentences and paragraphs. To highlight some facts, use arrow marks in a different colour, draw circles on key words, break the monotony by adding a few handwritten sentences etc.

7. **Create the desire:** The reader may want to know, "Why should I by this? What is there in it for me?" Your copy must give forceful answers to these questions by highlighting the benefits of the product or service being offered. Talk about your intended customers and their interest and not your own business. Remember that readers keep getting such mails. Your letters should stand out.

8. **Forceful action stage:** Tell the readers what to do next and the urgency of it – depending on what you want, give your telephone number, or ask them to visit your office. Give accurate directions to your office and inform them of your working hours. It's also important to urge your readers to take action right away.

9. **Enlist the support of the support staff of top management** if you intend to approach them with the letter. If the secretary to the CEO knows that you are sending the letter, it will be easy for you to follow-up.

VII. Circulars

A **circular** is a form of business communication aimed at mass distribution to a large number of people at one time. It is a communication meant to notify or convey to all the customers, business friends, shareholders and employees, certain fundamental changes or important information. A circular is a letter which contains common information about the business which is printed or photocopied in sufficient number of copies and sent to all the concerned parties.

They are used for giving relevant information to people within the organisation or for communication from the organisation to outside stakeholders. With the advent of computers and photocopying, they can be prepared only once, copies of which can be made for wider circulation. Each of these copies can look like the original. With modern technology, it would be possible to personalise them as well.

The audience for a circular can be widespread and the number depends on whom the writer intends to contact. Occasions when circulars are issued can be many. Some examples are:

(a) Establishment of a new business.
(b) Starting a new department.
(c) Business expansion, acquisition of new business, new collaboration etc.
(d) Downsizing, break-up in partnerships/collaborations ec.
(e) Change in business location.
(f) Starting of new branches of business.
(g) Admission of a new partner into the business.
(h) Announcing price changes.
(i) Clearance sale.
(j) Sale of a business

Circulars used for advertising and making public statements can be in the form of posters, leaflets or handouts that make people aware of a particular subject.

Example of a Circular

Giving Information about the New Price List to Franchisees

May 20, 2013

Sir/Madam,

We call your attention to the new price list of our product range, which we enclose. We are happy to announce that we have reduced the prices of some of our key products by 10% flat. This has been possible because of the strategic shift we have introduced in our inventory policy and also because of better logistic management. We have upgraded our capsule filling machine recently. This will help us scale up our production, thus ensuring seamless supply of these drugs in the coming years. This will help us service the market better.

We would also like to draw your attention to the technical specifications of items 4 to 7, where we have retained the old price, but there is vast improvement in the quality standards. We would welcome reactions from your customers regarding these products.

In view of the price reduction mentioned above, we have retained the credit period and payment terms as before.

You are welcome to visit our facility to understand firsthand the improvements we have brought in. That will give you an opportunity to interact with our marketing team

Please study our new price list and contact us if you have any questions. Your orders shall always receive best attention from us.

Yours faithfully,

ABXY Pharmaceuticals Ltd.

VIII. Covering Letter: Job Application with Bio-Data or Résumé

The first official communication related to your career is the job application. Since it starts your professional life, sufficient care has to be taken to prepare and draft the application. Until recently, the conventional method of drafting a job application was simple and straight. It was in the form of a letter addressed to the employer explaining or giving personal details such as name, address, qualifications, experience (if any) and references. This information used to be general and presented in a single page. However, the current trend is to make it into two parts, viz., the covering letter and résumé or a more detailed CV as attachment.

Difference between Résumé and CV: In the United Kingdom, a CV is short (usually a maximum of 2 sides of A4 paper), and therefore contains only a summary of the job seeker's employment history, qualifications and some personal information. It is often updated to change the emphasis of the information according to the particular position for which the job seeker is applying. Key words may be highlighted to attract the attention of the potential employers. A CV can also be extended to include an extra page for publications if these are important for the job.

In the United States and Canada, a CV is used in academic circles and medical careers and is far more comprehensive than a résumé, which is used for most other recruitments. A CV elaborates on education to a greater degree than a résumé and is expected to include a comprehensive listing of professional history including every term of employment, academic credential, publication, contribution or significant achievement. In certain professions, it may even include samples of the person's work and may run into many pages.

Some companies standardise the information they would like to receive by producing their own application form. They may or may not ask for a separate CV to be attached.

> *It is reported that some employers spend as little as 45 seconds skimming a résumé before branding it "not of interest", "maybe" or "of interest".*

The Forwarding Letter

Your covering or forwarding letter makes a lot of difference between your application being noticed and considered or discarded. It should be in a simple form addressed to the prospective employer. It contains your name, date, address to whom it is to be sent, the job you are seeking, the source through which the vacancy is known to you and a sentence indicating that the résumé is enclosed. The covering letter should not be a dull or lifeless note. On the contrary, a well-drafted covering letter reflects the personality of the writer, his attention to detail, communication skills and enthusiasm. Coupled with the résumé it helps the prospective employer to decide whether to invite the applicant for an interview or not.

Your cover letters should follow the basic format of a typical business letter and should address three general issues including why you are writing, what you have to offer and how you will follow up.

It will include a contact section, a salutation, a statement on why you are qualified for the job, an appropriate closing, and your signature.

A cover letter typically accompanies each resume you send out. Your cover letter may make the difference between obtaining a job interview and having your resume ignored, so it makes good sense to devote necessary time and effort to writing effective cover letters. Perfection matters when writing cover letters. Every cover letter you write should be customised for the job you are applying for, clear and concise, grammatically correct, and error-free. Make sure you do not send a standardised covering letter to all employers.

When you are sending an email cover letter, follow the employer's instructions on how to submit your cover letter and resume. Make sure that your email cover letters are written as well as any other correspondence you send, with appropriate opening, body and closing segments.

Tips for writing a good covering letter:
- (i) Use a good quality paper for the application.
- (ii) Type the letter neatly and properly unless a handwritten application is specifically asked for.
- (iii) The name and the address of the employer should be written carefully.
- (iv) Express desire to be considered for the position.
- (v) Mention the source of information regarding the vacancy, like an advertisement – press, online, former employer etc.
- (vi) Use an active and positive tone.
- (vii) Express enthusiasm and optimism towards receiving a favourable reply from the employer and an opportunity to discuss more details in an interview.
- (viii) Mention that the résumé and other documents, if any, are enclosed;
- (ix) It should be a formal letter.

Bio-data or résumé: The second part is the **Bio-data or résumé** presented in a table form covering different aspects of your personal details. It is also referred to as C.V. i.e. 'Curriculum Vitae'. This is the most important document in the process of job application as it provides an overview of your education, experience and other qualifications. Hence, this has to be prepared with utmost care. It should emphasise the details to show your suitability for the job you are applying for. Tabulation ensures disciplined and orderly presentation and allows no omissions. In general, the information to be included in the Bio-data is classified into the following five broad categories:

1. Personal details.
2. Educational Qualifications.
3. Extra curricular activities.
4. Experiences of work.
5. References.

1. Personal details

This should generally cover the items given below :
- (a) Name in full. Preferably in block letters, in the order of first name, middle name and surname. If specifically demanded, surname may be written first followed by first name and middle name.

(b) Contact details,
(c) Date of birth (In many companies which follow the policy of Equal opportunities, this is not required.)
(d) Marital Status (married or unmarried)
(e) Mother tongue (Peculiar to India, where there are many languages)
(f) Other languages known
(g) If applying for a job outside the country, include the following details :
   (i) Nationality
   (ii) Passport number
   (iii) Period of validity of the passport
   (iv) Knowledge, skill level and academic achievement in other languages

2. **Educational Qualifications**
   (i) A complete record of academic qualifications with ranking positions beginning with matriculation, giving details of institutions attended, universities from which diploma/degree obtained etc. The current trend is to begin with details of the highest level of education and projects undertaken.
   (ii) Additional courses, trainings.
   (iii) Awards, scholarships etc.

3. **Extra Curricular Activities**
   They may be relating to sports, drama, study circles, workshops, seminars etc. and prizes, awards, distinctions etc., achieved in those fields. These achievements add to your personality aspects such as teamwork skills, inter-personal skills, organisational skills etc. Note that companies appreciate team based activities more than individualised hobbies.

4. **Work Experience**
   (i) Current employment status and job description if applicable.
   (ii) Previous employment stating the name of the companies and periods of employment and job description.
   (iv) Significant achievements, if any.
   (v) Any voluntary work done, for any social, cultural, charitable organisation, short period work during vacation etc. This is important especially for fresh entrants to job situation.

   Useful tips for writing about work experience
   (a) Use action words, such as developed, organised, executed, spearheaded etc.
   (b) Do not mention routine work details. Aspects like working in a team, quality service, leadership role etc. catch the attention of the reader.
   (c) Try to relate the skills to the job you are applying for. A finance job experience involves numeracy, analytical skills, problem solving skills etc. Focus on persuading and negotiating skills if applying for a job in the marketing department etc.

5. **Interests and Hobbies**
   This segment should be short, and to the point. Show a range of interests. Bullets can be used to separate interests. Avoid writing about passive, solitary hobbies like reading,

listening to music etc. Hobbies which are out of the ordinary make you stand out. Any interest related to the job could help. Being the captain of a sports team or the leader of a biking group helps in demonstrating leadership qualities. Any activity with opportunities for demonstrating employability skills, such as organising, team work etc. will add to your acceptability.

6. **References**

Generally, two references are expected. One should be from the academic field, like a teacher, a guide, or a respectable individual in the society who knows you. The second should be a former employer in the case of those with work experience. Name, title, address and telephone number should be given indicating your relationship with them. It is necessary to obtain permission from these people to include their names as references.

IX. Email Etiquette OR Netiquette

Netiquette, short for "Network Etiquette" or Internet etiquette", is a subject for study as part of business writing, because the Net has taken the place of sending paper copies by post, fax etc. It is faster and very convenient for organisations as today the Internet is ubiquitous. Netiquette is the etiquette of cyberspace. Etiquette means "the forms required by good breeding or prescribed by authority to be required in social or official life." In other words, Netiquette is a set of rules for behaving properly online. Netiquette has a dual purpose, to help net newbies minimise their mistakes, and to help experienced cyberspace travelers guide the newbies. It realises that most people would rather make friends than enemies, and if a few basic rules are followed, the Net users can make many more friends than enemies. With social networking becoming more and more popular, etiquettes are being compiled for other portals. 'Twitter-quette' is one example.

Computer networks bring people together who would otherwise never meet. However, this medium is impersonal and so, the correspondence becomes less personal. It is said that humans exchanging email are often like those behind the wheel of a car. They curse the other drivers, make obscene gestures, and generally behave rudely. Such behaviour is hardly seen at home or at work, where people meet and talk. Since there is a machine in between, they think they can be at their worst. The purpose of Netiquette is to convey to users that such behaviour is not acceptable. The network should be used in a positive and constructive manner to express oneself freely, access a world of information, enrich themselves and explore strange new worlds without stepping on the toes of others.

The e-mail has replaced many functions of the business letter. Here are some tips on writing effective e-mail. Email has made a number of major changes in the way business functions. One of the biggest advantages in business is the convenience it provides. It is easy and costs nothing to send mail to many in the company. Even in education, cyberspace has the potential to be a tremendous resource for students and teachers at all levels.

Netiquette is described as a set of social conventions that facilitate interaction over networks, ranging from Usenet and mailing lists to blogs and forums. These rules were described in IETF RFC 1855 document. (The Internet Engineering Task Force (IETF), which develops and promotes Internet Standards.)

The USENET netiquette highlights using simple electronic signatures, and avoiding multi-posting, cross-posting, off-topic posting, hijacking a discussion thread, and other techniques used to minimise the effort required to read a post or a thread. Similarly, some Usenet guidelines call for use of unabbreviated English, unlike the instant messaging protocols like SMS.

Companies like IBM post their own netiquette guidelines for their employees highlighting the basic need for professionalism, amiable work environment, and protecting the company's intellectual property. Some companies limit the use of the Net in their offices, as accessing the Net and communicating on the social networking sites becomes addictive.

Like many Internet Phenomena, the concept of netiquette and its application keep changing, and vary from community to community. However, the basic Do's and Don'ts should be understood and followed.

It is often possible to contact powerful people directly, because many executives read their own email, rather than having it screened like their paper mail and phone calls.

> "I am the only person who reads my email so no one has to worry about embarrassing themselves or going around people when they send a message."   ... **Bill Gates**

There are some managers who do not know how to cope with email facility and are perpetually "email overloaded", while others may be so accustomed to it that they become "snail-mail ignorers", i.e., they forget or do not bother to read their paper mail.

Tips for email etiquette

In addition to the netiquette for exchange of mails among family and friends, there are a few additional conventions for email at work, which are distinct. *Please note that all the tips given above apply here as well.* Here are some tips:

1. **Do not get too informal:** The tendency when it comes to e-mail is to write less formally. Remember that you are still writing a business letter, except that the mode of conveying it is technology based.
2. Though professional email can still be informal, a lot of the humour and wit that is appropriate in a discussion group is out of place at work.
3. Do not discuss personal problems or company politics or criticise a colleague or boss on email or social networking groups. You never know where it lands and create problems for you.
4. Email etiquette forbids spreading of misinformation, personal or confidential information, or any statement that is needlessly damaging to the organisation and to others.
5. When you introduce yourself via email, you are not only making a first impression, but also leaving a written record. So use caution, especially when dealing with powerful people. Make sure that they do not mind receiving an email.

6. In order to ensure that people know who you are, include a line or two at the end of your message with contact information. You can save a ".sig" or a "signature" file and add it to the end of your messages. It takes the place of your business card. It should not exceed 4 lines. Generally signature files are not used in work email within the organisation. It is used only when the email is sent to external recipients.

   Keep the mail messages short! Do not exceed 100 words per mail, and 65 characters per line. But if the message is a lengthy one, prepare the reader by including the word "Long" in the subject header. Lengthier files can be sent as attachments. A good rule of thumb would be not to send a file larger than 50 Kilobytes.

   Remember that many people pay for connectivity by the minute, and the longer your message is, the more they pay. They would not appreciate lengthy mails.

   Be careful when addressing mail. Know to whom you are sending the mail. Unsolicited mail costs the receiver as well.

7. **Format:** Use the format provided by the software properly. The 'To' is for the individuals the letter is directed to. 'cc' segment is for those you want to have a copy and 'bcc' refers to those you want to send a copy but you do not want people to know that they are in. Fill in the subject line. The recipient will know the subject and accordingly open it immediately or keep it for later. It will also help him recall and bunch all mails pertaining to a subject. Begin the e-mail with a normal salutation.

8. **Contents:** As with the business letter, keep it brief. All the business letter essentials apply to the e-mail as well.

9. **Links:** If you are referring to a web site, provide the link.

10. **Follow the ABCs of communication:** Accuracy, Brevity, Clarity and Courtesy.

11. Remember, mails on the 'Net can be archived. It is easier to revert to electronic mails than to hard copies stored in files and stacked away out of reach. In short, take care what you send on the 'Net!

12. While forwarding or re-posting an official message, do not change the wording. You may shorten the message and quote only relevant parts, but be sure you give proper reference.

13. **Be tactful:** "Flaming" is what people do when they express a strongly held opinion with full flow of emotion. It gets immediate attention. It is a long-standing network tradition and can be a lot of fun for the writer and the reader. Netiquette does not forbid it, but does not appreciate its perpetuation, like a series of angry letters, most of them from two or three people directed toward each other, that can dominate the tone and destroy the camaraderie of a discussion group. They monopolise the bandwidth. It is unfair to the other members of the group.

14. Common rules for e-mail and USENET such as avoiding flame wars and spam are constant across most mediums and communities. (**Flaming**, also known as **bashing**, is hostile and insulting interaction between Internet users)

15. **Be conservative** in what you send and liberal in what you receive. You should not send 'heated' messages even if you are provoked, not even in response to 'flames'. Wait overnight to send emotional responses to messages. If you still feel strongly, use FLAME ON/FLAME OFF to indicate your mood.

16. **Try to avoid sarcasm:** It may be misunderstood and remembered. Be careful with slang or local acronyms.
17. **Use mixed case:** ALL UPPER CASE LOOKS AS IF YOU ARE SHOUTING. Instead use symbols like * for emphasis and underscores for underlining.
18. If you send encoded messages make sure the recipient can decode them.
19. Unless you are using a protective firewall, you should assume that mail on the Internet is not secure. Your email address can be subject to hacking. Never put in a mail message anything you would not put on a postcard.
20. Do not open unsolicited mail or mail from unknown persons or respond to request for personal information. Do not respond to unsolicited mail asking for information. It is unsafe.
21. Check all your *mail subjects* before responding to a message and respond to only those, which are directed to you. Make sure you respond to mails where you are the primary recipient and not cc'ed.
22. Watch 'cc's when replying. If it is meant as a 2-way communication, do not include others.
23. **Do not use emoticons:** There are two reasons for avoiding these. (1) While many net-savvy users are familiar with it, there are still a lot of people who do not understand the abbreviations and symbols used in emails. (2) You are writing a business letter and emoticons have no place in it. However, if the situation warrants, use smileys to indicate your tone of voice, but use them sparingly, and make sure the recipient knows what the character position stands for.
24. **Do not use Acronyms**: The acronyms may be misunderstood and result in a war of words.
25. It should be remembered that one's posts or can easily be made public. It can have disastrous consequences. Users generally take the privacy of their posts for granted. Even one-on-one communications, such as private messages on chat forums and direct SMSs, may be breached.
26. Emails can be forwarded easily and messages can spread faster than one can imagine, resulting in grave situations.

This is a true story of a company CEO who misjudged the situation. He observed for several days that the car parking lot was fairly empty at the beginning of the work day and even before the closing hours. The indignant CEO sent a group e-mail to all managers to enforce discipline among their subordinates or they would be sacked. The recipients forwarded this to hundreds of other employees with a warning. This leaked to the media and the public. This resulted in a catastrophic drop in the company's stock price by the end of the day.

---

27. Emails can be stored and retrieved easily. When you communicate through cyberspace via email or on discussion groups, your words are written and stored in such a way that you have no control over them. In other words, if your mail has not been worded carefully and has hurt someone's feelings, there is a good chance they can create problems for you.

28. Beyond matters of basic courtesy and privacy, e-mail syntax allows for two different types of recipients, such as the main recipient and the CCs. The primary recipient defined can be expected to respond. If you are a 'CC' recipient, you are not expected to respond. You have received the mail for information only
29. It is advisable to use the traditional mailing list than CCs, as it can be misused. The "reply to all" facility quickly expands the number of responses manifold. In extreme cases, if the number runs into millions, it can bring down the mail server. In cases like this, rules of netiquette require efficient sharing of resources.
30. Another rule for online behaviour is to adhere to the same standards of behaviour online that you follow in real life. In real life, most people are fairly law-abiding, either by disposition or because they are afraid of getting into trouble. In cyberspace, the chances of getting caught may seem slim and so people may think that a lower standard of ethics or personal behavior is acceptable in cyberspace. This is a wrong notion.
31. The writer should realise that the receiver of an email or a message is also a human being with his/her own sensitivities. When you communicate electronically, all you see is a computer screen. You do not have the opportunity to use facial expressions, gestures, and tone of voice to communicate your meaning. Whether it is an email exchange or a response to a discussion group posting, it is easy for the respondents to misinterpret your meaning. All the writer has is words, and they should be used judiciously and caringly. Every time they write a mail, the users should ask themselves: *"Would I say this to the person's face?"* Be pleasant and polite. Do not use offensive language or 'flame'.
32. *Breaking the law is bad Netiquette.* If something is illegal in real life, chances are it is also bad Netiquette.
33. While writing mails, mistakes like spelling errors or even flame may creep in. The writer may have asked an irritating or even a stupid question. Netiquette requires that the recipient overlook the mistakes and not criticise the writer. If it is a minor error, it should be ignored. Even if you feel strongly about it, think twice before reacting. If you need to, then point out the mistake politely, in a private email, and not in public online fora. No one has the license to correct everyone else. Give people the benefit of the doubt. Arrogance and self-righteousness will make the dispute go out of hand. To avoid conflicts arising out of mistakes, companies can develop their own codified internal manuals of style to set an acceptable limit for user behavior.
34. Respect other people's time and bandwidth. When you send email or post to a discussion group, you are taking up their time. Make sure that the time they spend reading your posting is not wasted. Bandwidth is the information-carrying capacity of the wires and channels that connect everyone in cyberspace. There is a limit to its data carrying capacity at any given moment. People pay for this.

35. People access the Net at their convenience. Do not expect instant responses to all your questions or your arguments. It should be worth the trouble.
36. People as a matter habit, CC mails to people whether it is necessary or not. This is rude, as they will be wasting their time reading unwanted mail. Ask yourself whether they really need to know. If the answer is no, do not waste their time.
37. Most discussion group readers are already spending too much time sitting at the computer. They will have other matters to attend to.
38. Make yourself look good online. You will be judged by the quality of your writing. Spelling and grammar do count. Pay attention to the content of your writing. Check your facts. Bad information spreads like wildfire on the net and may come back to you in a totally distorted manner. You are responsible for what you post and not for what anyone else does with it.
39. Make sure your notes are clear and logical. It is perfectly possible to write a paragraph that contains no errors in grammar or spelling, but still makes no sense whatsoever if unwanted irrelevant words are used. Keep it simple.
40. Whether your mail is for giving information or in response to a question, try to include all the necessary information without digressing or being incoherent. It is a good practice to edit your email and make it perfect before sending it. It makes you look good and the reader will also appreciate it. It is not a good idea to send supplementary emails for the same purpose to indicate corrections.
41. Swear words are not nice. If you feel that cursing in some form is required, it is preferable to use amusing, tactful substitutes for harsh words or the classic asterisk filler, like s***. The meanings of these are known to all. This playfulness is somehow appropriate to the net, and you avoid offending the reader needlessly.
42. Check your mail 'inbox' preferably three or four times a day, but at least twice a day. You should always check your mail in the morning when you come in to the office and in mid-afternoon, or an hour or two before you leave.
43. It is bad manners to constantly watch the computer or cell phone screen while talking to someone. It is disrespectful and non-productive.
44. If you are really too busy to check your mail that often, or if you are going to be out for more than a day, consider delegating the task by putting a temporary password. Some systems also allow you to set up a limited-access password for the person screening your mail. Another way to handle the situation is installing an "answermail" facility. The message tells your correspondent how long you will be gone and whom to contact if the information is urgent.
45. If you think the importance of a message justifies it, immediately reply briefly to an e-mail message to let the sender know you have received it, even if you will send a longer reply later.
46. If you come across someone who claims to be too busy to answer emails, the option is either not to send emails to that person, or have the return receipt feature on the system. If it is important, follow-up on phone. In extreme cases, send a follow-up

email and copy it to your superior even if it is going to make you unpopular with that person. But then your boss may view it as your incapability to work with that person, and form a negative impression about you. So, this step should be adopted with caution.

47. If people with whom you communicate are located across the globe, it takes time for the message to reach the recipient and for him/her to respond. Do not send reminders unnecessarily.
48. One way of using the Net is to enrich our knowledge. When in doubt about anything, one can ask questions online. Many persons may give intelligent answers. When you post a question to a discussion group that you do not visit often, it is customary to request replies by email instead of to the group. When you get all those responses, post the summary to the discussion group. That way, everyone benefits from the experts who took the time to write to you. Similarly, if you have researched a topic that you think would be of interest to others, post it. Sharing your knowledge is fun. It makes the world a better place.
49. Respect other people's privacy. Do not read other's emails. Even the system administrator has that power.
50. If there is a request for someone else's email address, take that person's permission and give it, along with work phone number if it is available.
51. Do not send an email notification that you have sent a document by post or any other medium. This is rude as it assumes that the intended recipient does not check his/her snail mail regularly, unless you know for sure that the recipient ignores paper work or the document being sent by post or courier. If the document is urgent, market it so and send it.
52. Many companies impose restrictions on the usage pattern of the Internet in the same way as they limit personal use of office telephone.
53. Some companies do not make it easy for their employees to send mail to everyone in the organisation. Employees may be designated for specific periods to screen every message that is sent out to all employees. Other companies have mail areas called "Junk Mail" or "Fourth Class Mail" that employees can use for classified ads, requests for general information etc. Such mail is separated from normal person-to-person mail, so that busy people are not bothered by it. If your company offers this benefit, use it, but follow the organisation's rules and check everything twice before you send it out.
54. Delete old and unwanted mail regularly. In most companies, mails are retained on the employee's computer only for a limited period. The main server of the organisation retains them. If there are important emails, save them in hard copy or on your own workstation. Make a list of situations where problems have arisen due to lost emails, and request the management to allow for additional storage facility.

The list is long. Net users should remember these tips and develop appropriate cyber world habits.

Significance of Internet access in India

We in India have taken to the Net in a big way, and the number of converts to this is increasing by the day. Obviously, it is cheaper and faster than postal communication. For some, it is a status symbol, to indicate that they are keeping pace with this communication marvel! For some, it is an addiction, especially posting, tweeting, playing games etc. For many, it is convenient to do all bank transactions, pay bills, buy products, stay connected with their friends and relatives through email and social networking portals and also find some entertainment. For many business managers, it is an essential facility, especially in these days of quick correspondence, telecommuting, and groupware, to share computer screens and work together. Whatever it is, the Net is here to stay and expand into all aspects of our personal and business world.

According to a survey conducted by JuxtConsult, an online research solutions consultancy, urban areas of India are home to over 30 million Internet users. Of these Web users, about 20 million users access the Web daily, and this is a significant number. Again, home usage accounts for 59 percent! Broadband reaches 77 percent of home Internet in urban India, and 74 percent of office-based Internet users. With the development of mobile communication technology of 3G (third Generation level), it is now possible to access the Net even on cell phones, as the Developed World moves to the 4G era, which helps in faster data transfer, both audio and visual communication. With cloud computing, optimisation of the networking facility round the world is being attempted.

Statistics like these generate a lot of interest. One way of looking at it would be to remark that the country has arrived on the map of 'Net users. However, it should be remembered that the initial users of the Net were technically minded, and understood the nature of the medium and the protocols. Today, there are many who are new to the environment and are unaware of the etiquette. They should understand to behave properly on the Net and learn how one should 'Post' or 'Send'.

■■■

Case Studies

1. Communicating the Company Policy

Our company, a pioneer in advertising, had earned a name for its professional excellence. Employees considered it a privilege to be part of this organisation known for its value systems and a very forward looking HR policy including flextime, working from home etc. However, it recently suffered a series of embarrassing and expensive exodus of clients. Their image was getting hit, as deadlines were not met. Employee costs were mounting. The senior staff, who were the backbone of an agency of this nature and were with them for a long period, complained that there was inadequate support from the 'behind the scenes' workers like computer operators and clerical force responsible for the smooth running of any business. Most of these employees were recent recruits. It was observed that they were not reporting for work at the right time, but were billing the company for extra hours they spent in the office.

The management decided that it has to introduce disciplinary measures. The first step was the introduction of a system of clocking-on swipecards for clocking in at the start and end of the shift. It was decided that this would eventually be linked to calculation of pay. To most members of the public this may have seemed a rather minor issue, but this was not the case with the employees. They responded in a negative manner. They refused to do any work beyond their duty hours, and dropped everything that they were doing at the end of their work day and left. If they had to be so punctual while entering, they would be so even while leaving. The senior staff responsible for client meetings and presentations became helpless. No ad agency can call all client meetings during fixed working hours.

The management was in a helpless situation. After several days of discussions between the employees and the management the card system was temporarily withdrawn and the employees went back to work. The disruption in work cost the company a lot of money, but it could not improve customer loyalty. Regaining is an uphill task for the company, but there was no resolution to the original problem of unresponsive behaviour of the junior staff.

Questions for discussion
1. Examine whether the problem faced by the company was largely due to poor communication within the organisation.
2. Do you think that the reputation and size of the company hindered the effective communication of this change in work practice?
3. What do you think were the barriers to communication? How could the company have improved internal communication?

2. A Typical Crisis Situation in a Hospital

It all happened towards the end of a normal working day at a hospital. This could happen in any organisation. The flow of events was as follows:
(a) The Director of facilities at the Hospital was on a routine inspection of the surgical wards at the end of the day. He noticed a leak in the water pipe in Operating Room 1.

(b) He sent an e-mail to The Director of Nursing, informing her of the leak in OR 1, and that it should not be used till the leak was fixed. He also requested her to make sure the leak was fixed first thing in the morning.

(c) The Director of Nursing forwarded the message to the on-duty nursing supervisor of OR 1.

(d) The supervisor had a long tiring day and so, wrote a message and pasted it on the notice board, stating that the operations scheduled for OR 1 should be shifted to OR 8 for the next day.

(e) The surgeon who had been allotted OR 8 for the day came in at the right time. He was annoyed that OR 8 was occupied and was getting prepared for some other surgery.

(f) The nursing supervisor for the day arrived at his usual time and found the surgeon frustrated that his patient was ready for the surgery but OR 8, which was allotted to him earlier, was not vacant. He was shouting at the hospital manager.

Questions for discussion

1. What were the channels of communication used by each person?
2. Were all the stakeholders adequately informed? Was the communication effective? Where did it break down?
3. Should a different channel of communication have been used instead?
4. What are the measures that can be taken by the hospital to prevent such confusing and embarrassing situations from occurring again?

3. Eliminating Barriers to Communication

For communication to be effective the message must reach and be understood by its receiver. Barriers to communication must be anticipated and avoided. Organisations seek to eliminate barriers to its communication through its well thought-out communication strategies.

The IT company, based in India, recently established a subsidiary in a European country. Through this, it was planning to service a number of new markets. It had anticipated potential language and cultural barriers as it ventured out to new areas. To minimise the risk of these barriers and increase the effectiveness of its communication, the company selected agencies with local knowledge and understanding of those countries.

Internally, the main office of the company created a central point or a Hub for all company-wide announcements and information for all its employees. It encouraged free interaction and discussions on the Hub. Initially, there were a number of confusing or mixed messages. Employees in remote locations needed a lot of support. Gradually, they settled down and the number of confusing messages reduced.

The company started analyzing all the past messages to understand: (a) the area-specific nature of the messages, (b) major issues that came up, and (c) the time they took to get their answers and settle down.

Evaluating past communication helped the business see where improvements could be made as far as the company policy towards employees was considered. They still had to address the social and cultural integration of the employees. A number of employees from the home base had been transferred to these remote locations and quite a few from those countries were working at the head office. Very soon, the company received a number of requests for relocation back to India, and it had to do something to address the issue of integration of employees at all locations.

Discussion points: Considering the multi-location operations of the company, suggest at least three effective internal communication strategies to improve employee satisfaction at all locations. Give your justifications. The objectives are: (1) To increase awareness of its key messages, (2) To build the reputation of the company in its new locations, (3) To ensure that the company values and culture are maintained throughout.

4. Computer-Aided Communication

Electronic mail has revolutionised the way communication takes place in organisations. E-mail allows messages to be rapidly created, changed, saved, and sent to many people at the same time. E-mail is a preferred channel for coordinating work and schedules. Messages can be clearly defined through concrete and specific instructions. For example, an e-mail can be sent to all managers informing them of a meeting. The message can inform the subject, the names or positions of the participants, time, place and person to be contacted. Thus it becomes a very specific message. There is no need to print and deliver.

There are several problems and limitations to electronic mail. The most obvious is information overload. E-mail users are overwhelmed by the number of messages received on a daily basis, of which many are unnecessary to the receiver. Another problem with e-mail is its ineffectiveness to communicate emotion. The tone of the messages can be easily misinterpreted, causing misunderstandings between the sender and the receiver. The reader can read sections selectively and skip the rest.

The following is an e-mail message sent by a manager in an engineering unit to all his subordinates:

"It has been observed that the department staff have been spending a lot of time outside after the regular lunch hours. This has to stop. There are complaints about delays in our delivery schedules. A meeting is fixed for tomorrow at 4 pm at my office to discuss discipline issues in the department. Please be present with your work targets for last 2 months you're your achievements."

At the meeting, two employees were not present. Enquiries indicated that they had not checked their e-mails, as they had quite a large number of unread e-mails. They were busy completing their tasks and so thought they would check the mails after the shift was over, but forgot.

Questions to be discussion
1. What does netiquette say about an e-mail in all capitals? Was the manager right in this case?
2. Did the manager make a mistake in sending the meeting notice by e-mail?
3. What is the tone of the e-mail? Is it specific? Has the manager obtained detailed information about the behaviour of his staff?
4. What would be the effect of this mail in the relationship between the manager and the staff?

5. Supply Management

Three departments of the company, viz., supply chain management, logistics and marketing, were operating from the same floor in the office. The supply chain assistant was a very pleasant lady, who was well appreciated by the management and the suppliers alike. She was responsible for calling the suppliers and ensuring all supplies were in place. This also included office stationery.

One day, the manager found her at her table, crying. He did not know what to do. After a lot of coaxing, she confessed that she had run out of ink cartridges and printing paper. She had forgotten to order supplies for the past three months and was regularly borrowing from the other two departments. Tired of her frequent requests, they were unwilling to lend her more. She confessed that she had called the suppliers once and even sent the list of the items she needed by fax, but had not followed through. This morning, when she contacted the company, she was told that they were out of business. She informed her immediate supervisor, who fired her for incompetence. In the meantime, staff members were getting impatient waiting for the supplies.

Questions for discussion
1. When was the beginning of the problem? When and how did the office assistant respond?
2. When did she communicate with the suppliers for her requirements?
3. What should she have done?
4. Using the elements of effective communication, discuss what should the immediate supervisor do now?

6. Nonverbal Communication

Nonverbal communication is sharing information without using words to encode messages. There are four basic forms of nonverbal communication: proxemics, kinesics, facial and eye behavior, and paralanguage. All these have been discussed in the chapter on Silent Communication. Face-to-face meetings have the highest information carrying capability, because the sender can use verbal and nonverbal communication channels and the receiver can provide instant feedback.

Case: It is the quality assurance department of a chemical company. The subject for discussion is the non-woven filter to be used and the issue is the new product which the vendor is importing from Korea. Filters are very important, in fact, critical in a chemical factory to assure quality and so far, the products in use got clogged in a couple of applications and did not last long. The company was looking for a better option.

As such, managers from related departments, such as purchase, finance and production, had been invited to look at the product, consider the quotation and give their opinion. All these are at a similar position in the company. The QA manager had invited two of his subordinates to join in the discussion. The room was small, and the chairs were haphazardly placed. The subordinates had already arrived and were seated in front of the boss. The QA manager, who was the convener, had a lot of paper littered on his table. As the participants sat down, as he was about to greet them, he got an e-mail alert and got busy attending to it. It was quite visible from his facial expression that he was distracted from some other issue. He just picked up the new filter that was on the table, and started reading from the catalogue. The participants were visibly disturbed by this. His subordinates were uncomfortable but could do nothing. The meeting was a brief one, with the convener promising to send them the catalogue for their comments.

Questions for discussion
1. Was that a successful meeting?
2. Was the setting right in the meeting room? Was it congenial for a detailed discussion on such an important issue?
3. What went wrong in the beginning?
4. Who should have been most interested in the product?
5. Did the QA manager give enough indication that it was a very important meeting?
6. Could he have done something better to get a feedback from the participants or arrive at some conclusion?

7. Communication Flows: Grapevine

This is the case of a 200 seat BPO office. There was a very congenial work environment, where employees from different parts of the country came together and worked as a well coordinated team, almost like a well-oiled machine. The clients from the developed world were happy with the service and so there was a continuous flow of business. As such all the employees had access to e-mail facility at work, both to receive and to send.

That was a Friday morning, and the employees were looking forward to a fun filled weekend in a resort booked by the manager. As usual, his secretary arrived before the manager did and opened her computer. To her dismay, she found an e-mail from her friend and co-worker, saying that the manager was found by the security lying on a bench outside the reception. The security allegedly reported that he was completely intoxicated and was shouting at some imaginary person. They rushed him home. His wife was completely disturbed to see her husband in that condition.

The secretary found this information interesting. She did not wait to get any clarifications, but added a little more spice and immediately e-mailed it to ten of her friends.

A little later, the manager walked in and as is his usual practice, greeted everyone as he reached his cabin. His behaviour was very normal. However, she kept quiet, observing him very carefully to find any trace of his previous night's behaviour.

Very soon, he called the night supervisor for a review of how the night shift work was and if there were any issues escalated to the supervisor's level. This lady, the night shift supervisor, was one of the recipients of the secretary's e-mail. She could not keep the information to herself. She confronted him and asked him how he could possibly face everyone after what happened the previous night. The manager looked confused until a copy of the secretary's e-mail was given to him by another staff member. After reading it, and hearing the supervisor, he became very angry at the secretary for spreading such a baseless story. But the matter did not end here. By then, the story had spread like a wild fire in the entire organisation.

Questions for discussion
1. What was the mistake of the secretary?
2. What should the manager have done when he saw the e-mail and had talked to the supervisor?
3. What can the organisation do to prevent the spread of gossip through the grapevine?

8. Communication Flow – Formal and Informal Channels

This is the story of Mr. A, the sales supervisor in an automobile sales and service organisation. He had worked under the same CEO for five years. In fact, the two had become good friends. They even met in the evenings after office to have a drink before getting back home. They often discussed their personal problems and sought advice from each other.

The service department was in charge of Mr. X, a very capable and reliable person who had joined about three years ago. Four technicians (M, N, O and P) reported directly to the CEO, and their time was allotted to the two departments according to requirement.

It was a busy day at the centre, but Mr. M had some personal work. He asked A if he could take leave for the second half of the day. Mr. A agreed and said he would inform the CEO later at lunch time.

Mr. P overheard this, and immediately went to Mr. X and complained that Mr. M was getting preferential treatment and that he wanted half the day off. Mr. X always wanted to make sure that the technicians were happy and so approved Mr. P's leave. But he did not tell anyone else about this.

Mr. P who is a close friend of Mr. O told him of his permission to go home early. Mr. O in turn, informed the CEO, who was quite unaware of the leave application of Mr. M. So he granted permission for Mr. P to leave early.

In effect, quite without the complete knowledge of the CEO, but with permission from Mr. A and Mr. X respectively, two employees remained absent for the same half day on a busy day at the centre.

Tempers started flying in the afternoon, as the centre was understaffed and the customers had to wait for long hours to get their requests addressed.

Questions for discussion
1. What are the different forms of communication flow taking place in this centre? Draw a diagram to show the flow of communication.
2. What measures should have been implemented to make sure that communication is smooth and the work does not suffer?
3. How should the CEO communicate his authority to the employees?

9. Downward Communication: Building Employee Morale

ABC Consulting Co.: A knowledge based organisation

There were about 35 senior managers in the department handling about 70 – 75 clients. They in turn, had their own subordinates and interns. The office was a buzz with a number of teams working in groups, a typing pool, a small, but well stocked library, an administrative officer, a receptionist and a couple of office assistants, who did all sorts of odd jobs. The accounts of the department were handled by the head office. There was competition among the senior managers, there were jealousies and insecurities, but at the end of the day, they all stood for each other.

One of the senior managers, however, was overambitious, and by maneuvering, and hobnobbing with the top management, became the head of the department. His former colleagues knew him and his weak points very well, and so he wanted to get rid of them. His strategy was to gradually make them resign and move out, so that he could have his own favourites there.

As a first step in his strategy, he would call all the senior managers to his cabin, have the 'Do not disturb' red light outside and talk them down for almost half the day. He went on deriding each one by turn and the senior managers were left with a situation where they could not tell him that they had deadlines or client meetings to attend. This went on for about two weeks. The more enthusiastic sat right in front and kept nodding their heads as they spoke. Many others preferred to sit in some corner in his cabin while he went on and on. They exchanged notes with each other, practiced left hand writing, mirror writing, doodles etc. Productivity levels nosedived, and he used this against the managers.

He also resorted to snooping. During lunch break, even the trash cans in each manager's cabin would be checked to see if they had tried to communicate among themselves.

He was so determined to have his way. One by one, within 2 weeks, 30 senior managers gave in their resignation papers. New people with absolutely no experience were appointed. The department head was satisfied that he had a set of people who knew nothing, so he could lord over them.

It did not take much time thereafter for the Chairman to sack the head of the department, but the damage had been done. The exodus had already taken place. The stable gates were closed after the horses had escaped.

Questions for discussion

1. What was the effect of this type of downward communication?
2. What should the senior managers have done? What was the scope for upward or horizontal communication?
3. What communication protocols could the top management have established to check the department head and stop the downward slide?

10. Case Study: Premium Courier Service

Prior to sending their load to a particular station, the general practice among courier and cargo companies is to send advance intimation by e-mail. This is called a pre-alert message sent to the cargo officers of various airlines so as to book the consignment. This includes details such as flight number, total number of bags, total weight of the bags etc. The cargo officers decide whether to pick up a load or not depending on the load already booked with them. For instance, if the load has to go from Bangalore to Pune, the duty Airport Executive at Pune airport receives the e-mail and accordingly retrieves the load and confirms the receipt of the load to the Bangalore office. This worked very efficiently for Premium and the arrangement was satisfactory.

However, one night, the person on duty at Pune airport observed that there was neither pre-alert nor any load from Bangalore. He tried calling the manager of the Bangalore office, but there was no response as the office was closed for the day. Even his personal mobile number was switched off. Thus, no contact could be established. He tried contacting the chief of the Bangalore office though it was very late in the night. Even the chief could not establish contact with the manager. Nobody in the Bangalore office knew where the manager lived, and so the chief panicked. He had to decide whether to do something immediately or to wait till morning.

Finally, the chief called the HR Executive and asked him to go to the office and find out the address of the manager from his personal documents. The HR executive went there in spite of the late hour, noted his address and gave it to the chief.

The chief, along with the HR executive, reached Ravi's house. It was almost three in the morning. Ravi was surprised to see his boss at his doorstep at that hour. When asked why he did not send any pre-alert or cargo to Pune that evening, he replied that the planes were all booked heavily that evening and as there was no space, none of the airlines would accept their load. So the question of sending any pre-alert did not arise. He however, explained that the load was booked for the morning flight.

The chief was very angry with the manager that he did not care to inform him about all this. He had woken up so many people, dragged the HR executive to the office in the dead of the night and had himself driven all the way.

Questions for discussion
1. What was communication issue that contributed to the problems that night?
2. What could the company do to make sure that such instances do not occur? Suggest the communication process that should be followed by the company.
3. How should the chief inform everyone in his office about the communication process?

Annexure

EXERCISES FOR PRACTICE

1. You are applying for internship in a company manufacturing rubber parts and components for automobiles, like rubber beadings for automobile doors and windows, wiper blades etc. The company is situated in the outskirts of Pune. You have done your research on the company and its product range.

    Your letter should give information about your institute and the duration for which you are available for internship. Inform why you are applying to this company, and the special field where you would like to work, such as supply chain management, logistics marketing etc. Also inform the company about your interest in joining them after your course.

    - Which department in the company will you send this letter to?
    - How will you organise the body of the letter?

2. You are the marketing manager working with a manufacturer of UPS systems for various applications. Recently your company has introduced some improved features in the UPS systems offered for computer applications. Write a circular letter to your distributors describing these changes and how they will benefit the customers. Inform them that their sales target for the current year has to be scaled up.

    Make the letter interesting and appealing. You can give fictitious names to suppliers of parts and components. You can add more product features.

    - The UPS has become very sleek. It looks good and requires less space.
    - The coils being used are of better quality. A new source of supply has been identified for the fuse packs. These suppliers have promised stringent quality control measures at every stage.
    - As a result, the average life of the UPS has increased to 4 years, due to which the company is now offering a 2 year warranty instead of the earlier one year.
    - Manufacturer discount is 3%. You are free to pass on any portion of this by way of discounts or gifts.

3. In an engineering company, Mr. X was a shop supervisor with over 20 years of experience. He rose from the level of a technical assistant to this position by dint of hard work and superior skills in meeting production targets. He was a mentor and guide to the next generation of shop floor workers. However, of late, there are a number of complaints about his impatience and short temper because of which, he has made many persons in his department, including you, unhappy. Write a letter complaint letter to your manager giving details, which according to you, are not acceptable.

4. You are working with a consulting company which offers various services, such as marketing research, advertisement impact studies, consulting in strategic management etc. Write a proposal to a prospective client bank offering a deposit mobilization study covering a specific city. Your proposal should indicate that you have done enough research about that bank and its competitors. Indicate how you are going to conduct the research, what your coverage will be and the type of analysis you would be doing. Inform him about your experience in that area and how the bank can benefit from this study. Invite him for a meeting to discuss and finalise the terms of the study. Prepare an impressive cover letter.
5. Prepare a presentation for the above client highlighting the salient features of your proposal.
6. You want to buy a book from Nirali Prakashan situated at 1312 Abhyudaya Pragati, Shivaji Nagar Pune - 411005. Write a letter indicating your requirements.
7. You are the owner of a shop that sells ceiling fans. You receive an enquiry letter from M/s Khanna Hotels, Shivaji Nagar, Pune, in search of information about the price and availability of fans. Write a letter in response to the enquiry made by M/s Khanna Hotels.

■■■